TRAIPSING
THROUGH
WONDERLAND

*Strange Times and Strange People,
in Another America*

Fred Reed

For Ava Carlyle Vernier, the most glorious, bright, lovely, and just plain fun five-year-old authority on dinosaurs in this or any nearby galaxy, from her unbiased grandfather.

Coverr photo: Fred, Vutch Jones, Don March, sometime in the Sixties

CONTENTS

INTRODUCTION

These are chronicles of a disordered life, a type satisfying to its practicioners, though not always comfortable. Included are accounts of a Southern boyhood, BB gunned and barefoot, of a car-crazed adolescence in rural Virginia, of the years of solo hitchhiking as a devotee of the long-haul thumb, of curious recruits in Marine Corps boot camp, of hopping freight trains on the Eastern seabord, of years as a police reporter for the Washington Times, of scuba diving the deep walls of the Caribbean and sitting on the conning tower of a sunken German U-boat at 115 feet, of the fleshpots of Asia and time as a war correspondent in Southeast Asia and on staff for Soldier of Fortune magazine and...well, you get the picture. It is intended to throw light on odd nooks and crannies of life that I have thought of note. The reader will find an America that was but never will be again, an age of innocence. Some of it may be oof sociological, or perhaps, psychiatric, interest, as for example the Moonie hive in Hyattsville or the biker bar in Denver. But it is meant to be good-humored, largely devoid of politics and, well, just fun. If you enjoy it, I will have succeeded.

Guadalajara, Mexico, 2021

UNTITLED

1 MEN AT WORK

In Which Embattled Manhood Rassles a Carburetor, and Is Discomfited

The abyss is everywhere, the unknown chasm that lies beyond the world we think we understand. Especially in carburetors. The other day I went to the back yard to change the main jet on the carburetor that engages in respiration for my '67 Dodge. It is a simple device, having none of the incomprehensible swirls of anti-pollutional hoses that festoon modern machines like malign linguini. Changing the jet is a simple matter of unscrewing one sorry little metal doughnut and replacing it with another. All you need is a screwdriver, long skinny fingers, four arms, and an ability to see through sheet metal.

Okay. I advanced on the old bucket with a box of tools and a *Soldier of Fortune T-shirt*: modern American manhood at its clear-eyed, technically adept finest. I scowled. I endeavored to look masterful. No office-serf like me can do anything practical without (a) a sense of wonder that it actually worked and (b) a giddy exultation at his prowess. Whenever I successfully repack the wheel bearings, I have an urge to put my foot on a log, beat my chest, and utter a long quavering shriek. Unfortunately, the neighbors, jealous types, would send for a struggle buggy and a couple of big orderlies.

The hood went up. Say "Ahhh." I am the equal of anybody in my mastery of hoods. The float bowl came off easily. Anything mechanical comes apart easily, often leaping spontaneously into more parts than you knew it had. The Second Law of Thermodynamics, which insists that the universe tends to disorder with devilish single-mindedness, was no doubt discovered by a physicist working on his carburetor.

The old jet came out easily. The new one screwed in simply... well, almost simply, if only my fingers would fit behind the float, but there was no serious problem. I'd just take a long screwdriver, hold the jet balanced on the tip, turn it slowly.... Actually, there was no great difficulty at all. I merely put my foot on the battery for balance, holding a small flashlight in my mouth to shine into the carburetor, held the float with one hand and guided the jet with the other. Easy. Unfortunately, it didn't leave a hand to hold the screwdriver. The solution was really quite simple. All I had to do was....

After 45 minutes, my wife came out. She is by profession a harpsichordist and has the eye-hand coordination to disassemble a watch while bouncing on a trampoline. She does not, however, understand masterfulness. She tried to insert the jet a few times.

"This is ridiculous. Are you sure this is the right part?"

It was the wrong question to ask of embattled prowess.

My father came out to try. He had been skulking about, waiting for me to fail entirely so that he would be more impressive when he succeeded. He assumed a masterful expression and had at the vile device with the deft touch of a trained surgeon.

"Damn!"

"What?" I asked.

"I dropped it."

A principle of automotive mechanics is that all parts smaller than a tire look exactly like gravel. I put the patient jalopy in neutral and we pushed it back a yard to look beneath it. We got down on our knees and began peering at the driveway trying to convey by a sort of panicked casualness that we were in command of the situation. Nothing. I began throwing gravel piece by piece into the woods on the theory that whatever remained would have to be the jet.

Judging by the sun, we had about three hours of daylight left.

Having found the thing at last, my father impaled it by its slot on an outsize screwdriver and began poking it at the carburetor like a dirk. He certainly looked masterful. I imagined him as a sort of latter-day D'Artagnan crossing swords with the enemies of the Crown, and leaving them with carburetor jets screwed into their breasts.

"Is it working?" I asked.

"Nothing to it. Used this trick for years, putting number-10 screws into junction boxes. Damn!"

We rolled the car back again and began searching for the jet. Five minutes later we did it again. My father looked down the driveway with a masterful expression that was beginning to be tinged with realism. "I calculate we've got about 600 more feet of driveway," he said.

Automotive repair breaks into two phases-the first, in which the mechanic wants to fix the device, and the second, in which he wants to kill it. The difference between an obstacle and an enemy is about an hour and a half. Rage builds. It begins as a sort of interior itch accompanied by a desire to flex the large muscles. Then the fingers begin to curl uncontrollably. They are wondering what part of a carburetor might be the neck. Yet you still have to work delicately, precisely, or else call a mechanic. We tried.

"Damn!

2 DANCING ON THE BAR

Degradation and Horror in Mexico

T he night Pancho Tequila nearly poisoned my daughter in the Mexican port city of Manzanillo is one that will make me forever remember Ninja, or at least her legs.

Macon, nineteen, had come to learn scuba. She wanted to dive because she was afraid to be underwater and had a phobia about fish. Her response to fear is one of bull-headed aggression. She doesn't like being afraid. It annoys hell out of her. She goes at a fear like a bulldozer at a stump.

She took diving lessons with friends of mine at Neptune's Diving. After her first pool. session George, her instructor, was not sanguine. "I don't know, Fred. Maybe she should take up golf. She doesn't ...I don't know."

I didn't know either, but I suspected.

On her first checkout dive, kneeling in sunny rippled sand at twenty feet, she was running on guts alone. Second dive, more comfortable. Third, wandering around looking at fish (Yes, those: the hated enemy).

By the end of the week, with me watching like three hawks, she was doing 80-foot canyons at Carrizales, afterwards hollering, "Oh, *wow!* Dad! That was neat! Can we find some *really big* fish?"

That evening some of the dive crowd went to Colima Bay, a boisterous night spot where the poisoning nearly took place. They were celebrating because it was Wednesday, or maybe because it wasn't. I was celebrating a daughter. Meanwhile, Ninja....

Let me back up. Ninja was a woman I'd been on several dive runs with. She was smallish, looked Asian but spoke good Spanish, dove like a dream, and did full-contact karate for a hobby. And kinda cute. We'd agreed to meet that night to dance.

The crowd got there, but no Ninja. Colima Bay is your standard glass-ball disco—dark, with rotating ball hanging from the ceiling covered with mirror fragments, splashing reflections everywhere, and music at 12,000 decibels and lots of sober people, all of them somewhere else. We got a table in the thumping murk and ordered exotic fish dishes because that's what they eat in Manzanillo. The young Mexican guys all wanted to dance with Macon. She's blonde. In that room full of dark hair and coffee-colored flesh, she stood out like Rasputin at a convention of Quakers.

Further, she was in her shrapnel phase, with funny-looking pieces of metal stuck in portions of her anatomy. It's what kids do. She looked as if a bomb had gone off in a barbed-wire factory and she should have been several blocks farther away. It's hip. The Mexican kids wanted to be hip too, so they flocked around.

(Once Macon called me from San Francisco and said solemnly, "Look, dad, you aren't going to like this, but, well, I just got two tattoos on my face. And my brain pierced.")

Still no Ninja. I was disappointed. "Ninja?" said one of the dive mob. "She goes to the gym to work out for a couple of hours in the evening. Maybe she'll show later." Oh.

Instead, Pancho Tequila showed up. He was about three feet tall, a genuine midget, wearing a sombrero several yards in diameter and crossed cartridge-belts on his chest. Pancho had a magnificent moustache you could have hung clothes on. He looked like the Cisco Kid, only somebody had hit him on the head with a rubber mallet and shortened him by half.

Except that the cartridges were shot glasses. Pancho worked for the house. His job was to wander around and pour shots of tequila down the guests. Since there was no charge, there was no resistance. He noticed Macon, who looked like a sunflower. He bore down on her with a clear intent to tequilate.

I didn't care about the kid's getting a shot of tequila. She was legal in Mexico. She had spent a year in serious art school in San Francisco before deciding that she wanted an education, and had lived in the Tenderloin. She was pretty and could do charming, but for fragile innocence, for shy vulnerability, she was up there with boot soles and tank treads. But we were still in the daddy-daughter state when she hadn't told me all the crazy things she had done, and I was pretending I didn't already know.

Thing was, her mom did something about Substance Abuse. If word got back that I'd taken our precious offshoot to a den of Mexican dwarves wielding tequila and branding irons (stories like this one, well, mature with age), I'd be dogmeat. I wondered what rentals might cost in Tierra del Fuego.

At midnight Ninja showed up, causing me to catch my jaw in both hands. She had looked nice on a dive boat, with salty hair and a shorty wet-suit. Gussied up with a tad of makeup... yeesh. I thought gentle and sophisticated things like, Hoo-ahh! and took deep breaths.

Two a.m. rolled around and the place was starting to rock. Little blips of colored light raced around like rabid moths and the music actually began to sound good. Better living through chemistry. Macon was happily dancing with some kids she had found. They couldn't understand each other, but it just seemed to give them something to talk about.

Then Ninja hopped onto the bar and started gogo dancing. I guess she thought it the best thing to do. Nobody seemed to care, certainly nobody male. She was all plum glitter and nice legs. Thus began Macon's notion that her dad dated hot-ticket go-go dancers in weird foreign bars. It wasn't quite true, or only sometimes, but most of the best things in life aren't. The young are perennially surprised to find that their parents already know about sex. I don't know why Macon insists that I danced on the bar with Ninja. You can't prove it, and anyway I damn near fell off.

In a moment of temporary exhaustion we were sitting at the table again and here came Pancho Tequila with, of all things, a watering can. Or maybe a teapot. I'm not too technical on domestic apparatus. Anyway it was made of clear plastic and full of (are you ready for this?) tequila punch. Pink.

Pancho would just pull some victim's head back and pour punch into his mouth, gunk, gunk, gunk, for as long as seemed to him a good idea. Which varied. It was scary. With some brands of tequila, you can get cirrhosis just by reading the label. Pancho was engendering a lot of cross-eyed people.

I'm not sure what else happened. Things didn't seem to get any clearer as the night wore on. My impression was that something was wrong with the air-conditioning and it began to emit blurry air. Not my fault. Actually, I wasn't there. I just heard about it later. That's my story anyway. Plum, though, will always be one of my favorite colors.

3 HANT I

Hant, the Law, and Moonshine:
True Tales from West Virginia

'T other day late in the afternoon I went down the holler to get Uncle Hant to explain to me about law and order. Hant knows nearly 'bout everything, more than anyone in West Virginia, even Bluefield. He makes the best shine for three counties, and sells it to yups from Washington. Hant can do pretty nearly anything. I guess he's one of them Renny's aunt's men.

I've always wondered who Renny was.

I followed the rail cut through the woods down toward North Fork. Since the mines went busted the trains don't come any more. The rails are rusty and weeds try to grow in the track bed. It was late in August and the air was warm and soft as a hound in the sun and bugs was hollering like crazy, trying to find girlfriends before winter came and they froze. I feel that way sometime too.

Hant was by the still, pouring stove polish into a barrel of shine. He's tall and scrawny and getting old now so he ain't as limber as he used to be. He still wears that old floppy hat that looks like a cow made it and he's got a jaw like a front-end loader. He says the hat makes him look authentic. Yups won't buy shine from you if you don't look authentic.

"Say, Hant, I come so you can tell me about law and order."

"Too damn much of it," he said, like there wasn't any more to say. He let the last bit of stove polish drip into that barrel of shine. He doesn't believe in wasting things. "You want a drink, boy?"

"Not that pizen you make. I ain't that dumb."

I didn't go to school just to carry my lunchbox. 'Course, I'm not sure why I did go.

He sat on a stump, stiff, like a Buck knife folding and pulled a jug out of a bush. "I wouldn't give you any of that yup exterminator," he said. "This here's pure Beam."

"I reckon I will then." He passed the jug and I took a sup. "Hant, I saw this tow-headed gal on TV and she said we needed more law and order in West Virginia."

He looked thoughtful and hove the stove-polish bottle into the woods. He's always trying to find a way to give his shine a little extra kick. He tried wood alcohol but the yups went blind on the way home and ran into telephone poles. It was bad for business. The phone company said it would sue if he didn't stop. Then he tried LSD, but they kept trying to drive up roads that wasn't there and kilt themselves. Brake fluid didn't work either. I hoped stove polish would do the job.

"Gimme that jug back," said Hant, who knew what mattered to him. "More laws? Never had much use for the ones we got. Maybe some people ought to leave other folks alone." He took a three-gurgle hit and looked satisfied. Hant gets along fine without laws.

Hant don't actually exist. He's a Literary Device. We got lots of them in West Virginia. Mostly you find them in damp spots in the woods.

I said, "She allowed as how we ought to get rid of guns, and keep our dogs on a piece of rope when we walk around, and don't never smoke, and a bunch of other stuff that didn't make sense."

"Get rid of guns?"

You could see he was rolling the idea around in his head, trying to get the flavor of it.

"Then what you gonna shoot road signs with? Damn, you can't use a bow'n'arrow out a car window, leastways not over eighty mile an hour. I guess that lady don't got the sense God give a possum."

The county wasn't a good place to be a road sign. It wasn't a good place to be a cat, either.

"What the hell you want to keep a dog on a piece of rope for? Dog don't like it. You don't like it. Don't make sense. How's Jif, anyway? Still hid out?"

It's hard to keep Hant pointed in the right direction when you talk to him. He meant Jiffy Lube, my girlfriend. Her real name is Jennifer Imidazole Ferguson, but we call her Jiffy Lube.

"She's doing good. Sheriff says she can come home now."

A few weeks back she got in a fight with Jimmy Jack 'Callister at Red's Billiards and laid him out cold with a pool stick. The sheriff said he might have to give her a ticket if he could find her but he couldn't and he said the Statue of Limitations on smacking somebody as no-'count as Jimmy Jack was about two weeks.

"She said as how you didn't have enough shine for the yups last week and you might need another still."

He looked sorrowful. "That's me, a day late and a inch short. Maybe I'll put in another cooker."

"Hant, that television lady said we needed to shut down moonshiners."

I figured that would get his attention. It did, too. He looked solemn as a undertaker that's wondering where his shotgun is.

"That ain't law and order," he said. "That's meddlin.'"

That's what it looked like to me. When Willy Bill Jenkins came back from Chicago, that's in Pennsylvania, he said you couldn't even have a dog if it didn't have some piece of paper, and kids gotta wear crash helmets if they ride their bikes and the law makes'em wear shoes. Now, I figure Willy Bill's stretching it some. I don't believe dogs can read, even in Pennsylvania. Still, it sounded to me like somebody needed to get smacked upside the head.

I saw why Hant was worried. His business is pretty good now. So many yups come out of DC that he pretty nearly needs a parking lot. He says drinking authentic shine gives a yup a sense of adventure so he feels like his life means something, which of course it don't. They pay forty dollars for that rust-cutter of his, leastways when he puts it in these authentic mountain stone jugs he gets in bulk from Taiwan.

And I could see Hant wasn't going to tell me much about law and order, except it was people meddlin' where they didn't have any business meddlin'. I knew that anyway. Maybe that's all there is to say about most laws. I took another hit of that Beam and headed back. Hant's old three-legged hound Bird-shot walked with me a ways. I scratched his ears for him. Bird-shot's a fine dog. Don't meddle with anybody.

4 A COP'S WORLD

Tales from my nine years as police reporter for
the Washington Times

Police aren't like other people–not after a year on the job. Urban cops live in what amounts to a parallel world, in the city we all know but somehow a different city, sordid, hidden from the respectable middle-class, dangerous, peopled by creatures who seem barely human. It changes them.

Cops see the grotesque, the inexplicable, the scarcely credible. On a hot night in August we found the guy in the bushes near National Airport who two weeks earlier, having lost his girlfriend, had put a bullet through his head. The stench was awful, a rancid sick reek. The guy's face was sliding off his skull and his spine was a white rod visible through his chest. Some of the cops were breathing through their mouths to avoid gagging.

They hide in black humor. Do do reporters who like them.

"Think mouth-to-mouth would save hie?" I said.

"You're sick, Reed," said the sergeant in charge. It was a compliment.

Months later one of them told me, "The only way I kept from puking was, no way was I going to do it in front of a reporter."

A cop sees people at their worst, even good people: the banker, stopped for speeding, huffing and puffing about how important he is; the woman hiking her skirt and flirting; others lying, lying, lying. A cop never goes where good things are happening. A woman doesn't call 911 to say that her husband hasn't had a drink in five years, the kids aced their SATs, and she passed her mammogram. He goes into homes on domestic calls and finds couples glaring at each other in hatred while the kids cry in the corner because mommy and daddy are fighting.

So much of the cop world is ugly. You answer a check-on-welfare call and find an old woman passed out on the floor with her husband wandering around bumping off walls. Really: Dazed shuffle, bump, startle, turn and shuffle till he hits another wall. Maybe dementia, maybe Alzheimer's.

Or maybe knows he's losing his wife of fifty years, and just turned his head off.

Fire-department med-techs arrive. The woman's blood pressure is something like 240/180. You could rupture a truck tire with that. They carry her out. "Pressure's rising," says the paramedic in the ambulance.

DOA in progress. She's not going to last. The radio says a gang fight is developing, so off we go.

This happened.

How does a cop handle it? It never stops. You go to the hospital to interview the rape victim, age fifteen, because you need a description. She's sobbing hysterically, half out of her mind. They're sedating her. The dirtball really knocked her around: bad facial bruises, split lip. Every cell in your body wants to find the guy and beat him until he doesn't have an intact bone. Brutality has its appeal. It really does.

You have to turn off, not get involved. It only sort of works.

Americans are insulated from death. Cops see a lot of it. So do others in the street trades: shock-trauma surgeons, ambulance crews, fire departments, ER nurses. It isn't pretty movie-death. It's the grandmother who stroked out in the bathtub three days ago, and the flies beat you to her. It's the teenage Cambodian gang-shot in the head, still breathing, with brain tissue swelling out of the hole like obscene lips.

DOA in progress.

You turn off. You have to. I remember a wreck at a brightly-lit intersection in suburban Maryland. Some idiot had been speeding real bad and flipped his pickup. He didn't roll it–the sides weren't scratched. The truck went airborne and landed on the top. The driver came out through the windshield.

There were a dozen squad cars and several ambulances. The street was blocked off with police tape. The bar lights on the squads flashed *red-blue red-blue*. The med-techs, two guys and a gal, were working on what was left of the driver.

DOA in progress. Red mush was coming out of his mouth and they were trying to intubate him and pump his chest at the same time. Waste of time. They knew it. You gotta try. It's one of the rules.

Another med-tech, a woman, knew the cop I was with. She smiled and called to him. I remember the question: "Bob! How's your wife?" They chatted. Ten feet behind her the rest of her team were losing this guy. *Pump, pump, pump.* The woman in the group dived into a medical bag for something that wouldn't work either with the tight, controlled speed they get when everything is on the line. And we were laughing and telling stories.

Self-preservation. Do the job, but don't get involved.

The kids are the worst. Old people are going to die anyway. Adults–well, they're all grown up. But the ones that really get to cops are kids deliberately hurt. Lots of cops refuse to work in kid-abuse units because, they say, "I'm afraid I'd kill somebody."

There a cop learns things he doesn't want to know. He learns, for example, that if you splash boiling water on a three-year-old girl, you get pink swollen splotches. If you hold her hands under boiling water, you get puffy pink lines of demarcation between burned and unburned flesh. These are called "immersion cuffs."

It happens. Usually the mother does it. Men commit far more crime, and almost all of the violent crime, but women do more of the child abuse. Their dirtball boyfriends do a lot of it too. The father doesn't--usually.

You don't have to ride long in a squad before you recognize that "scum" is a real social category. It isn't a politically correct category. You can't speak of scum in newspapers. They exist.

For example, the derelicts who urinate on the sidewalk in plain sight of children, or break into an unoccupied house and live there, using one room as a toilet. The child-molesters. And worse: The couple (it happened, right here in the nation's capital) who kept their small daughter tied up for months, causing rope-burn on unhealed rope-burns, tortured her, fed her so little that she was thirty-nine pounds underweight, and then stuffed her in a closet, tied in a jacket with the hood turned around backward. She suffocated.

Scum. They're a cops world.

5 THE TRUMP MONSTER

It Cometh from the Pit, and Hath a Knout

Once upon a time there was a fairy kingdom that lived inside a place called The Beltway, and was surrounded on all four sides by a land called America. The Beltway was aligned with another kingdom called Manhattan, inhabited by disembodied heads that spoke from the walls of bars, and with yet another closed kingdom called Hollywood, the abode of half-educated narcissists. These kingdoms were in eternal political syzygy, and spoke not with the people of the surrounding lands, of whom they knew nothing. The following is a chronicle of what befell them, and why.

After years of peace, the Kingdoms were taken greatly aback by the rise of the Trump Monster, their surprise being proof that they knew nothing of the surrounding lands. They knew nothing for good reasons, of which there were two. The first was that they passed their lives with each other and among each other and talking to each other and writing about each other and reading about each other behind the high walls of their kingdoms. In organs like *National Review* and *The Weekly Standard* they endlessly wrote stories of the form "A soothsayer in Manhattan replies to what some other sayer of sooths said about yet another's attack on someone else."

They had all dwelt in monasteries called Harvard and Princeton, where they learned that they were the wisest of men, and inerrant. They had no idea that they were hated in the strange lands without the walls, which on their maps were drawn as fog with notations such as "Here dwelleth dragons." They did not know that there were people who agreed not with them. For were they not right about all things?

The other reason for their puzzlement was a powerful spell called "Political Correctness." This strong magic prevented the outlanders from saying anything that the Three Kingdoms did not want to hear. Anyone who engaged incantations called "slurs," which were truthful thoughts about sacred tribes, or who said Inappropriate Things about a certain little country whose only importance was being that little country, was thrown into durance vile. Thus the Three Kingdoms never heard anything they didn't like, and so believed that almost everyone without the walls loved them. They had scarce an idea what furies were roiling and boiling and stirring under the surface of the Outer Realms.

Now, until the Trump Monster appeared, America was ruled by a pseudo-democracy of one bicephalous party with two names. The Only Party consisted of blackguards and Quislings and pickpockets bought and paid for by the plutocratic oligarchy of large corporations, AIPAC, and the very rich. These told the two halves of the One Party what to do. Every four years there was played a great tournament in which candidates of the Two Names of the One Party engaged in the most savage combat imaginable. This was to distract the people outside the walls. Afterwards nothing changed and all went on as before, though the division of the spoils shifted a bit.

And in their ignorance and pride the Three Kingdoms engendered a monster called Trump, and it bit them.

The Only Party had always controlled the villeins because it controlled the choice of pretenders to the throne. A pretender gained the Presidency by buying it, and the rich who provided that money controlled as vassals those who accepted it. The pretenders were as straw and melons sold in a market.

Furthermore, the scribes and oracles of the Kingdoms said aloud only those things that were meet for the surrounding peasantry to hear. The puissant spell of Political Correctness amounted to a societal mute button and prevented the Holy Orders within the Three Kingdoms from noticing what stirred without.

Until the Trump Monster came raging, slouching toward Bethlehem, with which the Kingdoms confused themselves.

And there was afright and desperation and rending of teeth and gnashing of hair for many were the rice bowls threatened.

The darkest of horrors was that the serfs might come to choose the manner of their government. For long years the Bicephalous Party had presided over that most desirable form of democracy in which the people had no power. This laudable state they had maintained by never talking about anything of substance, such as unending wars in remote lands beyond the edges of the maps, or the importation of slaves from curious and unwholesome countries or the manufactures of all things by foreign dwarves.

A great broil ensued. The people saw for the first time a chance to manage their destinies and rose up for the Trump Monster. Inside the Beltway, the Wise and Good–for did they not so denominate themselves?–were greatly astonished. "What manner of wight can this be?" they asked in wonder. They said that the Trump Monster was beguiling fools, the cracked, and those who represented the worst in America. And the scribes and oracles were sore afraid, for most of the outlying populace appeared to belong to these tribes.

One of the Two Names of the One Party, the Democrats, sent forth a dreadful creature called Hillary to fight in single combat with the Trump Monster. Her very visage turned men to stone, it was said. She was held to be of one blood with Boadicea, Jeanne d'Arc, Lucretia Borgia, and Bonnie Parker.

The Three Kingdoms were at one with her, as she was corrupt, mendacious, criminal, and ugly, as well as suffering coughing fits and dizzy spells. Surely, said the scribes and oracles, any monster must fly screaming from her mere presence.

Yet it seemed that the Trump was no common monster. Every time he was beset by the scribes and oracles of the Beltway, he grew stronger, and a sulfurous smoke breathed from his mouth. With drawn swords the Trump Monster and the crumbling ruin yclept Hillary circled each other.

And beyond the parapets and crenellations of the Three Kingdoms the sky grew darker. Inside the Beltway and in Manhattan, the disembodied heads railed and raged, but with every blast the helots jointed the Trump Monster in larger numbers, for they hated the Insiders. In Hollywood the Half-Educated Narcissists said ever stupider things, but these had not their usual effect.

In their pride the Three Kingdoms had engendered Nemesis, and they watched in terror behind the ramparts as the sky grew darker and strange shapes twisted in the looming clouds and the Trump Monster strode ever nearer, breathing fire.

6 ALLAHU AKBAR!

Attack of the Tuirbanate

This was written when a series of murders by Muslims were much in the news but their perpetrators never identified as Muslims

In May of 2018, the second year of Mrs. Clinton's administration, national puzzlement was high over the continuing wave of mass killings. A week before, nineteen children had died in the Blaintree Kindergarten massacre in San Francisco when Mohammed Shah Massoud, Faisal ibn Saud, and Hussein al Rashid burst into the school and began firing.

As in the shooting three months earlier of thirteen in Washington by Mohammed Faisal and Sala al Din Hussein, and in the preceding fire-bombing of the Hancock Tower in Chicago by Farouk ibn Mohammed, experts struggled to make sense of events. The head of Homeland Security, Chupamela Sanchez-Jones, explained it succinctly: "It is almost impossible to prevent attacks when they have nothing in common. What do you look out for? What is the connection between killing children, firebombing a restaurant, and flying aircraft into buildings? There is none. It is baffling."

Everyone of importance—the *New York Times, MSNBC, NPR,* the *Huffington Post, Mother Jones*, and *Salon*—agreed that there was no obvious motive. Time and again for many years attackers had come from nowhere and killed for no reason. There was no pattern except the strange cry, "Allahu Akbar."

Mrs. Clinton's Secretary of Defense, Wilhelmina "Creepy" Crawley, offered an explanation.

"My staff at the Pentagon have determined that "Akbar" is a combination of "AK," automatic Kalashnikov, which I am told is a form of gun, and BAR, Browning Automatic Rifle. This shows an unwholesome fascination with guns. We are investigating links to the NRA."

Logic indeed urged control of guns. In October of 2017, three gunmen—Mohammed Massouf, Mohammed Ali ibn Hussein, and Abu Bakr ibn Saud–had shot and killed fourteen people at Starbucks in Philadelphia. They too had shouted about Browning Automatic Rifles.

Priscilla Latvi-Germond, Director of the FBI, offered another possibility. "We think the killers may be white-supremacists, perhaps linked to the KKK." When it was pointed out that few of the terrorists were white, she said that this was evidence of a dangerous spread of White Supremacism to people of color.

Some suggested that the killers were troubled youth who had suffered the trauma of broken homes. Others suspected the aggregate effect of microaggressions over the years.

Desperate to find some common thread, scholars looked to historical events. For example, on November 12, 2015, at a school for retarded adults in San Bernardino, Syed Rezwan Farook and Tashfeen Malik shot dead 14 people. They too had shouted the mysterious "Allahu AK-BAR."

Then-President B. Hussein Obama was as puzzled as anyone else by this massacre.

He said, "It is possible that this is terrorist-related, but we don't know; it is also possible this was workplace-related," adding, "we don't know why they did it."

But there were clues. Rachel Maddow summed it up thusly, "What do all of these shooters have in common? Guns. Whenever someone is shot, a gun is involved. It's a hundred percent."

It was inarguable.

Yet inconsistencies persisted. When Omar ibn Osama Mohammed suddenly cut the throat of little Martha Clark, age nine, on the streets of Santa Cruz, neither AK nor BAR was involved. Yet he shouted "Allahu Akbar!" California authorities suggested that the heinous act might be a cry of desperation from a man, so impoverished by an unjust society, that he couldn't afford a Browning Automatic Rifle.

Investigation revealed that the young men who had shot up the Starbucks in Philadelphia were of the 150,000 Syrian and Afghan refugees brought in by former President B. Hussein Obama. Perhaps the stress of immersion in a racist white society had proved too much for them, said *Salon*. Perhaps slow service at Starbucks had produced unbearable frustration. They were responding the only way they could.

The inexplicable bloodshed continued.

In Paris, Ahmad Al Mohammad, Bilal Hadfi, and Brahim Abdeslam among others conducted a murderous rampage, but again no motive, no commonality could be found. Were they out of work and sunk in despair? Were they recently divorced?

Mrs. Clinton's Attorney General, Lasagna Woodley-Park, said, "As a woman of color I deplore these killings, but I think we need to remember that some of these men were suffering from recent trauma reflecting cultural insensitivity resulting from colonialism, White Privilege, and institutional racism."

She was referring to the death of Al Mohammad's daughter of septicemia following a botched genital mutilation, and of Hadfi's daughter, whom he had been forced to drown in an honor killing after finding the seventeen-year-old kissing her boyfriend.

Psychologists agreed that drowning a daughter might cause PTSD, but most of the killers in recent years hadn't drowned their daughters, only mutilated them. Once again, there seemed to be no commonality.

At Harvard the sociologist Barbara Levin-Oslieber said, "Some studies suggest that it is a matter of malignant hyper-masculinity caused by addiction to violent video games."

Or perhaps, as B. Hussein Obama had suggested, the killings were due to problems at work. People having disagreements at work often shot up schools and firebombed restaurants. But many felt that there must be some other underlying cause, some pattern. Drug addiction? Extended use of methamphetamines sometimes triggered violence. Failed marriages? Schizophrenia? Bullying in middle school?

Michelle Obama, then the First Lady, had a novel explanation of the Twin Towers that demonstrated the value of a Princeton education. "I think they were trying to land those planes. They weren't very good pilots, and those big planes must be very hard to fly."

This actually made a great deal of sense. The Pentagon is close to National Airport. A terribly inexperienced pilot could easily miss the runway.

Mrs. Clinton, not yet a candidate, had made an impassioned plea for control of box-cutters. "We cannot allow these vicious devices to be used to kill thousands of innocent Americans," she said. The Association of Department Store Managers pointed out that without box-cutters they would not be able to unpack Chinese merchandise. Mrs. Clinton had replied with a magisterial "Unopened boxes are a small price to pay for national security."

On November 5, 2009, at Fort Hood, Major Nidal Hasan shot and killed 13 people. Outraged, President B. Hussein Obama said that it showed the insanity of the Second Amendment and argued for disarming the military.

Finally a break came. Roberta Prangle-Dinwiddie, head of the

American Psychological Association, said in a press conference, "We keep searching for a common thread, but there seems to be only one: perpetrators are all male apart from the ones who aren't. In a post-colonialist society in which men—*ugh!*–can no longer batter people of color, their innate aggressiveness seems to be fueling this."

In his retirement home in Jakarta, Hussein Obama returned from prayer and said that the incident was "regrettable, but understandable in light of the history of oppression and colonialism, and that guns need to be outlawed."

That, everyone agreed, must be the case, as the killers otherwise had nothing in common.

7 A GRAND ADVENTURE

Wisdom's Price

He grew up in the woods and rivers of the county, fishing and swimming and hunting under sprawling blue skies and driving his rattletrap car insanely and lying on the moss with his girl and watching the branches above groping the sky and marveling as the young do at the strangeness of life, and the war came in a far country. It doesn't matter which. It was just a country.

His father, an angry man emitting the foul stench of patriotism, said his duty was to become a soldier and kill whoever it was in the far country, wherever it was. His father didn't know or much care. It didn't matter. Somebody would know. A man's gotta do what a man's gotta do. It would be a grand adventure, an uncle said.

He enlisted. In the aching humid heat of a hot state he drew toothpaste and seven-eighty-two gear and green clothes from supply and learned to march in squares while a sergeant said Lef-rye-lef-rye-lef. He felt the sense of power and invincibility that comes of rhythmic camaraderie with thudding boots. He learned to use grenades and flamethrowers and the proper placement of a bayonet in a kidney. He learned obedience and various forms of likely suicide, but it was for his country, dulce et decorum est, and he sang fierce cadences on the march. If I die on the Russian front, bury me with a Russian cunt, lef-rye-lef-rye-lef-rye-lef. It was a grand adventure, calling to a young male's desperation to defy existence, to cross the mountains, to see the dragon, to overcome. The colonels at Training Command had calculated this nicely.

He felt the romance and variety and absurdity that men love in the military in time of peace, and collected the stories that soldiers tell in bars. See, we was in TJ at the Blue Fox, and Murphy was getting a lap dance from this senorita with frigging water-melon tits, I mean those hangers just wouldn't quit, and this owl flies in, some kind of freaking bird anyway, and she screams and falls on Murphy and... He felt the freedom of being away from the county, in wild bars nobody back home had ever heard of. It was the life.

Then he was on the late-night tarmac of the airfield, staging out for the remote country of which he knew nothing. Wind swirled and jet wash smelled of aviation kerosene and he was fit and hardly noticed the weight of his pack. Heavies roared in and out, taking troops. He savored a new phrase, FMF WesPac. Fleet Marine Force Western Pacific, alive with hormonal appeals of armies on the march, of foreign legions and Marcus Aurelius on the Rhine-Danube line, though he had never heard of the man, and he was part of huge events happening in the night.

On the first day in-country he went to his posting in the remote land, in a convoy of open six-bys. The heat and strange people along the road exhilarated him and he was really, truly out of the county and he took it all in with wide eyes and the mine went off under the lead truck and the driver landed screaming by the road, his legs gone. Mines do that. Marines ran to him and said Jesus, oh Jesus. Fuck. Fuck, fuck, fuck. Get a corpsman. Oh shit. Oh Jesus. The screaming stopped, that being the nature of femoral arteries.

Three months passed. He now hated the people of the remote

country, though he still knew nothing of it. Soldiers hate. He killed some enemy soldiers and some who may have been enemy soldiers and then some he knew weren't but who were in the wrong place after his platoon took casualties from a sniper. It didn't affect him, not that he knew. Dead people were just dead people, so what. He hated the scuttling cockroaches anyway. Light'em up. Light'em all up. Let God sort'em out. He had never heard of the Albigensians, but soldiers vary little.

One day the platoon approached a town and a sniper fired at them. "Light'em up" said the lieutenant, who hated the locals. Ten minutes later thirty-seven villagers were dead and the reporter who had been there got pictures of it all. They appeared around the world. The platoon didn't know why they were being picked on. If villagers didn't want to get shot, they shouldn't let heavily armed insurgents come into their village. At a thousand legion halls, members said war is war, people get hurt. You gotta expect it. The press are wimps, comsymps, unrealistic idealists. We need to unleash the troops, let them win.

Officers, knowing that reporters were the most dangerous of their enemies, said that it hadn't happened, that the enemy had really done it, that it was an isolated incident, and that there would be an investigation. The commanding general in what interestingly was called "the theater" had presidential aspirations, and so sacrificed the lieutenant, who eventually received three months house arrest.

The soldier from the county almost made it. He was approaching PCOD, Pussy Cut-off Date, determined by the germination time of gonorrhea, when his truck hit the mine. Nothing new here. Men in agony, exposed bone, crushed lungs, and the dying crying out for the trinity of the badly wounded, mother wife, and water. This time the soldier from the county was half gutted.

It was a grand adventure, though.

On the ward where they removed a length of his intestines, he saw many things. He saw the soldier with his jaw shot away who fed through a tube in his nose. He watched a high-school girl of seventeen from Tennessee as she saw her betrothed, stone blind, his face a hideous porridge that would gag a maggot.

Johnny...Johnny...oh Johnny.

He left the hospital with a colostomy bag and instructions never to eat anything he liked. Women do not like colostomy bags, so he had time on his hands. He read. He thought. He came to hate, to hate with a shuddering intensity that unnerved his friends, who learned not to talk about the war. Like soldiers since before time existed, he learned that the war was not about the noble things it was supposed to be about, God and country and democracy, but about money, power, contracts, and the egos of the men who, on the principle that shit floats, always rise to the top. For the rest of his life, he would really, truly, want to kill.

He had come a long way from the county. It had been a grand adventure.

8 GREEN KID ON THE LOOSE

First Taste of a Wide Country

Green Kid Loose in America: How We Were During high school I lived aboard Dahlgren Naval Proving Ground, on the Potomac River in what was then rural King George County, Virginia, where my father was a mathematician. Dahlgren existed to fire enormous guns downriver, including sixteen-inchers that rattled our windows most wonderfully. The county was Huck Finn territory. People farmed and crabbed in the Potomac for a living. The country boys spent their time driving disintegrating wrecks at unwise velocity, lying about how much poontang they hadn't come close to getting, wandering through the woods with rifles and shotguns, and swimming in Machodoc Creek. It was what boys were supposed to do. We did it.

I wanted to go on the road, a drive that I've never shaken. I had a literary bent as well as a rifle and a decent jump shot, and had read Kerouac. A sense of urgency was upon me. I was getting old. Running away at seventeen was almost reasonable; at thirty-five, I sensed, it would be ridiculous. After my junior year at King George High I began surreptitiously packing a duffle bag with what I thought people needed in the wilds of America: Canned food, a jungle hammock, my prize Panasonic multi-band radio, a razor I only barely needed.

I wasn't running away from anything, but toward something. I just didn't know what. Nor was I sure where I was going. South. That was easy because Route 301, then the major north-south artery, was maybe three miles from my front door.

Various subterfuges served to keep my parents from suspecting. Fortunately, like all teenagers I knew far more of life and the world than did my parents, which made it easy to fool them. For at least three years I believed that my preparations weren't plain as warts on a prom queen.

I'd never hitchhiked at all. Starting on a June night from the crossroads of 301 and Route 206, I hung my thumb out. My first ride was a black guy, queer as a three-dollar bill, who kept going down back roads and showing me a notebook of photos of a fag party. I understood at last and said no thanks. A nice enough guy, he said ok and took me to Fredericksburg. Then a late-night ride with the drunk in the '61 Fury who between Warrenton and Roanoke nearly drove head-on into a gasoline tanker. Then....

I thought these were adventures. Actually they were the everyday coin of the roads, known to all long-haul thumbs. I didn't know that yet.

But that's not what this is about.

A few days out, on a rainy night somewhere in the coastal flatlands, I found myself beside a deserted rural highway. At this point I'm not even sure what state it was. The region had been cleared a couple of years back and was growing over in pines not much taller than I was. They glistened with recent drizzle that threatened to start again. The only thing of human provenance was an Esso (I think) station glowing a hundred yards away in an otherwise empty night. I had the world pretty much to myself, which I would learn to like. I think a lot of us did.

I was lonely, but not unhappy. A couple of years later I would find that solo on the big roads worked for me. I wasn't antisocial but...self-contained. I went far enough into the pines not to be seen and, with a little fumbling in wet needles, the jungle hammock was up. I walked over to the Esso station to get a couple of cokes.

I don't remember anyone working there, though someone must have. The blue-white glow of the pump island bathed everything, and the bottles clunk-lunked out of the drink machine. There was no traffic, just dark woods and Standard Oil.

It was...my world. I was accustomed to the woods, had lived for a summer in a jungle hammock at a camp in Maryland, and had spent high-school vacations working at Kriegstedt's Esso on Route 301. It fit me somehow.

Back in the pine flats I climbed into the hammock after stuffing supplies for the night inside. A jungle hammock has mosquito-net sides that droop so that you can keep light objects in them, as well as a rain tarp and a double bottom so that the rain doesn't soak through. I was just in time. The drizzle picked up, not a rain but a pitpitpit on the tarp. The night was chilly but I had a sleeping bag.

I lay there with an open can of tuna fish on my chest, an orange soda gripped between my legs, and a roll of crackers in the mosquito netting. It was mighty satisfying. Cold rain an inch away engenders appreciation of a dry sleeping bag. It gave me a feeling that I was getting away with something. Having eaten, I plugged the earphone into the radio. Even then I knew it wasn't wise to call attention to myself at night.

For I don't know how long I tuned into the web of stations that covered Dixie, the late-night country stations listened to by a thousand truckers on the empty highways beyond midnight. Night on the radio is a curious world of affable DJs talking to people they understand and almost know. The cab of an eighteen-wheeler becomes almost a living room. So does a hammock.

What sticks in my mind was a delight in self-sufficiency, in being warm and dry on a wretched night out in the great sprawling expanse of America, making it on my own. Soon it would be commonplace. I and thousands like me would stand by the highways, rocking in the windblast and whine of the big trucks, living out of backpacks, dropping into an arroyo with a bottle of Triple Jack when we got tired of waiting. Not yet. It was a stripling's first time out. And it was great.

We haven't gotten to what happened in Myrtle Beach. Another time.

9 ROUTE 301

A Report from the Dark Side of Mars

Three a.m. in August of 1962, on US 301, still two-lane, through rural Virginia. The night was humid with vapor from the nearby Potomac River. Bugs shrieked and keened in the woods, like bearings that needed lubrication. Gus's Esso glowed in the night, brash and red as a Budweiser sign. Route 301 was still the freight route to Florida. Interstate 95 had not yet gone through Fredericksburg, stealing the long-haul north-south traffic and killing businesses on the highway.

After midnight, traffic was mostly big trucks. They roared past the dark forest, roadside trash blowing in the blast, tires whining as mournful as lost dogs. Miles away, they coughed, downshifted, gathered themselves to blatt their way up the grade to Edge Hill. Hour after hour they sailed by.

The country boys worked shifts in the county's gas stations, six days a week at seventy-five cents an hour. For the most part we were wiry, slightly crazy, with bad complexions and the empty minds of thirteenth-century peasants. At night we worked alone. Crime had not yet engulfed America. For a stripling of sixteen it was a big feeling. The big roads at night were not a kid's world. We liked that

I'd sit in the office, door open, and listen to the radio or just to the silence. Outside, above the fluorescent lights of the pump islands, insects swirled and jittered. The forest brooded dark around. Once a green luna moth landed on the outside of the plate glass. It was about the size of Batman. I walked over and peered into bulging dark eyes inches away. A bug like that can make you think the world is stranger than they tell us, with maybe more to it.

It was another time and a smaller world. The Sixties hadn't started. We kids lived in rural isolation, knowing nothing of the growing tumult in the Middle East, of which we had never heard, or of the coming war in Asia, where some of us would die, or anything beyond the bounds of King George County. Drugs didn't exist. There were as many malls in the county as there were Bactrian camels. We knew only what we saw, what we did: the woods, creeks, fishing, crabbing on the river, guns, sock hops, innocent attempts at lechery and, especially, cars.

In a dispersed land, with people living in remote farms and tiny towns, some of them not even wide spots on the roads, cars were important. We lived and dreamed them, craved the forged pistons we couldn't afford, the milled heads and magneto ignition. A boy automatically cataloged cars that streamed by on the highway: fitty-six Fly-mouth, '48 Chev, *ba-a-ad*-ass 61 Vette, exotic confections like a Studebaker Avanti.

It was funny how a kid could bond to his car almost as he might to a favorite pooch. Your mosheen was part of who you were. Butch wasn't Butch. He was, for all time in memory, Butch of the '53 Ford painted white with barn paint. When you parked in some deserted lane in the darkness of Saturday night, you had a fond appreciation for what your crumbling rust bucket could do, such as, usually, start.

A gas station was a natural home for us.

You learned funny things: where the gas cap was on every car ever made. (Try a fitty-six Chevy.) Mostly it was just "Fillerup? Check y'awl?" squeegee the windshield, maybe trans fluid, tires. Self-service stations were in the future. People were courteous.

In the late hours a seriousness fell over the highway. At four a.m. we got travelers who meant it, running on caffeine and maybe no choice, faces blank with a dozen hours on the road. They'd slow from a steady eighty. Past midnight the cops were sparse and didn't care anyway. Get fuel, hit the rest rooms, and blow on out in five minutes. At the pumps the mufflers ticked and creaked as they cooled and there was sometimes a momentary camaraderie between people out in the lonely night when nobody with sense was. I've felt the same thing on the bridge of a carrier on a late watch.

Strange things happened. Others were said to have happened. A tall skinny senior we called Gopher worked shift at Gus's. Gopher was a bright but odd country kid with a perpetually puzzled expression. You had a feeling he wasn't always sure where he was. Being immensely tall and wearing a Norfolk and Western cap, he looked like a lighthouse disguised as a railroad engineer.

One day (I was told, and hope it is true) a woman pulled up to the island in a Corvair, a car, now extinct, that was shaped like a bar of soap and low to the ground. The car was as short as Gopher was tall. From altitude Gopher asked, "Can I help you, Ma'am?

"Do you have a rest room?"

The distance was too great. Gopher thought she had said, "whisk broom," and responded, "No, Ma'am, but we could blow it out for you with the air hose." In the resulting turmoil, Gopher had no idea why she was yelling at him.

The roads were a course in humanity. We picked up a jack-leg sociology that, later, years of thumbing the continent would verify. The better the car, the worse the people in it. Owners of Cadillacs were awful snots, but people in old pickups would go out of their way for you. That sounds too cute, but it's true. Cadillacs didn't impress us anyway. There was just something wrong with those people. Now if they'd had a huge Chrysler hemi with pistons like buckets and cross-bolted bearing journals....

One night a smoking, rattling wreck of a former school bus pulled in. Migrant workers. Fabric showed on the tires. They were going north to harvest some crop or other. They were not Latinos, as we had not yet opened the southern border. I could tell they were down on their luck. They were ragged, wore bandannas and crumbling jeans, and just looked tired. Two dollars gas. The driver politely asked if they could use the rest room as if he thought I might say no.

I gave them a couple of quarts of used oil. More correctly, reprocessed oil. Kids didn't steal from their employers as they do now, and it was the only time I did it, but, well, those folk needed oil, and they didn't have money. It was thirty-five cents a can.

A different place.

10 POTTIFYING THE NAVY

Loons Assault Innocent Urinals

*H*oo, the Navy has gone funnier than when Junior put his tadpoles in Aunt Lu's milk. It's wonderful. Headline, the *Washington Times*: "Navy admiral wants to get rid of urinals."

On aircraft carriers. Yep. See, urinals aren't good for gender-equity, which is what the Navy is for.

Best I can tell, the admiral figures urinals make the girls aboard feel plumbing-challenged. It gums up their self-concept. And life, remember, is already tough for gals on warships. It's bad enough having those boomy old gun thingies everywhere, and those smelly airplanes. They make a hostile environment and all. But the worst is those disgusting white patriarchy symbols, stuck threateningly to bathroom walls.

Think about it. Every time a woman goes to the men's room, there they hang, row on row, in silent reproach, telling her she isn't Fully A Person.

The horror.

But now help gallops over the horizon, thumpety-thump. The help's name is Admiral John Nathman, and (incredibly) he's a naval aviator. Yes indeed. Potty John, the Carrie Nation of urinals, is going to make it all better. He wants "gender-neutral water closets."

When I was a Marine, I always wanted a commander who had an interest in urinals. None of them did, and they probably still don't. But the Navy, as Marines have always suspected, is a little different. And apparently getting differenter.

Personally I don't think Potty John has gone far enough in making the military resemble a sorority house. For example, a gal on ship stands out by virtue of having breasts, which must create a hostile work environment. (In fact I've never met a sailor who was hostile to breasts, but I'm being socially progressive here.) I think that as a simple matter of consideration for our warrioresses, men in the services should be required to have breast implants. Gender equity. This is, after all, the New Navy.

If compulsory surgery seems extreme this year, at the very least silicone strap-on mammaries should be mandated. Think of them as pre-loaded bras. Since servicemen have to wear uniforms anyway, minor additions could do no harm. Infantrymen carry packs, don't they?

I figure breasts might become insignia of rank. Enlisted men would get small ones. Officers would have big mommas. Potty John, being an admiral, would have three. The Chief of Naval Operations would wear an udder.

Look, I'm just trying to be helpful.

Let's be honest. Many unnecessary hardships are inflicted on women by the Navy. It's so military. I figure the Navy might consider renaming a carrier or two in a more woman-friendly manner — the USS Daycare comes to mind, or the good ship Terrycloth. Then there are family separations. I'm agin'em. So I figure a carrier's hangar deck could be divided into a labor ward and a nursery. Granted, weapons would have to be sacrificed, but all they do is encourage violence. (Onboard counseling might help to reduce this lamentable side-effect of testosterone. We could have caring, sensitive fighter pilots.)

Fact is, I admire Potty John for his willingness to be different from all those stodgy old male admirals we used to have. Can you imagine Bull Halsey (I guess today he'd be Heifer Halsey, or maybe Steer Halsey) focusing on urinal equity as he led the fleet against the Japanese? How about David Farragut: "Damn the torpedoes, full speed ah...Wait! Let's stop and talk about gender equity!" No. No urinals for them. They were fixated on violence.

My father spent four years at sea during World War II, first aboard the USS Greer in the North Atlantic, and then in the Pacific on DD-554, the Franks. He didn't talk a lot about it. He was there for some of the big assaults, doing close fire support with 5-inch-38s. Those were ugly days when blood ran on the decks and the kamikazes screamed in and you red-barreled everything you had at the nacelles and hoped you hit a fuel tank before the pilot hit you. I bet those sailors, mostly dead now, all of them forgotten, would be proud to know about Potty Consciousness.

Truth is, the military needs to be stripped of all manner of gender-unfriendly trappings. What could be more phallic than a tank gun? The very thought must be offensive to women, and make them Uncomfortable. Submarines are nothing but nuclear-powered phallic symbols. (With a propeller, which is a disturbing thought.) I reckon we ought to have gender-neutral, cubic submarines. Flowered wallpaper would add a homey feel and, if you got rid of those awful male torpedo-things, there might be room for a shopping deck.

The potty problem has reared its genderishly inequitable head for years in the mascara military. You just get in trouble for talking about it. Consider urinals and the Army. They were never a problem, because men regard the entire earth as a urinal in waiting. The side of the road, the middle of the road, a tree, the ocean--they don't discriminate. The way feminists see oppression everywhere, men see urinals. It's a design feature.

Which means that if a battalion of trucks is maneuvering in the desert, guys don't care. Anywhere is as good as anywhere else. Women see things differently. They're embarrassed. They want a bush to go behind. In deserts there aren't any bushes. That's how you know it's a desert.

So they want all the guys to stand on one side of the truck while the ladies retire to the other. Of course, if the truck is in the middle of a group of trucks, this doesn't work. And if some dimwitted guy forgets he's not really in the military, and thoughtlessly goes to the wrong side of the truck to check the oil — that's sexual harassment, buddy. Firing squad to the fore.

I'm dead serious: Research has been done on ways to let female soldiers pee standing up. If that's not gender equity, it's at least comic relief.

I have to agree with Potty John: For many reasons, none of which I can think of, men should not be allowed to stand comfortably while making a sacrifice to the Porcelain God. However, the Navy shouldn't simply write off its investment in urinals. Surely unmasculine uses can be found for them.

They would make splendid planters for flowers, for example: They have a robust watering system and good drainage. The lighting would have to be replaced with grow lamps, but this requires a mere changing of bulbs. Easy. We would have a win-win situation: Feminists would get even with men for being able to use urinals, and men would have flowers to look at. A window-box arrangement around them with drapes would be lovely.

See why I tell guys, Don't enlist in this silly circus?

I've gotta run. To my stockbroker's, to invest in implant companies.

11 DIVE, HE SAID

Going Seriously Boom: Aboard a Nuclear Missile Submarine

This originally appeared in Harper's Magazine.

We stood, the captain and I, high in the sail, the rounded steel dorsal fin that used to be called the conning tower, as the sun rose red over the Cascade Mountains of the Pacific Northwest. A bitter cold wind raced over the Hood Canal, leading to the open Pacific; the water was black and troubled. Below us, for 560 feet, stretched the USS Florida: a ballistic missile submarine, SSBN 728, third ship of the Ohio class, our newest and deadliest. From our position above, she looked ugly and industrial, the dull black of steel mills and railway cars--yet, in her odd way, lovely. Submarines are an acquired taste.

Should there be a next war, it is with such bleak ships that we will fight it, firing stumpy missiles that hide beneath the waves. The joy of battle has given way to the conventions of the board room, the dream of martial glory to the peculiar satisfactions of remote, anonymous, abstract death. The world has for years been moving away from a glamorous notion of war, first to the squat green ugliness of tanks and now toward computerized bombs that go it alone in their eerie search for targets. The Florida is the best and, just possibly, final artifact of the new anti-chivalry. If and when the call comes to kill the enemy, the crew of the Florida will never see them. This suits the clinical impersonality of our times.

American submarines, virtually all of them nuclear-powered, fall into two categories: missile boats, unambiguously called "boomers" in the Navy, and attack boats, which hunt other submarines. The United States now has ninety-six attack boats and thirty-six missile submarines, including eight of the Ohio class, which have twenty-four launching tubes for missiles. The boomers spend their days loitering quietly in launch zones that put them in range of their Soviet targets. Their job is to not be found, and they are indeed hard to find.

On the deck, if the rounded surface of a submarine can be called a deck, sailors readied the Florida to cast off from the dock at Bangor, Washington. A ship displacing 18,700 tons of water when submerged and costing a billion dollars does not take lightly to the sea.

"Single up all lines." "All lines single, aye."

When the last lines were heaved ashore, sailors turned the cleats to which the ropes had been attached upside down and flipped them into the hull to present a smooth surface. Any projection causes flow noise. The crew of the Florida do not fear the Soviets, nor the terrible pressure of the depths, nor the acts of a hostile god. They fear noise.

Captain Robert Labrecque, a likable and thoughtful fellow in his early forties, father of two, chatted with me on the deck about torpedo technology and sonar while the mountain peaks turned molten pink and the wind whistled over the windshield. The windshield, along with radios and an antenna, detaches for diving. Looking down, I noticed how very little wake the Florida left. Wakes are turbulence, and turbulence is noise.

Sailors in bright orange weather suits, their faces masked against the wind, kept up a constant chatter with the control room. "Helm bridge left 10 degrees, steady course 270." "Bridge helm, steady 270, aye." Captain Labrecque took little part. American naval practice relies on training and the delegation of authority; enlisted men of twenty-five often bear major responsibility for the safety of the ship. The crew continued their steady patter of commands.

"Mr. Reed," the captain said, "it is time to go below. We are going to dive."

We climbed down one frigid metal ladder after another, through a narrow vertical pipe, and debouched into the brightness and warmth of the control room. The contrast was startling. Men in shirtsleeves sat at panel after panel of switches, dials, gauges, and a complex array of glowing indicators. From this small room the Florida is controlled, her speed, course, and depth determined; her twenty-four missiles, (carrying 192 nuclear warheads) launched on their 4,600-mile trajectories. Only by massive preventive maintenance can such ships be kept in running order.

"Coffee, sir?" asked a sailor. I nodded, still chilled. The courtesy, the ordinariness of these men, was in the context somehow curious. There is nothing ordinary about the Florida. She is after all a doomsday machine.

The helmsman and planesman sat at their controls, rather like those of airliners; the diving officer sat behind them and gave orders in quiet tones. The atmosphere was attentive but relaxed. For them, the day was like any other. There were taking a billion-dollar ship, easily the most powerful weapon the planet has ever seen, down to the frigid depths where light is dim and color flees. Nothing interesting was happening, but sailors nonetheless watched the gauges with care. There are m any things one wants to know when submerging a submarine, as for example whether one has closed all the hatches. The point is not facetious: submarines have been lost because of open hatches. The deep sea is not a forgiving place.

Men passed through the control room on the way to other destinations. The Florida is roomy for a submarine, being forty-two feet wide, and she carries a lot of men, 165 normally. American naval philosophy discourages automation. The Navy believes that machines make more mistakes than people do. At depth, a mistake can occur quickly and cause a shattering implosion that strews wreckage for miles. At thirty-four knots and a depth of 900 feet, typical figures for modern submarines, a faulty computer controlling the diving planes of an attack submarine could drive the ship below crush depth in seconds. The emphasis on safety pays off. The United States has lost only two nuclear subs, the Thresher in 1963 and the Scorpion in 1968.

"What do you think?" asked the executive officer, noticing a certain impassioned expression on my face. I am a certifiable technophile. Viewed purely as a machine the Florida seemed to me the pinnacle of human achievement, and a very pretty pinnacle at that. Yet if I considered its purpose, I would think it a spectacular embodiment of abject stupidity.

"I'm in love. I think I've got a First-Amendment right to own one of these things."

The officer smiled. "All ahead two-thirds."

"All ahead, aye."

Hands went to switches, indicators changed color, and soon the ballast tanks began to fill. The tone was easy-going, congenial. In the confined quarters of a submarine, congeniality is essential. But on long cruises, edginess starts about two weeks out. First, some men get irritable and snappish, then they calm down and others take it up. The Florida is a comfortable iron pipe, but an iron pipe nonetheless.

Minutes later we were submerged, a fact making no appreciable difference except on the gauges. A submarine is a closed world, normally unaffected by outside conditions. My escort officer was Lieutenant Edward Wilson, a pleasant young man who never seemed to be out of arm's reach. We walked through long corridors, the temperature unchangingly cool and the lighting unchangingly pleasant. The cream-colored walls of a submarine are lined with cables and pipes, sprinkled with valves and gauges. The ship hummed-barely, by design-with air-conditioning and other very slight noises of machinery.

I am an amateur of submarine technology, and so I asked Lieutenant Wilson to show me the silencing measures. He did, but by prior agreement this article was submitted for security review, and much of what he said did not survive that review. The Navy was unfailing friendly throughout my trip, and indeed extended the invitation unasked. Yet there were many things the Navy would not let me write about, and others that it asked me not to write about.

Silencing is both an art and a science. Tiny accelerometers detect any vibration in rotating objects, whereupon the offending object is immediately replaced. Hydrophones on the outer hull listen to the ship itself to hear whether anything has begun to make noise. Lieutenant Wilson pointed out the omnipresent rubber washers, inches thick, separating everything from the hull. Most equipment rests on rubber, never touching the hull.

Noise to a submariner is not the simple matter it is to others. Flow noise, caused by the passage of water over the ship, is similar to the sound of wind over a moving car. It can be reduced by moving more slowly, by eliminating all protrusions and openings from the hull, and by using hydrodynamically streamlined shapes. Propeller noise can be reduced by careful design and precise machining (a chip in the propeller can produce a whizzing sound). The worst propeller noise is caused by cavitation-the formation of bubbles or partial vacuums, which occurs when a high-speed propeller moves away from the contiguous water faster than the water can follow. The cavities immediately collapse with a thunderous racket. A partial solution is to use larger propellers, which turn more slowly. Another is to go more slowly, and another, to stay deep enough that water pressure prevents cavitation.

Machinery noise is another matter. A nuclear reactor produces steam, which turns turbines, just as wind turns the propeller on a child's beanie. Turbines produce a terrific whine. Reactors also produce heat, so cooling pumps-which make noise-are needed, at least at high speed. There are also air conditioners, compressors, footsteps, dropped tools. If these sounds reached the hull they would be transmitted into the ocean.

Near the end of our quick walk through the ship, Lieutenant Wilson led me through the missile bay, where huge red cylinders rise in neat ranks three feet apart. He stopped to show me a sailor's berth, nested between a pair of missile tubes, one of the earth's more esoteric bedrooms. He knocked first and asked permission to enter. The military believes that enlisted men have a right to privacy in their living quarters. Nobody was there. Inside, we found bunks with curtains, small lockers, and jacks for plugging headphones into the ship's entertainment system of several channels-usually rock, country and western, and a religious channel said to be widely listened to. The blankets are army-camouflage, which struck me as ridiculous.

"So the Soviets can't see you?"

He laughed. "No. We used to have wool, but the lint clogged the air filters. These don't make lint."

We traipsed through the sub and found a wealth of details that a civilian wouldn't think of. For example, how does one get rid of garbage at depth? There is the TDU--Trash Disposal Unit (everything military has to have an acronym to be taken seriously). The TDU, which resembles a vertical torpedo tube, ejects packets of garbage weighted to sink. Leaking hydraulic fluid can cause a visible slick, so the periscope uses a special soluble fluid. We stopped by the oxygen generators that produce oxygen by electrically hydrolyzing water. The result is gaseous hydrogen that is dumped overboard through a diffuser that breaks it into very small bubbles. Big bubbles might be visible on the surface.

The last stop on the tour was the crew's mess, a reasonably large room with a Coke machine, orange and cream walls, and checkered table-cloths. A Coke machine on a doomsday boat seemed incongruously human.

"What do you do for amusement?" I asked a lanky, dark sailor sitting alone at a table.

"Sleep," he said-the black humor of GIs.

"Sounds bleak. Why did you take this job?"

"I ask myself that."

"You going to get out?" "No...no."

Such answers are common in the military, particularly in the undersea services: I hate it but I love it.

The Navy would say virtually nothing about the Florida's sonar. In particular, it would not say whether the Florida has a towed array, which is a long cable trailing far behind the ship and carrying hydrophones. All modern submarines that I have knowledge of use towed arrays because of their superior sonar performance. A photograph of an Ohio-class submarine published by the United States Naval Institute purports to show the stowage space for a towed array in the rear fins. The Navy will simply not confirm or deny anything about sonar. One might assume that the Florida, working in the same water as other submarines, uses the same technology. But I don't know.

In the sonar room a half-dozen men sat in near-darkness in front of screens. Luminous green sand drifted slowly down the screens, each grain representing a slight blip of sound. On submarines today one watches sound instead of listening to it. Small red and green lights glowed on indicator panels connected to powerful computers and to hydrophones outside the hull. Day in, day out, complex mathematical programs race through elaborate computer circuitry, adding this ghost of a whisper to that hint of a noise, analyzing, inferring, best-guessing to quantify almost no sound at all. Rows of switches control the equipment, but their labels would never pass security review. From this room the Florida gropes her way through the weird, deceptive hall of mirrors that is the acoustic ocean.

A submarine is blind, able only to listen, yet listening is not the simple thing it seems. Sea water is eerie stuff, rife with structure and peculiarities, less a substance that a place with semi-predictable corridors and ambiguous echoes. For example, warm water heated by the sun forms a "surface duct," its thickness varying with the time of year, in which sound is trapped as if in a pipe. Thermoclines-boundaries between warm and cold layers-reflect sound the way mirrors reflect light; a submarine below a thermocline usually can't be heard from above.

At roughly 4,000 feet is the "deep sound channel"; sound travels at that depth for incredible distances, sometimes halfway around the earth. Strange things happen. Sound refracts-that is, bends-in the direction of lower velocity. It travels faster in warm water and faster in water under pressure. The curious result is that sound goes down into the deep sea, then comes back up, then goes back down as sinuously as a snake. The points of surfacing are called "convergence zones"; in the open ocean these are about thirty-five miles apart. Thus, a ship can be heard when it is 35, 70, 105, or 140 miles away, but not at 20 miles. All of these qualities vary with temperature, which is to say with the time of year, and with salinity. All can be measured and recorded. Navies do not have oceanographic vessels because of an interest in the ways of fish.

All of this matters to the crew, who are hunted every day of the year by their Soviet counterparts-who to the rest of us are chiefly budgetary justifications. The likelihood of survival is measured in decibels. "Three db down and I've got his ass," is a typical statement about an enemy's prospects. He who is heard first tends to be dead.

My escort and I went to the crew's lounge, a tiny space with a VCR, so I could talk to the enlisted men about submarine life. The Florida has a library, barely, but videotapes are the preferred off-duty amusement. Like most military men, these sailors were at first embarrassed by the here's-a-reporter-now-perform atmosphere, but they quickly adopted the reticence of starving used-car salesmen.

"Okay, you guys, give this gentleman straight answers," said my lieutenant.

"How do you like submarine life?" I asked a fellow from the reactor section.

"It sucks."

"Why?" I asked for the sake of journalistic propriety, having heard the answer a thousand times.

"I want my children to recognize me."

From the others came a chorus of "yeah" and "no shit." A cruise lasts roughly seventy days, followed by thirty days when the ship is in port. Each boomer has two alternating crews, Blue and Gold. This system results in sailors' spending about five months a year at sea. The strain on marriages is enormous, the effect on children, who cannot understand, worse. (The Navy's divorce rate is the highest in the military.) Young children desperately want their fathers to stay at home, and sometimes think that daddy's absence is their fault.

"My little boy-I can't figure how-decided that the reason I had to go away was because he wasn't potty-trained. When he finally got things under control, he was real happy because he figured Daddy would stay home now. It wasn't fun when he found out I was leaving again."

"My kid kept worrying because I must get wet and cold underwater, and how could I breathe? I had to bring her aboard to show her, and she got over it."

"It's like a divorce twice a year. This is my last cruise. A lotta guys are getting out."

During cruises the Navy wife becomes accustomed to independence, to making decisions, and taking care of business. Then the sailor comes home, and thinks that he is in charge. Just when they get it straightened out, off he goes. Not uncommonly it comes down to the Navy wife's ultimatum: "Look, sweetheart, you're married to me, or you're married to that goddammed ship. Which is it?" In a menage a trois with a pretty young wife, a submarine tends to be the weak link, and the civilian world gets a splendidly trained technician.

If I were a Soviet submarine captain ordered to hunt the Florida, I would pray fervently that I not find her: these ships are decidedly armed.

The Florida carries four torpedo tubes in the bow for Mark 48 torpedoes. These weapons, long bright cylinders, rest in racks in the center of the gleaming torpedo room. I have watched torpedoes loaded on attack boats, and it is an awesome thing. The crewman opens the tube door and that big fish slides smoothly in with deadly silence. A placard on one of the Florida's tubes warns, "Warshot Loaded." Live torpedo, ready to fire.

Modern torpedoes are usually guided most of the way to their targets by wires that trail behind them to the submarine. The range of a Mark 48 (the Navy says nothing, but published sources are available) is thirty-eight miles Consequently the Old-World War II aim-by-eyeball is impossible. For reasons grounded in the laws of physics, a large receiver is needed to detect the very low frequencies that constitute much of a submarine's radiated noise, and also to get accurate bearings. The ship's sonar can guide the torpedo. When it nears its target, the torpedo pursues autonomously, using "pinging" sonar. One does not so much use modern weapons are merely supervise them, making, as it were, suggestions of a general nature.

Firing a missile requires several officers to have several keys to which no one else has access. Should Captain Labrecque develop a brain tumor and acquire Napoleonic aspirations concerning the Soviet Union, nothing would happen. Not only are several people required to agree to fire, but several different people must agree that an order to fire has been given. In the cryptography room, continuous contact is maintained with command posts on shore (radio waves of sufficiently long wavelength will penetrate sea water), and any message to fire missiles would appear in code. The order must be independently looked up, decoded, and verified by more than one person. The ship must then be brought to the proper depth for firing. Because firing missiles requires the concerted action of so many people, there is no way a few crazed crewmen could launch a missile. A boomer does not accidentally go boom.

To my surprise, the captain let me watch a simulated launch. The drill begins in the control room, where Captain Labrecque stands behind what looks like a symphony conductor's podium. Labrecque chooses which tubes to fire, orders "Denote twelve," then "Fire twelve."

Down in the missile control room, other men sit at other banks of switches and indicators. The ship is so ridden with computers and sensors that it just misses being alive. The crucial switches, the ones that do spectacular and irrevocable things, are all locked. Again, the sequence is simple and quick; this part of the process is thoroughly automated. But the simplicity is deceptive. A few switches can cause a large number of things to happen in the ship's great banks of semi-sentient circuitry. When a missile has been selected for firing, the computer must be given the target's location. The ship carries several extremely precise inertial navigation systems that give an accurate fix on position. Since the submarine is always moving, for maximum accuracy the information must be fed to the missile's own computers at the last moment before launch. The missile's guidance system is itself fearfully complex and precise.

The Trident I missiles aboard the Florida are easily accurate enough to hit cities. Before a missile can be fired, however, the gyros in the guidance system must be "spun up" and allowed to stabilize. This takes a good many minutes, although the missiles can be fired sooner with decreased accuracy.

The actual firing takes place at a fairly shallow depth. The first step is to pressurize the missile tube to a pressure equal to that of the surrounding water; otherwise, the missile hatch cannot be opened. The big circular hatch over each missile swings up, leaving the missile dry in its air-filled tube beneath a breakable plastic cover. A gas generator then produces sufficient pressure to drive the missile through both the plastic cover and the water to the surface, where its motors ignite and, no longer under human control, it flies off to kill a few hundred thousand people. Missiles can be fired quickly. All twenty-four can be dispatched in the time it takes to get a hamburger at McDonald's when the lines are short.

Crewmen talk among themselves about the possibility of having to kill tens of millions of people they have never seen, in a country they have never visited and know next to nothing about, in order to defend the West against communism-something few of them can discuss intelligently. No one wants to do it, so perhaps it doesn't matter that these sailors have little notion who they would be killing. The psychological protection they employ is to believe they will never have to do it, and they are almost certainly correct. A common saying is that if the Florida ever fires, she will have failed to do her job.

But of course there is no escaping the awful what-if. The missiles exist and seem to work. In this world anything can happen. What would the crew do after firing, knowing that their families would very likely be dead, or knowing that there wouldn't really be any place for them to go that would be worth going to? One imagines sitting in the unchanging cool and quiet, everything functioning as always, missiles tubes empty. The unseen world out there is ending, the submarine bases-as priority targets-destroyed. What now? There are plans, escape zones, all the rest, but...so what? No, the best thing is to say that it will never happen.

Personally, I have wondered how many of the subs would actually fire. If America has been obliterated, what purpose would be served by burning to death millions of bewildered Russians who have no more interest in war than do the crew of the Florida? These are difficult questions. I, too, stick with the thought that the ship is a deterrent, and therefor won't be used. The afternoon was edging toward dusk as we approached the pier at Bangor. Again I sat in the sail while the crew went through the delicate job of docking the ship. Countless small adjustments were needed.

"All ahead two-thirds."

"All stop." "Easy, easy."

To my eye, none of these instructions changed the ship's motion, but the pilot could read nuances of wake hidden to me. The huge hulk crept into her berth. Below, a hundred technicians, none of the wanting to hurt anybody, worked the machinery of continental incineration with the quiet efficiency of operating-room technicians. Somewhere out in the fathomless oceans, Soviet technicians did the same in their own launch centers and undersea board rooms. Behind us on the hump formed by the missile bay, the dark circles of the missile doors lay in outline. The wind was again turning brisk.

12 STORM SEWERS

Storm Sewers and Bottle Rockets: How We Were

I will tell you of my days as a tunnel rat.

It was, I think, 1954, not a decade removed from V-E Day. We lived in Arlington, Virginia, where my father was a mathematician designing warships for the Navy Department. It was a time of intense tranquility. After the war, people wanted prosperity, washing machines and, above all, to be left the hell alone.

The post-war economic boom was in full flood. Fathers worked, mothers stayed home, kids read Hardy Boys books by thousands and played with fifty-bottle Gilbert chemistry sets. Prosperity came in standard units. Houses were identical, comfortable, and laid out in a griddle, like those square iron warts on a waffle iron. People watched Ozzie and Harriet. Consult your paleontologist.

I was nine, a virtually instant product of my father's return from the Pacific. He had spent four years trapped on a destroyer, the USS Franks, with men who, he said, became exponentially uglier by the month. Seen in those terms, the Baby Boom wasn't surprising.

I digress. War. We were three: Mincemeat, Dukesy, and I. Mince. His parents believed him to be John Kaminsky. He was a crew-cut blond who could outspit anyone. Spitting was an art. You did it sideways, casually, as if you were really thinking about something else, perhaps 12,000 suicidal Japs storming ashore at Wake. Spitting suggested ironic defiance as you fused your last artillery rounds. Dukesy--Michele Duquez-- was a darkly handsome kid of Frog extraction. Later he joined the Foreign Legion and terrorized the Silent Quarter of Arabia.

Well, maybe he didn't, but he should have.

We played baseball, endless baseball, on the sloping plains of North Jefferson Street. Home plate was a manhole cover, first and third the bumpers of cars. On the day of The Great Discovery, the ball was an old and ratty one, coming unstitched. Flaps of horsehide hung from it like a spaniel's ears. It wasn't much of a ball. It was, however, the only ball.

Dukesy smacked a long liner that rolled into the storm sewer at the bottom of the hill.

"*Geez, lookit!*" we all hollered, because that was what you hollered in times of stress or wonder. We ran down and peered into the opening. We could see nothing.

There, in the eternal sunlight of 1954, we pondered. The ball was in the storm drain. We absolutely weren't supposed to go into storm drains. On the other hand, nobody was watching. We were boys. If you are wondering what happened, you need to get out more.

Once inside, we realized that we had to pull the manhole cover back over the hole, or else we would be caught, perhaps by someone falling on top of us. We buttoned-up, and found ourselves in that most splendid of boy things, a Fort. There was a concrete platform to sit on, and the opening at gutter level to peer out of unseen, and, below, a forbidding concrete pipe, half the height of a kid, leading into pitch dark nowhere.

And nobody else knew about it. A private world.

The entrance to that pipe was dark and yawning. It was echoey. It was musty, forbidding, and probably dangerous. Rain might come, and trap us. Scary things with teeth probably lived inside. Cave-ins were a near certainty. It would be foolish to go inside. Obviously the thing to do was get candles and explore. We did.

Above ground, mothers baked, grass grew, the sun shone. Below, in the entrails of Arlington, trickling with water, we crept through flickering darkness. A boy of ten can bend in ways that would cause early arthritis in a garter snake. We crouched in more-or-less the shape of paperclips and spraddled through the sewers, splonk, splonk, splonk. That *splonk*, the rubbery slap of sodden Keds on concrete, is known perhaps to only three people. And one of them was crushed by a falling camel in the Silent Quarter.

Probably, anyway.

Ayer's Five and Dime, the ten-cent store in the shopping center at Westover, may have wondered about the surge in sales of candles. We crawled and duck-walked and splashed our way through a widening network, finding a storm drain opening onto Washington Boulevard. We staged sandwiches there, and pea-shooters, the kind with the little bowl on top to hold lots of peas. You can't have too many peas, not when cars are whizzing by two feet away with hubcaps to shoot at. Around the Fourth of July we sent bottle-rockets slithering and ricocheting into the murky distance. We had to stop the space aliens who were attacking from the center of the earth.

If you were to look on Washington Boulevard for that storm drain, which exists to this day, you would find on the roof, written in candle smoke, the initials of our gang, "SSI." I can't tell you what they stood for, because we pledged not to. But they're there.

I was going to tell you about war.

We discovered an outflow that was beyond our supra-terranean territory, so we didn't really know where it was. A larger pipe, perhaps three feet in diameter, debouched into a grassy trench with high walls. Thereabouts older kids, perhaps fourteen, played. We snuck out, showered them with rocks, and yelled, "*Nyaa nyaa nyaa,* your mother's a queer!" We weren't sure what we meant, but it was universally held to be an insult. Then we dove into the tunnels.

The leviathans were too large to follow us. And we knew it. No drug can equal the excitement of fear devoid of danger. "Nyaa-nyaa-nyaaa! Come get us. Dare you!" *Splonksplonksplonk.*

Ah, but the Rat with Red Eyes that we found under Westover. The world may not be ready for this. We discovered a place where the round pipes gave way to a huge square drain, where we could stand up, and the water became ominously deep. Light filtered in from somewhere. There was a curious smell, like earwax. We got half-inflated inner tubes, squashed them through the smaller pipes, and floated on them a short distance to a sort of subterranean beach. It was the exit, now buried by development, to Westover.

There, crouching on the shore, was a vast Rat with red eyes. As I remember it, the beast was about the size of a St. Bernard, and probably radioactive. It whiffled its whiskers and eyed us with, we thought, carnivorous portent.

Sewer rats don't have red eyes. We agreed that this one did. We didn't go back. There are limits. Even the Foreign Legion will tell you so.

13 SUNRISE, YET

A User's Guide to the Supervision of Morn: The View from the Malecoón

Written in 2020 in Chapala, Central Mexico

Lake Chapala at sunrise never looks the same twice. Colors flame and shift. Though it is late in the season and should be chill, we do not seem to be having winter this year. The *golondrinas*, swallows, seem confused and have not migrated as early as they usually do. This year they sat in their thousands, three inches apart, on overhead cables and seemed to wonder what to do. Finally they left.

Before light we awake. The dogs, knowing that they are going for a walk, leap and twirl and bounce and make nuisances of themselves. Violeta brews coffee to rekindle the guttering flame of life. (That's poetic. Like Milton.) We attach their leashes. They jump into the back of the CRV with enthusiasm. Vi bluetoothes her phone to the car's sound system, surprisingly good, and we head out to Beethoven or Louisiana blues.

The world is another place before dawn, towns along the lakefront blank and lifeless, stop lights mindlessly changing in the absence of traffic, and existence belonging exclusively to ourselves. Lights glow in Donnas' Donas–Donna's Doughnuts–as the staff gets ready for the morning rush. A few cars wait in the parking lot of the all-night pharmacy.

The *malecón* along the water in Chapala is a wide boardwalk of patterned cement, sometimes fifty feet broad, with benches and trash cans running from the park to the end of town, much of it lit by street lights. It is not quite deserted. Early morning runners are out, and the street sweepers, and others walking their dogs. Still, there is a sense of solitude. We have become regulars and there is much *"Buenos-dias"*-ing. For a little over an hour we walk at a rapid clip, the dogs wanting to sniff everything and Charlie, a he-dog, signing trees and posts as is right. As the horizon begins to glow we often encounter Arturo, the bartender at the American Legion post, and his wife, who also walk and supervise the arrival of day.

Often in the dimness before dawn there will be a pickup truck or a couple of parked cars with music blaring and much laughter and several young standing around and drinking beer. These are *trasnochados*, "all-nighters," men and women, who have spent the night partying. Drinking in public is illegal. So are a lot of things. As long as they cause no trouble, which they don't, the powers that be somehow fail to notice them. It is a sensible arrangement.

On weekends Chapala swells with tourists from Guadalajara and stalls go up on the sidewalk paralleling the malecón, selling hats and coconut juice and purses and fried this and fried that. On Sunday night the stalls go back down and the town empties. It is as regular as a heartbeat.

There is a statue of Mikey Laure, a noted guitarist and singer born in Chapala and popular in the Sixties. On the road into town is a statue of Pepe Guize, also of Chapala, who wrote *Guadalajara, Guadalajara.* In Rosario, a town far to the northwest, there is a statue of Lola Beltrán, the queen of ranchero, in her birthplace. And in Guanajuato, a statue of Don Quixote and Sancho Panza. I think people here have their priorities straight. In statues I much prefer Sancho to some goddam general.

With coming storms, the lake has a darker face. The wind

comes up, chill and moist with droplets and there is a sense of things going on above our human paygrade. Sunrise never looks the same twice no matter how often we and the dogs inspect it.

Another statue is of Jesús Pescador. Jesus, Fisher (of men). I am not sure to what extent how many people believe what, but the Church is part of what they are and they are content with it. Many of the young are not observant, but this means only that they are not observant, not that they want to abolish their culture and history.

OK, maybe I am getting tedious, but I am an obligate inspector of sunrises. I have been advised to consider therapy for it, but I would rather have hemorrhagic tuberculosis.

Finally, dogs. La Coyota, África, and Charlie. As we used to say in Alabama, they ain't got the sense God give a crabapple, but they are good hearted beasts. Years back, Africa crept under my stepdaughter's gate as a nearly dead puppy suffering from full-body mange. Natalia being Natalia, off they went to the vet. There we learned that while few things in life live up to their billings, mange dip works like a mad sonofabitch. Africa turned into a long, low-slung pooch, apparently a cross between a Border Collie and a fire hose, and currently flourishes.

We leave, going by the market for oranges to squeeze for juice in the morning. Mexicans believe that orange juice should have departed an orange no more than an hour before breakfast. This alone is sufficient justification for living here.

Anyway, them's mornings in the Reed-Gonzalez household. I cannot doubt that people in their millions have been wondering, "What do Fred and Violeta do in the morning?" I am glad to have supplied this yearning.

14 HANT II

*What Thomas Jefferson Needed to Know, but
Didn't*

The other day I went up the holler to talk to Uncle Hant about Democracy. Hant knows everything. Well, nearly about everything.

He lives just past the creek in a double-wide with a satellite dish and his old dog Birdshot. You could call him a mountain man. He's tall and lank, like they made him by the yard and sawed off a piece, and wears this floppy slouch hat, and when he sits down he looks like a hinge folding.

For West Virginia, Hant is pretty rich. Years back he told the Feddle Gummint that he was a one-legged Injun Princess named Sighing Cloud with black lung, over ninety years old, and partners with a African American running a AIDS clinic.

Now the gummint sends him truckloads of money. He had to resurface the driveway so they could park.

Anyway, he was setting under his favorite tree with a plastic gallon of Coke and a bottle of Wild Turkey. Birdshot was lying next to him, scratching and watching squirrels. Hant's kind of slow and quiet, and doesn't get excited about much. Ain't much to get excited about in the hollers.

"Hant, explain to me about Democracy," I said.

"Ain't any."

He seemed to think that covered it. Hant's not a man of many words.

I tried again. "I don't reckon that's what that school-lady used to say. Remember her? She came from Wheeling and she went to a real college. She said democracy was the American way, and all advanced, and these old Greeks did it."

Of course, the Greeks did a lot of things you could get shot for where I live.

"Pass me that Turkey."

He did. But he didn't say anything. I wouldn't quit, though.

"She said it was noble, and these important guys like George Washington liked it so much they wouldn't do their laundry without it. She said the best thing about it was that it let the common man run the country."

That got Hant's attention. He thought a little.

"That was the best thing about it?"

"Yeah."

"What was the worst?"

Hant could be hard to talk to.

"Well, she said it was better than stewed rabbit, and how it taught us to respect the wisdom of the people, and the Average Man."

He took the bottle back. No flies on Hant.

"Boy, the average man barely got sense enough to find his way home at night. I guess we're in deeper trouble than I thought."

I got to worrying about it. About the common man, I mean. There's this show on TV about this enormous fat lady who's always doing specials on things like Dwarves with Three Heads and the Women Who Love Them Too Much, which would be at all. But what was scary was the people that came to watch. They didn't have much shape to'em, and they laughed sort of *hyuk-hyuk,* and breathed through their mouth like they been inbreeding too much. Whenever that fat lady said something uncommon stupid, they'd yell and clap and stomp their feet, and the women would shriek. I told Hant about it.

"That'd be Oprah," he said. "Did she look like five hundred pounds of bear liver in a plastic bag?"

When Birdshot heard the word "liver," he perked up like a Democrat that's discovered a unwatched treasury. I know people with less sense than Birdshot.

"There's another one of them ladies, though," said Hant, trying to remember. "Makes you think of a plaster wall with legs."

I thought about the common people I knew around Bluefield and North Fork. Nice folk, at least until after the thirteenth beer, but, being from West Virginia, they mostly had three thumbs and didn't know who the President was. On the other hand, some things it's best not to know.

Anyway, there was old Robert Weevil up the holler near Crumpler, and Mrs. Weevil, and all the little Weevils. A sociologist lady from Washington D.C. came to give them some kind of test to see how smart they were. I hear they had to put her in a rest home afterward.

I guess I was getting upset. I'd come to tell Hant how good democracy was, and he wasn't having any.

"Hant, what that school-lady said was, elections are like a town meeting, and the candidates express their ideas, and then the people choose the best one. Ain't that better than a Duke or some musty old King?"

I figured I had him now.

"Think about it, boy. 'Bout a million years ago, they had kings lying all over the place like dead cats, and nobody had much. The only way a king could get more than he was worth was to steal everything from everybody else and put it in a pile. And they still couldn't get cable. That's why they had revolutions.

People wanted to get their stuff back. They didn't care about freedom and democracy. Still don't.

"Thing is, now everbody's got a four-by-four and 500 channels on the satellite. Hell, they mostly don't even know what kind of gummint they got, long's as it doesn't outlaw beer and NASCAR on Sunday. They don't want democracy. They want to sit loose and stay dry. It's all they want."

I figured I needed to stop talking to Hang too much.

He wouldn't stop though. "Well, think about the last ten presidents," he said, and got a satisfied look on his face. Then he said, "I reckon if you went to Willy's Beer and Lube and caught the first ten people who came in, you'd do better."

He passed me the Turkey and I took a big hit. Birdshot cocked his eye at a squirrel on the ground, hunting acorns, but decided against it and went back to sleep. That old dog was comfortable. It was enough.

15 HANT III

Hant Ponders Furrin Policy: Can't Be Worse'n What We Got

'Tother day in the afternoon I went down the holler to ask Uncle Hant about this here Eye-rack. One of them blonde gals on TV that looks like they've been hit on the head or maybe drank Drano and didn't have her mind working right, if she had one, was talking about it. I didn't much understand. Hant, he knows everything. Hell, there's people in Wheeling even that don't know as much as he does.

Hant lives out in the woods and makes moonshine to sell to the yups from Washington. He says Yankees are dumber than retarded possums and it's the only way to make a living without working. He doesn't much like working.

I walked down the rail bed from Crumpler, that's a little place that used to be a coal camp before the mines died and the trains stopped coming. It was all peaceful and the bugs shrieking like they do so they can get laid and the sun pouring down like lit-up maple syrup and all the plants was so green you'd think they had batteries in them.

Sometimes I figure bugs got more sense than people do. All they care about is gal bugs and food. I'll still take my girlfriend Jiffy Lube. Sometimes she gets upset and maybe smacks somebody with a tire iron, but bugs got six legs and I don't think I could get used to that.

I turned up the cut in the bank where Hant has his still and found him pouring Clorox into the moonshine. Hant's more'n six feet tall and kinda stiff, 'cause he ain't been young since God was a pup. When he sits he sort of folds up like one of them yaller rulers that you measure things with, if you're a carpenter. He's got a face like a lantern and this hat that looks like a cow pie that the cow stepped on.

"Say, Hant," I said, by way of starting a conversation, "Tell me about this Eye-rack thing that they're always talking about on the television. They say we got a war going."

His eyes lit up and he almost dropped the Clorox jug. He said, "The South done rizz again? I *knew* it would," and he grabbed the deer rifle that he mostly keeps leaning against the cooker. Sometimes he has to shoot revenue agents. He never did like it when West Virginia joined the Feddle Gummint in the war agin cotton. He always figured West Virginia guessed wrong when the Yankees started meddling with everybody. Considering the results, I reckon he had something.

Most usually he has a jug of Beam handy. He sure ain't gonna drink that snake pizen he makes for the yups. He keeps putting stuff into his shine—brake fluid, LSD, cocaine, stove polish—to give it a kick. Mostly it kills the yups before they get back to Washington. Ain't hardly a telephone pole between Bluefield and the Yankee Capital that don't have a dent in it.

I said, "Naw, the South ain't rizz, least I don't guess so. This sort of pole-axed looking tow-headed gal said we had to drop bombs on these people in Eye-rack."

He took a hit from the Beam jug and passed it to me. His eyes got squinty and he said, "*Eye*-rack? Where the hell's that?"

I didn't know. That Beam sure was good. I sat down against a stump and said hello to Birdshot, that's Hant's old dog. Birdshot's only got three feet because he stuck a paw under a lawnmower once to see what was making all that noise. Sometimes it don't pay to wonder about things too much.

I said, "This ol' gal said Eye-rack blew up some buildings in New York."

"What's wrong with that?"

"That's what I thought you'd tell me. Gimme 'nother hit off that jug."

He passed it to me, but kept an eye on it. He knows what matters to him. Then he looked into the woods the way he does when he doesn't know the answer to something.

"Too dam' many yups coming to buy shine now. Clorox seems to give it a pretty good zing, but I'm thinking about bug spray for the next batch. How's Jiffy Lube doing?"

That's my girlfriend.

"Pretty good, I guess. Still talks about getting married, but I figure I can hide in the next county. I still want to know about this war, Hant."

"Exactly what *is* a Eye-rack?" he said.

"Best I can tell, it's someone that wears a fender-cover on his head, and his wife wears a black bag."

Hant chewed on that for a moment. I could tell it moved him. "All right. I see it now. Bombing them is a good idea. It's putting them out of their misery...It's the Christian thing to do I reckon...Figure they'd like a little shine before they go?"

"This gal said they don't drink shine."

"Must be a uncha dam' comminists," he said.

Birdshot put his head on my leg and watched a squirrel that was hunting acorns in the woods. He didn't really care. He knew he was supposed to chase squirrels, but he didn't really want one. He just watched from a sense of duty. I guessed it was like patriotism, that they kept talking about on TV. You didn't really want to kill whoever it was, leastways till you found some reasons maybe, or at least who they were, but you owed it to your country to do it anyway.

Hant pulled a Buck knife out of his pocket and started cutting on a stick. It's what he does if he's trying to figure out something that's too much for him.

Finally he said, "Well, if they don't drink shine, what do they do?"

"Mostly they blow up furriners, gal says."

"Then why don't the furriners go away? I would."

"That's what I'm asking you. You're supposed to know everything, ain't you?"

He pondered. "Yeah. But maybe that part slipped my mind a little. Sometimes it gets hard, knowing everything. I expect a little Beam would help." He took a three-gurgle hit and looked powerful satisfied.

"These Eye-racks planning on coming over here?" he said.

"Not that I know about. I mean, people with fender-covers on their head is hard to miss."

"Then I say leave'm there. Yankees is always meddling where they don't belong...Hoo, I'd sure like to see you tell Jiff she gotta wear a black bag." He gave this let's-you-and-him-fight chuckle he has when he wants to see someone else get in trouble.

"Not just now, Hant," I told him, thinking about that tire iron Jiffy Lube has. "Gimme that jug."

16 OUR VOLE

The Wind in the Willows Comes to the Reed
Household, and Is Welcome

We have voles. At least, we had a vole–or it may be that a vole had us. It is hard to tell with voles. The having and the had are separated, in the case of voles, by a point of view only.

The weather was frosty the other morning. The fire had died overnight in the stove, so I stumbled into the kitchen to start coffee, without which life is impossible in the Reed household. As I reached into the sink to fill the pot, a portion of the sponge turned black, skittered to a corner, and then hid beneath the stopper. Readers may doubt this, but I assure them that I saw it happen.

The transformation of sponges awakens my natural interest in poltergeists and fairies. I have always believed, or at least hoped, that things in kitchens might turn into interesting creatures-teapots into small dragons that would hiss in corners but get out of the way of the broom.

Anyway, the little fellow was the size of a mouse who had been on short rations. He had only the barest points of eyes, suggesting that the places he liked best were all underground, and had the longest, twitchiest pink snout, which he poked from beneath the stopper in frantic investigation. His tail was an embarrassment-a stubby and rather accidental-looking arrangement, such as one would leave at home on a Sunday walk. The beastling was shivering horribly because there was a half-inch of water in the sink and he had been unable to get out. One would expect an animal born of sponge to do rather well in water, but in fact he didn't.

I scooped him into a quart jar by way of rescue, and discovered that the scooping raised a question I hadn't fully anticipated. What does one do with a quart jar of madly scrambling-what? Clearly not a mouse, not a rat, not a mole--the forefeet were too small--not anything else of which I knew.

We decided that he was a vole, or at least that he would henceforth be a vole. To this end, we avoided looking in the dictionary so as not to be disappointed. My wife suggested that, rather than stand there forever in the manner of a zoological park, I should put him in a large clay casserole. We did, adding shredded newspaper for him to hide under and dry out in. (I know "dry out in" will offend the linguistically fastidious, but in times of crisis prepositions must fend for themselves.) I added a dog biscuit. Shortly an energetic crunching issued from the casserole. With voles, it seemed, mere panic does not get in the way of eating.

The acquiring of a foundling vole involves rather more than simple removal from the sink. Small animals are not evanescent. They last. One must do something with them. What? Throwing a scurrying furry animalcule into the snow to freeze was not something we were going to do. On the other hand, letting him go in the house did not seem the best thing. He might eat books. He might make more voles. He would almost certainly make more voles. My wife set forth to buy a cage.

Meanwhile, I dug beneath the snow for leaf mold, warmed it, and put it in the casserole. Our charge disappeared beneath it with much squeaking and crunched industriously on his dog biscuit. A sheet of quarter-inch screen weighted with a brass frog seemed to ensure his continued presence. Seemings are much to be watched.

My wife returned with an over-priced, uptown, chromed cage with an exercise wheel. It was the sterile sort of cage that would attract a vole accustomed to a high-rise with an elevator. Homey cages are not to be had nowadays. I spent an hour assembling it according to inscrutable instructions, during which I invented several new kinds of cages–cages with flaps pointing in unusual directions, cages with double walls and no roof.

Alas, our vole had left the casserole. How he did it is a mystery, although an animal that began as a sponge can doubtless do many surprising things. We sometimes see him rushing along the baseboards, attending to various errands. One such errand is the removal of beans from a stuffed duck, followed by their storage in the pocket of my armchair. Maybe he means it as a token of friendship. I suppose we will invest in a live trap to get some use out of the cage. Meanwhile, we have our vole, and he has us.

17 NEKKID IN AUSTIN

Times Now Ain't What They Was, Then

T he day carnivorous reptiles almost ate me in the skin bar in Austin was hot and breathless, with a relentless sun hanging over the city as if ready to drop. It was maybe 1971. I'd hitchhiked in from New York or maybe Minneapolis to see my friend Carol, who lived in a shack on Montopolis. Her boyfriend, a psychology student of some kind, suggested that we grab a cold beer, and several of its friends and neighbors, and grandchildren and second cousins, at a girly bar he knew.

Cold anything worked for me, though I only went to girly bars to read the articles.

The brew and view, which was on a densely trafficked main vein through town, was called the Wigwam or Tipi, or anyway one of those Indian words you live in.

The place was a certifiable western bar that could have gotten a USDA stamp: dim, smoky, with sprawling curved longhorns mounted on the wall, a cherry-red Bud sign that looked as if it meant it, and cowboys. A purple jukebox twanged about how momma done got runned over by a damn ol' train. The cowboys were big, rangy, and broad-shouldered, like Robocops in Stetsons. Texas has never quite figured out unisex. They were hootin' and hollerin' and swilling cold ones and telling lies. It was, like I said, Texas, than which it don't git no better.

Pretty soon the bartender got on the stage, which was six inches high, and said that now the "internationally known exotic dancer Kandy Pie" would entertain us. I think that was her name, though I once knew a stripper named Noodles Romanoff. You can't strip west of the Mississippi if you're named Mary Lou Hickenlooper.

Anyway, this clippity-clop music started and Kandy Pie came out wearing a horse. I guess it was plastic. It looked like she'd stolen it from a merry-go-round and had a hole where the saddle was so she could wear it around her waist. That horse was about all she was wearing.

She wasn't too exotic, but she was pretty near nekkid. I had to give her that.

Which had its appeal. Kandy Pie was a bodacious blonde who looked like a watermelon patch in Georgia, except she wasn't green. She was also on the wrong side of thirty-five. The make-up didn't hide it. She drooped where she should have perked, and had a few more pounds than she needed, and just looked tired. The cowboys didn't like it. Catcalls erupted.

They were louts, I guess, but they weren't really mean-spirited. Thing was, they hadn't paid to see an enactment of the Onslaught of Middle Age. Yeah, they should have been more gentlemanly. She should have found another line of work five years earlier. Fact is, Kandy Pie seemed to be on the receding cusp of her international career. Which probably spanned three cities in central Texas.

She clipped and clopped and the horse grinned its idiot's grin and the catcalls increased. She bore up under it, but you could see the pain in her face. It wasn't fun being laughed at for fading looks when looks were all she had. On the other hand, there's something to be said for knowing when to quit.

She clopped and bounced and hollered things like "Yippy Yi

Yay" and "Kyocera," and then pulled cap pistols and fired them in the air.

Blam!

Kandy Pie froze. I believe she thought a cowboy had shot at her. Actually a light bulb had fallen from the stage lighting and exploded.

That was all for dancing in a horse. She stepped out of ol' Trigger and just walked off the stage.

And came back with a cobra.

About two feet of cobra, gray, with hood flared. It had cold black eyes that augured nothing good and a low, empty forehead like a network anchorman. It wasn't a happy cobra.

Dead . . . silence . . . fell, thump, like a piano from a tall building. Nobody had expected a cobra. I supposed a sign somewhere averted to Kandy Pie and Her Merry Scary Animals, but I hadn't seen it, and apparently neither had the cowboys.

Kandy Pie was suddenly a different woman. Sort of goddess-like. She held that death-rope up and peered into its eyes, let it wrap around her neck, and peeled it off. A confidence had come over her, as though she were somehow in her element. Then she put the cobra on the stage. It set out toward the cowboys. Apparently it had plans for them.

Thirty chairs scraped simultaneously. Another second and those cowboys would have climbed the supporting poles and hung there like bananas. I planned to exit through the nearest wall.

Sure, I knew the beast had been defanged. So did the cowboys. Probably, anyway.

Just before that length of gray extinction left the stage, Kandy Pie put out her foot and gently pinned its tail.

"Anyone wanna hold it?" she said softly. It was a challenge. *My turn now,* she was saying.

Cowboys have their virtues, such as courage, and they really weren't bad people. In fact, they were actually pretty good people. One said, "Shore." He did hold it. You could tell he thought it was a really *fine* snake, even if it looked like Dan Rather. Others followed. Soon Kandy Pie was surrounded by masculine hunks who had decided she was quite a lady. I thought somehow of Tom Sawyer whitewashing the fence.

Turns out she was an act unto her own self. Soon she took the cobra backstage and returned with a boa constrictor. I won't tell you it was 400 feet long. I'll tell you it *looked* 400 feet long. A lot of fire trucks would have envied that thing. We all took turns draping it around our necks. About sixty pounds of it.

"Whatcha feed it?"

"Chickens."

"Live'uns?"

She smiled. "Yep."

The final act was a tarantula, big hairy orange-and-black sucker, like a yak hair pillow on stilts. Did I want it to crawl up my arm? No, but I said yes. It was a manhood issue. She put it on my wrist. Those rascals are heavy. She poked it so it would crawl. I knew it was going to bite me and carry me off to a hole to lay eggs on me. The cowboys clustered around, enthusiastic. *They* wanted a tarantula to crawl on them too.

I don't think it could have happened, except in Texas: One bearded long-haul road freak, buncha cowboys in dressy boots, large blonde in, if not the altogether, at least the mostly together, and a sprawling tarantula the size of a tennis racket. It was splendid, I tell you.

18 LANC

Conversations with Lanc, the Which There Won't Be More Of

Ages ago, for reasons of parental misjudgement, I studied at a small college in rural Virginia, Hampden-Sydney. While surprisingly rigorous, being resolutely Southern and as yet untouched by the foolishness that now degrades schools, H-S was also relentlessly preppy. The studentry tended to be vapid future bankers in small towns and pre-meds who would go to the Medical College of Virginia in Richmond. I loathed them, and they, me. At night, to escape, I walked wooded roads under the stars to smell the honeysuckle and listen to what the insects had to say.

One night I found Lanc's store. Lanc--Lancaster Brown--was an old black man, in his eighties I'd guess. At any rate he had gone to France in a labor battalion in World War I and spoke of the beer gardens and other wonders. He was pretty slow by the time I met him. His had been a long life and not always an easy one.

The store was tiny, old, worn, and unpainted, with battered glass cases of candy and bubble gum, unpainted plank floors and, in the back, a potbellied stove that always had a fire on chilly evenings. The counter had a big jar of pickled sausage, behind it a box of Moon Pies--the credentials of Southern ruralhood. A Camels poster from about 1953 was tacked to the wall. From it a full-lipped and busty honey-blonde in a cowboy hat smiled down at the world.

Lanc was alone that night, sitting on the old church pew across the back wall that served as bench when company came. I asked for a coke. He got it for me. He was not dark-skinned, more earth-colored, being about the shade of the dispirited floppy hat he habitually wore. I think he was embarrassed by being bald as an onion. With a freshman's sense of anthropological exploration I made conversation.

My grandfather, retired then, had been professor of mathematics and dean at the college. It proved a telling credential. As soon as he realized that I was Dean Reed's grandson, I became almost family. Like many people in the region, Grandpa (as I always called him) didn't like the racial situation, though he didn't know what to do about it. But when a local black woman had needed extensive dental work, Grandpa had quietly paid for it. This was not unknown to local blacks.

He wasn't at all what would today be called a liberal. He had none of the *amour propre*, not too much respect for scholarship, and believed in personal integrity. Worse, he read Latin. He just had a sense of what was right and what wasn't.

I soon got in the habit of dropping in on Lanc during my nocturnal tours of inspection. He usually sat on a broken-down chair, I on the pew. Light, what there was of it, came from a bare bulb hanging on a wire. On bitterly cold winter nights the store was warm and smelled comfortably of wood smoke and I was glad to be there. Lanc liked to roast apples or fry baloney on top of the stove. I ate vinegary sausage.

I was then known as Ricky but, mysteriously, he always called me Mickey. I supposed that oncoming deafness accounted for it. "Hey there, Mickey," he would say when I appeared, "You come on in, sit right down. Yes sir, you sit right down." He extended me credit and depended on me to keep track of the amount. I was Dean Reed's grandson. He knew I would never short him. You can bet I didn't.

We were a strange pair. I was very young, and knew nothing of life other than the small towns of Virginia and Alabama and what I had read in books. Lanc had grown up black in a countryside then more remote than it is now, a world with different rules and different people and utterly another place. And then found himself in Paris.

He would shake his head and smile bemusedly, as though still after so many years trying to understand France. Why, the beer gardens there, why you could go day or night—*day* or *night*—and the lights and how the people were dressed, and the women. In his time a black man didn't talk about white women if he was wise, and Lanc didn't much, even with Dean Reed's grandson. Still it dawned on me that he hadn't always been eighty years old, and that Paris wasn't Atlanta.

I was very young.

I couldn't talk to Lanc about much, I guess. The intricacies of differential equations and ancient victories in the Saronic Gulf were beyond him. I wasn't sure how he had learned to read. None of this seemed to matter. We discussed whatever we could, mostly Paris and the army and local lore. Occasionally blacks within walking distance came in for bread or Spam. One night a high school girl came and asked Lanc where Jimmy was.

"He out coon hunting," said Lanc.

"Two-legged or four-legged kind?" she asked, then saw me and giggled with embarrassment.

Things were not as Uncle Remus-ish as the evenings of fried baloney and Dr. Pepper might make them sound. There was real anger and hostility toward whites, but they knew better than to show it. One year I sublet a room from Ben Hairston, a black teacher at the local school. (I *really* didn't like preppy snots.) Ben was in his mid-thirties, drove an old hearse he had picked up somewhere, and had slightly screwed-up eyes from having accidentally gotten drunk with wood alcohol. He had lived all over the eastern seaboard and definitely qualified as sophisticated.

Which may be why he misjudged things. One night he told me that he was going to a party, and would I like to come? Sure. Shortly afterward we walked into the basement of a house nearby, where a dozen people were dancing. It was instantly obvious that I was not welcome. I think it surprised Ben more than it did me. Five minutes later we were gone.

The years passed. In summer the fields and woods behind the store glowed with fireflies, or lightning bugs as I will always believe they are properly called, and frogs creaked in the marsh. From time to time came the quicksilver fluting of a whippoorwill. Lanc was always be on his pew, frying his baloney. For a while he seemed eternal, and the store a place not really in the surrounding world. One year after graduation I went by and the store was closed, Lanc's house nearby locked. Dead, I suppose.

19 LIFE WITH BOB

A Weird but Instructive Interlude at Soldier of Fortune

This originally appeared in Playboy

I came into the weird mercenary vortex of Soldier of Fortune magazine when the phone rang in 1980. The voice on the other end was low and conspiratorial, the vocal cords sounding as if they had been ravaged by gargling gravel. Something in it whispered of far places and dark secrets too evil to be told.

"Hi, Fred, you asshole. I need a writer. Seventeen-five and bandages. Interested?"

I had been bumping at arm's length into Bob Brown, the eccentric Special Forces colonel who founded *SOF*, ever since the heady days of the fall of Saigon. Bored after Asia, he had started the magazine in 1975 with about $10,000 as an excuse to go to bush wars. The first press run of 8500 copies looked as if it had been mimeographed in his bathroom by poorly trained gibbons. The photos were badly enough exposed, the grammar wretched enough to give an impression of authenticity—a correct impression.

The first issue contained the famous photo of an African who had taken a 12-gauge blast just above the eyes—say "Ahhhh." Horror erupted. Across the nation, every pipe in the moral calliope began honking and blowing and, exactly as the old outlaw had expected, sales went straight up. This would become a pattern. Brown played the press like a piano.

"Hmm. Lemme think about it."

"OK. Ciao." Click.

I didn't think long. I was barely earning a living in Washington by free-lancing about the gray little men who run the world. A chance to be honestly shot seemed desirable by comparison. Life really hadn't amounted to much since Phnom Penh, and *Soldier of Fortune* had an appealing renegade reputation. What the hell; you only live once, and most people don't even do that. My wife and I packed the convertible.

Crossing the Beltway and setting sail through Maryland into West Virginia, I wondered what we were getting into—not that it really mattered as long as it was out of Washington. Was *SOF* what it purported to be? Was it really the professional journal of questionable adventurers with altered passports, of scarred men of unwholesome purpose who met in the reeking back alleys of Taipei? Of hired murderers who frequented bars in Bangkok where you could get venereal diseases unheard of since the 13th century? Or was it a clubhouse for aging soldiers trying to relive their youth? Or was it, as one fellow in Washington sniffed, "an exploitation rag catering to the down-demo extinction market?"

We crossed Kansas in the old Sixties blear-eyed, coffee-driven, unsleeping push and entered the People's Republic of Boulder, a lovely city of transplanted East Coasters who had gone West to escape the evils of Jersey and taken Jersey with them. *Soldier of Fortune* had its offices at 5735 Arapaho, in a park of egg-yolk-yellow warehouses where people made things like bowling trophies. I had expected a pile of skulls, barbed wire, a minefield or two and maybe a couple of prisoners staked to the earth to dry. Instead, I found a door with a small sign: STOP! BEFORE ENTERING, FILL OUT A CARD SAYING WHERE YOU WANT THE BODY SHIPPED. OTHERWISE, IT WILL BE

USED FOR SCIENTIFIC PURPOSES.

Must be the place, I thought.

A suspicious—and good-looking—secretary answered the buzzer lock in shorts and running shoes and took me through the warrenlike improvised offices to meet Brown. The walls were lined with pictures of commandos, guerrillas, and Foreign Legionnaires sweating over heavy machine guns in the deep Sahara. In an office, I glimpsed a short, weathered fellow who looked like Ernest Hemingway. Above him was a photo of a Vietnamese Ranger crossing a paddy, holding a severed human head by the hair.

Yeah, I thought, this is the place.

I stepped into bob's office, the Moon Room, and there he was in bush hat, camouflage shorts, and running shoes, legs propped on the desk and a T-shirt that said HAPPINESS IS A CONFIRMED KILL. The office had previously been leased by a minor aerospace firm, and the walls were covered in a mural of the surface of the moon, a crater of which formed an improbable halo above Bob's head. A pair of H&K 91s—wicked West German rifles—leaned against the wall with night sights on them.

"Fred! How the fuck are you?" he bellowed, his only way of talking. Bob is deaf—artillery ears—and seems to figure that since he can't hear himself, nobody else can, either. Actually, when he talks in his normal voice, people in Los Angeles can hear him. He is also so absent-minded that he is lucky to remember who he is. (This brings out the maternal instinct in women. As a staffer put it, "I never know whether to salute him or burp him.")

"Sit down. Listen, I want you to brief me about some things in Washington." He didn't talk so much as bark. "This is close-hold, real sensitive, but we've got some stuff out of Afghanistan that's going to blow...Washington...open."

The "stuff out of Afghanistan" lay on his desk: shattered instrumentation from a Soviet MI-24 helicopter gunship downed, if memory serves, by Hassan Galani's men and smuggled out through the Khyber Pass into Peshawar. Brown is always getting terribly important trash from odd places. A staffer once brought in an emptied Soviet PFM-1 antipersonnel mine—the butterfly-shaped kind they drop by thousands on the trails near the Pak border—by wrapping it in a plastic bag and telling Customs that it was a broken asthma inhaler. Anyhow, part of today's booty was a bright-red box, bashed up by the guerrillas in tearing it out of the wreck, with a 13-position switch labeled ominously in Russian.

"Probably the central weapons-control computer for the MI-24," Bob growled. "The intel agencies will pay a lot for this. We beat the Agency hollow on this one. Hehhehheh." Splash.

Bob splashes. He chews Skoal and spits into a water glass—sometimes, inadvertently, into other people's water glasses. You keep your hand over your coffee cup.

Why, I wondered, was this den of caricatures selling more than 170,000 magazines a month at three dollars a copy?

Popular myth notwithstanding, there aren't any mercenaries today in the accepted sense of the word: small bands of hired white men who take over backward countries and fight real, if small, wars for pay. The reason is that any nation, even a bush country consisting of only a patch of jungle and a colonel, has an army too big for mercs to handle. The pay is lousy, the world being full of bored former soldiers. Brown himself is not a mercenary but an anti-Communist Peter Pan and, for that matter, has never killed anybody (although he once shot an escaping Viet Cong in the foot.)

True, there are shadowy categories of men who might be called mercenaries, but the word is hard to pin down. Are the hit men and cocaine pilots of South America mercs? Are the Americans who joined the Rhodesian army and served with native Rhodesians? Men working under contract for the CIA?

You do find a few men such as Eugene Hasenfus, recently shot down flying cargo runs in Nicaragua. Pilots are in great demand as mercs because, while training soldiers is fairly easy, even for backward nations, flight training is hard to provide. Finding out who these men really work for is not easy: the employers tend to be curious corporations, possibly but not provably owned by intelligence agencies.

So who reads *SOF*? Marines, Rangers, and unhappy men, mostly blue-collar, who are weary of the unimportance of their lives. What the magazine sells is a hard-core smell, a dismal significance, a view of life as a jungle where the brutal stand tall against the sunset and the weak perish. *SOF* may be the only one-hand magazine whose readers hold a surplus-store bayonet in the other hand.

The magazine understands this and fosters it. The stories are mostly first-person accounts of scruffy little wars or how-to pieces on various techniques of murder but always with an undercurrent of approval and written in a low, throaty whisper as of old mercs talking shop. The classified ads in the back, for example: "Ex-Marine lieutenant requires hazardous employment overseas...." 'Merc for hire. Anything, anywhere...." "Pyro supplies." "Young man seeks apprenticeship under master spook...." "Uzi accessories." "Merc will do anything, short-term, hi risk." "Laser weapons, invisible pain-field generators...." "Ex-platoon leader, dependable, aggressive, fearless...." "Night-vision scope." "Chemical lance." "Savant for hire, an expert on weapons and demo. Prefer Central America."

Most of these ads are nonsense. A journalist who once tried answering them found that most were placed by poseurs. A few are real. Dan Gearhart, a would-be merc killed in Angola in 1976, got his job through *Soldier of Fortune*. At this writing the magazine is being sued because some mercenaries placed ads

("Gun for hire") and, apparently, were hired to kill a law student at the University of Arkansas.

They botched the job, several times. Almost all mercs who get publicity prove to be clowns. The trade is notorious for attracting neurotics and cowboys and people who think they are James Bond. Being a merc is not a reasonable way to make money. You could do better managing a Burger Chef.

The intriguing thing is the glorification of unprincipled ruthlessness, not of killing per se but of sordid, anonymous killing. The readers do not imagine themselves as knights jousting for damsels in fair fight, or as lawmen in Amarillo, facing the bad guy and saying, "Draw." They want to shoot the bad guy in the back of the head with a silenced Beretta. Brown had discovered antichivalry. There's a lot of it out there.

Yet, although the idea was brilliant, the magazine barely hangs together. Despite Brown's proven capacity for doing the impossible, as for example starting a magazine about mercenaries, he has a boundless talent for mismanagement. The staff stays in a state of turmoil and turnover, mistreats its writers and loses them, and barely gets issues to the printer, largely because Bob doesn't pay attention. He won't run the magazine himself, and won't hire a competent editor who will.

Although it may seem odd in a man who sneaks into Afghanistan the way most people go to McDonald's, he is too insecure to delegate authority yet is unwilling to stick around and exercise it himself. For example, at one point, Bob insisted on approving cover photos, but did not insist on being in the country when it was time to do the approving. Typically, everything would halt while frantic messages went out to the bush of Chad. The result made chaos seem obsessively organized.

Time and again, Bob would meet some drunk in a bar who wanted to write for *SOF*. "Oh, yeah, sure, sounds great. Send it to the editor. Terrific idea." Then he would forget to tell the editor and would go off to Thailand for a month, where-upon it would turn out that the guy couldn't write, and Brown couldn't remember what the assignment was anyway, and the editor wouldn't know what the hell was happening. Any adventurer with a good line of bull can con Bob out of airfares to distant places and live well for months at his expense until somebody finally figures out that the magazine is being taken for a ride.

Bob doesn't really read *SOF*. He once told me, "Hey, Fred, I really liked that Spectre gunship story you did. We could use some more like that." The story had been published a year before.

Bob misses appointments. He doesn't answer his mail—not surprising, because he doesn't read it. Mail requires decisions and he can't make decisions, preferring to put them off until the problems go away. Sometimes they don't. If the office were burning down, Bob would want to think about the fire for a few days before putting it out ("Yeah," he would say in that hard mercenary voice, eyeing the flames. "I don't want to be hasty. Let's kick it around in our heads for a while, see what comes out.")

As I stood looking into that crafty face pocked by shrapnel wounds, lined by many wars, some of which Bob has been to, I began to recognize the horrible truth. *SOF* is not phony exactly—the staff members really do the things they say they do—but neither is any of it exactly real. The magazine is a playground for half-assed adventurers, and Brown was having fun, that was all. I had come to work in Colonel Kangaroo's Paramilitary Theme Park: Step right up, hit the Kewpie doll with a throwing knife and win an Oriental garrote for taking out those troublesome sentries. Cotton candy at the next booth—in camouflage colors, of course—and.... That was the key to understanding *SOF*—realizing that Bob is not in the business of putting out a magazine. He is in the business of being Bob. He likes being the international mercenary publisher, likes playing Terry and the Pirates, and the magazine is merely a justification. Trying to understand *SOF* as journalism merely leads to confusion.

This explains the odd pointlessness of most of what the man does. For example, take the time he and the green creepers sneaked into Laos to see the anti-Communist brigands. In bush wars, they're all bandits, so you choose which bandits will be your bandits. It was a short trip, barely across the border. All that came out of it was photos of the rebel village with a huge satin *SOF* flag (DEATH TO TYRANTS) floating over it—silliest goddamn thing I ever saw. They really went, but it really didn't matter.

On the other hand, they have the guts to do it.

The mystery is how anyone as inept as Bob can survive while doing the things he does. In the Special Forces, he was known as Boo-Boo Brown because he couldn't get a drink of water without breaking his leg, losing his wallet, or setting off NORAD alarms. It's hard being a deaf commando with no memory. Bob once left an open bag full of cash in an airport in Bangkok—just forgot it, the way normal people forget a paperback book. Many who know him think he really needs a mother, or a keeper, and the incident suggested that he may have an invisible cosmic sponsor: The money was still there when a traveling companion went back, which is impossible in Bangkok.

He thrives on conspiracies, but most of them do not quite exist beyond the confines of his skull. I once spent three hours in a hotel suite while he and his ambient maniacs discussed some minor bit of information, so trivial that I can't remember it, whose revelation they thought would prevent the reelection of Jimmy Carter. But you can't blame Bob for not having much idea how the real world works. He has never lived there.

Neither he nor *SOF* can even begin to keep a secret, unfortunate in a man whose hobby is conspiring. I have seen him begin a plot to overthrow a scary foreign intelligence agency by inviting 13 people, including several strangers, into his office to talk about it. The magazine once taped some telephone conversations with me, neglecting to tell me that it was doing so. The editor then sent the transcripts to Thailand, where they ended up in the hands of a buddy of mine who was running cross-border operations into Laos—this was the attempt by Bo Gritz to free some POWs believed to be there. When my friend came back to the States, the FBI photocopied the transcripts. Oh, good. Bob is the Great Communicator, a sort of one-man CBS.

If, as someone said, the intelligent man adapts himself to the world, but the genius adapts the world to himself, Bob is a genius, living in a world he has built to his own specs. A fantasy world, yes, but Bob knows where reality begins and usually stops short of getting into trouble. He is crazy by choice, when it suits him—the world's oldest and most successful kid of eleven, with the kid's tribal mentality, deeply loyal to his adventuring buddies but to no one else, playing games in Uncle Bob's sandbox, which happens to be the world. I remember his lying with his head in the lap of his wise and patient girlfriend, Mary, when someone brought up the subject of railroad trains. "I've always wanted to be an engineer," Bob said, looking off into some interior distance. "Maybe I can buy a train. Can I buy a train, Mary?"

"You always want to be everything," Mary said. She understands him.

Mary stays with the old rogue (this is going to be the only real breach of confidence I will commit in this article, for which Bob is likely to have a brigade of assassins come after me) because he is a nice guy. I once asked one of his best friends, who are very few, how vicious Bob really was.

"Well, if you insulted his ancestors, poured beer on his head, and swindled him out of the magazine," the guy said thought-fully, "Bob might punch you out."

For a few days, my job was to edit the usual nutcake stories for publication, mostly human-interest stuff. There was one about how to weld razor blades to the bottom of your car so that a crowd trying to turn it over would have their fingers cut off, and another explaining three handy ways to make napalm with gasoline and simple soap flakes. Most of the staff—smart, funny people—knew the whole business was madness and en-joyed it. A few thought it was real.

The working level lunacy was plentiful. For example, glancing into red fire-extinguisher boxes, I found loaded 12-gauge riot guns with the safeties off. It seems that the SDS at the University of Colorado had threatened to storm the office, a cata-strophically bad idea. You should never storm a den of armed paranoiacs when there is no back door, especially when the paranoiacs have the firepower of a Central American army.

I heard about the SDS threat from Craig Nunn, the art director, a former Special Forces sergeant and street fighter out of Chi-cago with equal affinities for Bach and blood. To listen to the Brandenburgs, Craig always wore headphones on a long cord in the art room so that he looked like a deranged pilot flying an easel. Speaking of the attack by the SDS he said with subdued longing, the wistfulness of a man who hasn't shot anybody since lunch, "I think they should attack if they believe in it. God, hard times and body bags. I'd like that better than bubble gum."

The assault didn't take place. A local motorcycle associ-ation, allies of *SOF*, walked through campus in field dress—scars, missing teeth, gloves with fishhooks on the knuckles, I.Q.s dragging low around their ankles like skivvies at the dip. They announced that if any Commie pervert bothered *SOF*, which was a righteous and patriotic magazine, the bikers would break his arms in 14 places before getting down to detail work. One remark in particular—"Honey, you got pretty eyes. I'm gonna put 'em in my pocket"—is said to have directed revolutionary fervor into other channels.

One day I was sitting in the office with Harry, a hulking right-winger who worried a lot about the Trilateralists. Oddly enough, most of the staffers were liberals. Harry was a prop. (I divided the staff into workers and stage props, the latter being those who twitched, usually couldn't spell, and arrived in the middle of the night. The workers, mostly women, put out the magazine.) A glass wall separated the secretary from Harry's office, where he spent the day roaring and fuming like a volcano. His office was stuffed with guns, one specifically for fending off the SDS.

"Look at the bullets," he said. I did. Green plastic.

"Hollow. Filled with oil and tiny buckshot. They kill but don't penetrate glass. If a left-wing shit-head comes in and I miss him, I won't kill the secretary."

Harry was ever a gentleman.

After much negotiating, we got a Russian language expert through the university to come translate the writing in the red weapons-control computer. She was a tall, horsy lady, obviously unsettled by being in the lair of these horrible killers. We all sat around expectantly, awaiting an intelligence coup of a high order. It looked like a Big Deal. The MI-24 gunship was largely a mystery in the West. The translator picked up the red box and read, with solemn emphasis:

"In case of fire, break glass."

It was a fire-control computer, sort of. Oh, well.

Harry, the savior of secretaries, was strange, but he wasn't alone. The staff crawled with real lulus. There was Derek, a brilliant fellow who had been in a spook outfit in Nam (S.O.G., Studies and Observations Group, death-in-the-weeds people. Those in it are called Soggies.) Derek talked to Saint Michael, the patron saint of warriors, and Saint Mike answered. You would be driving along with the guy and he would be saying, "Mumblemumble, Saint Michael, mumblemumble," with his eyes rolled skyward, and you would say, "Ah, er, nice day, huh, Derek?" "Mumble...yes, quite true, thank you, we are blessed, mumble mumble, Saint Michael...." Vietnam is a hot, sunny place, and maybe there weren't enough hats to go around.

At nine P.M. at the Scottsdale Hilton Resort and Spa, under the puzzled skies of Arizona, the annual *Soldier of Fortune* convention flowed in full throbbing lunacy. The locals were upset: You could see it in their eyes. Across the city, police were alert, parents no doubt sitting up with .22 rifles and the family spaniel to guard their daughters. After all, *Soldier of Fortune* reeked of mutilated bodies in Oriental hotel rooms. It was the trade journal of lurching men with knife scars across their faces and faint German accents. One expected terrible things from it.

And got them. Sort of.

On the parking lot, lit by strategically placed headlights, several hundred conventioneers in jungle cammies gathered to watch Dave Miller, a tiny, fierce martial artist, pull a pick-up truck by a line tied to spikes through his biceps. The conventioneers, by and large, were the biggest collection of hopeless dingdongs to trouble this weary earth—twerps, grocery clerks with weak egos, various human hamsters come to look deadly in jump boots, remember wars they weren't in and, for a weekend, be of one blood with Sergeant Rock and his Merry Psychos.

On the tarmac was a cluster of shave-headed Huns, martial dwarfs, and minor assassins—the staff. The hamsters watched, agog. The conductor of this mad symphony was John Donovan, a muscular 270-pound skin-headed ex-Special Forces major who, it was rumored, manually broke up motorcycle gangs for a hobby. Miller stood with his arms upraised for the spikes, which were actually sharpened bicycle spokes. Nobody asked why he was going to do this. It would have been a hard question to answer. The crowd wanted deeds of desperation and sordid grit, not intelligence. An Oriental guy—of course—swabbed Miller's arms with alcohol.

That afternoon, I had gone with Dave to get the necessary paraphernalia. Dave was the kind of little man who figured that if he couldn't be big, he could be bad and went at it systematically: the Army, Ranger School, Pathfinder School, Vietnam, a dozen martial arts with names like Korean breakfast cereals, knife fighting, all the trinkets. *SOF* attracts large, tottery egos. Dave and I got along. He explained that you couldn't use rope to pull the truck because it stretched, and somehow tore the muscles. You needed fabric. So we sent to a fabric boutique, where the nicest young man, appalled, asked, "What do you gentlemen need?"

Counseling, I thought.

There we were, in worn tiger stripes and jungle boots, bush-hatted, with vicious specialty knives hanging on our hips, all sorts of commando badges and paramilitary nonsense stuck to us. We looked like stamp collections.

"We'd like to see some cloth."

He brought us a hank, or whatever you call it, of lavender-flowered stuff, whereupon Dave told me to hold one end and, unrolling 20 feet, began violently pulling on the other end like a frantic badger to see whether it would stretch. The nice young man nearly went crazy.

Back on the parking lot, the Oriental pushed two bicycle spokes through Dave's flesh ("Oooooh! Ooooooh!" moaned the hamsters) and connected the cloth to the bumper. Meanwhile, a twist had been added. The truck was on boards like rails so that it would roll across some guy's stomach to show how tough he was.

Miller went *"Unngh!...Unngh!"* and pulled like hell. The truck...yes...no...yes...rolled slowly onto the guy's stomach and stopped there. Miller had guts but no mass. The guy under the truck was real unhappy. Nobody had said anything about parking the goddam thing on him. He hollered in a rising scream, *"Oaaghgettitoffgetitoffgetitoff!"* and Miller tried (*"Ungh! Ungh!"*) Nothing.

Donovan the Man Mountain walked over, gave the tail gate a little tap and the truck shot off the guy like a squeezed watermelon seed.

Not everyone took this stuff seriously. At the first convention, in Columbia, Missouri, I and the usual bunch of camouflaged impostors had walked downtown one night in search of a bar. A college girl, not too impressed, asked, "Why are you wearing that silly stuff?"

"It's camouflage," I said, "so we'll be invisible."

"Oh," she said. "I thought you were a potted plant."

One day I went to work and saw someone looking at a peculiar piece of wreckage. More stuff from Uncle Daffy's Used Helicopter Lot? No. It was a Nikon, shattered in a way that didn't make obvious sense. A piece of leather had been driven into the lens barrel and stopped where the mirror usually is.

Brown had gone to Rhodesia and left his camera bag in a shop, which you don't do in times of terrorism. The shopkeeper, reasonably enough, had called the bomb squad. Those gentlemen had tied a long rope to the strap, pulled the bag carefully into the street, wrapped it in det cord—TNT rope, sort of—and blown hell out of Bob's camera. He now owned the only Nikon in the world with the case on the inside.

For a while, Brown espoused survivalism. Survivalists are the folk who dream of burrowing into Utah with radiation suits and submachine guns, awaiting nuclear holocaust. The do not so much fear an atomic war as hope for one, so that they can Survive It, making them the only people on earth with a vested interest in nuclear war. There are entire colonies of these squirrels out West, filling their basements with beans packed in carbon dioxide and arming themselves.

Brown briefly put out a magazine called *Survive*, which didn't. It folded partly because of amateurish management and partly because survivalists are too paranoid to let their addresses go on a mailing list. *Survive* croaked early, remembered chiefly for its cover photo of a cow in a gas mask.

Anyway, Bob decided to build a survival shelter. He duly found some land and had a phenomenally expensive bunker started. He did this with his patented tight secrecy, which meant that everybody in Boulder was talking about it—except to Bob, because people knew he wanted it to be secret. He began choosing people who would go into it and survive while everybody else bubbled into grease and flowed away in the gutters. He approached those elect (I wasn't one) and said approximately, "Are you saved?" Then he told them about Bob's Box. Someone calculated that six times as many were saved as would fit into the shelter.

Unfortunately, it seems that the floor had been badly poured. Water leaked in. And it turned out that the water was alkaline. Bob was the only survivalist in America whose survival shelter contained six inches of poisoned water.

Colonel Kangaroo and his madmen were once playing war in El Salvador. (War in Central America is great for *Soldier of Fortune* because there isn't any jet lag.) They were out drinking one night with one of the Salvadoran battalions, and things were getting woozy and intimate. *SOF* wasn't viewed as foreign press; it was part of the war effort, so its reporters got to go places that other reporters never saw. So pretty soon it was *amigo* this and *amigo* that, with all the intense comradeship of a war zone, and the wiry brown captain said to someone whom I will call Bosworth, "Come, *amigo,* I show you something very dear."

The captain proudly flung open a long blue cabinet, revealing row after row of preserved skulls. It seemed that the battalion contained a lot of Indians who hadn't lost their folkways —taking heads, for example. The captain grinned like a child showing his rock collection. Bosworth was charmed: This was the kind of thing he could appreciate. Why, the skulls even had painted on them the names of their former occupants. "Wonderful!" Bosworth said, warmth overwelling him.

"You like?" said the captain. "I give you!" Whereupon he handed Bosworth a pair of gaping beauties.

So Bosworth went back to the party holding Pancho and Jose in his hands and announced that he was not to be parted from the skulls. He meant to go through life with them. Brown, no fool, stared with an "Oh, shit" _expression, foreseeing problems in the afterlife. Customs, for example. ("These? Oh, I found them. No, nobody was in them.") How do you get human skulls into the US?

Finally someone came up with an idea. They mailed them to Bosworth with a note, "This is what happens to you if you come back to our country. "¡Viva la revolución! Partido Comunista."

I once went to Powder Springs, Georgia, to cover Mitch WerBell's Cobray school of counterterrorism for the magazine. WerBell, who died in 1983, was a legend in the mercenary racket, a veteran of obscure wars back when there really were mercenaries, and he had retired to a small palatial mansion.

Cobray purported to teach the death-dealing arts to professionals (who, in fact, would already know them.) For several thousand dollars, the student got a week or so of training in the arcana of the new antichivalry. The instructors—I got to know them—were real, but the courses weren't quite, which didn't matter at all to the students. In the morning, they got Introduction to Small Arms ("The bullet comes out of this little hole here. Point it somewhere else.") In the afternoon, they got Advanced Small Arms and Sniping. Subjects like these take months of study.

So I landed and was met by a former S.F. colonel and went to watch the classes. Among the students were a podiatrist from Miami, God help us, and his wife and two bratty teenagers.

I saw what had happened. Too many years of serenity and other people's feet had gotten to him. He, like the readers, wanted a taste of dark, adrenal-soaked desperation before arthritis set in—his quarter hour with mortar flares flickering in low-lying clouds like the face of God and the nervous click of safeties coming off along the wire, *pokketa pokketa*. So here he was, $12,000 poorer, with a tolerant wife and bored kids in Calvin Klein jeans, learning Night Patrolling. Women put up with a lot.

When I got there, Footman and the Powder Puffs had already studied Hand-to-Hand Death Dealing. The instructor, Marvin Tao, had told Footman that he had an unusually good radish position, or some such Oriental sounding thing. This consisted of standing sort of knock-kneed and pigeon-toed, while turning the palms out and bending forward. Marvin couldn't have been serious. Anyway, Footman was charmed, because here was something he could do. A genuine Martial Artist from Hong Kong said so. So every time I turned around, there he was—bent over, pigeon-toed and grunting dangerously.

All this yo-yo needs, I thought, is a string.

Three a.m. at the convention in Scottsdale. Most of the conventioneers had turned in. Brown and a few cronies sat by the blue glow of the pool, drinking and telling war stories. "Remember that hooker with three thumbs in Siem Riep?...." "So Barrow stood on a moving tank at Pleiku and shot at a dog with an AK. Fell on his head, tried to get disability..." "What ever happened to Jag Morris? I heard he got it in the head north of Au Phuc Dup...." Adventurers at least have stories to tell.

Green smoke was pouring out of one window and somebody was getting ready to rappel from another. I said, "To hell with it," and turned in. A muffled thumping meant the Brown was firing his .45 underwater.

A bit later, I woke up. Derek was handing me an FN rifle. "Found it," he said, and walked off, talking to Saint Michael. I curled around it and went to sleep. It made as much sense as anything.

20 TALKING WITH HANT IV

Hant Defends West Virginia: Terror in the Backwoods

I reckon it was nine in the morning and my girlfriend Jiffy Lube ran out to hide from the sheriff again. The day was slow and lazy as a coon dog on a porch. I figured I'd go down the holler and see Uncle Hant and get drunk. I mean, it was Saturday.

I walked down the old rail cut, mostly weeds since the mines closed in West Virginia. There was bugs flying around and making a racket and clouds way up in the sky, just hanging there. It was the kind of day when you don't want to do nothing. 'Course, that's how I look at most days.

Hant has his still in the woods up a ways from the old tipple that's rusting away now that there ain't no work. He's the biggest moonshiner in five counties. He sells busthead to yups from Washington who want a moonshine experience. If he has any left over, he gives it to the funeral parlor in Bluefield for embalming fluid. If he doesn't have enough, the funeral parlor gives him embalming fluid to sell to the yups. It's just how people are in the hollers. Friendly.

I turned into the woods past the big rock where I used to come with Jiffy Lube. It's because she's real...well, friendly. Her name's really Jennifer Imidazole Fergweiler, but everybody calls her Jiffy. She hadn't come out in sight for two weeks. She was at LouBob's pool hall when some feller got smart with her and she laid him out with a pool stick and ran like hell so he couldn't testify against her when he came out of the coma. The sheriff said the statue of limitations was about two weeks and then she could come back. I don't guess it matters 'cause the victim still ain't talking.

Anyways, Hant. The old scoundrel was standing next to the cooker, emptying a bag into it. He's tall and scrawny with a jaw like a front-end loader that needs a shave and when he sits down he kind of folds up in sections. He don't really exist. He's a Literary Apparition. West Virginia's full of them. Some folks say they come out of the old mine shafts.

"What you dumping in that brawl starter this time?" I asked.

"Mothballs." He looked real close into the cooker and started stirring it with a stick. He don't always say too much. I knowed why he was doing it. He likes to give that death juice of his a little extra kick for the yups. He's tried brake fluid, wood alcohol, rust dissolver, everything.

"Oh. I bet you got a jug of Beam somewheres. You got that crafty look about you. Gimme a hit. You hear the Feddle Gummint's done put in a six million dollar A-bomb finder at Lou Bob's?"

They did, too. I saw it. This eighteen-wheeler came in from Washington and they put up this thing that looked like a big door you had to walk through to go into Lou Bob's Beer, Bait, and Tackle. I didn't see why. The door Lou Bob had seemed to work just fine. These three men that wore blue suits and had one ear plug, 'cause I guess they couldn't afford both, looked at everybody. I got tired of it so I went around back and used the other door.

"Yeah? What they do that for?" He reached under a log and pulled out a bottle of Beam. He don't drink them bobcat squeezin's he makes. He may be a apparition, but he ain't a damn fool. I took a three-gurgle hit and felt better.

"So nobody could blow up North Fork with a A-bomb. I never thought of that."

He was nursing so hard on the Beam that I thought he wasn't listening. But he was.

I said, "Crazy Ray Wiggens come in wearing that radium watch he got in the army in Germany and all these horns blew and they took him off to jail."

Hant thought for a bit and said, "That's just good sense. A radium watch ain't nothing but a arpeggio A-bomb." Then he looked smug.

"Dammit, Hant, you're getting out of character again."

"Oh hell. It ain't as easy as it looks, being a Literary Apparition. Gimme back that jug."

"This blonde gal on TV that sounded like something had hit her upside the head said as how the Feddle Gummint's gonna drop bombs on Eye Ran. It's so they can't blow up North Fork with a A-bomb."

"How they gonna do that if LouBob's got that bomb-finder thing? It don't make sense to bomb'em. Better to sell'em bust-head."

Hant's always thinking.

"Can't, I reckon. The blonde gal says they're all tee-total. It's their religion, she said. I guess they're Pentecosts or something."

Hant looked up like he'd just got the horrors.

"Don't drink?"

"Naw. That's what she said, anyway."

"Well, hell. Let's bomb'em."

"That's what I figure. It just ain't American."

He grabbed a one-gallon stone jug from a crate of them and started filling it from the still. He sells all his death sweat in authentic mountain stone jars that he gets from China. He says a yup will drink battery acid if you put it in a stone jug. He knows 'cause he tried it once, but he said it wasn't good for repeat business.

I tried to get him back to A-bombs and all. Hant knows nearly about everything, but sometimes you gotta pry it out of him.

"Hant, I was watching TV at Lou Bob's and one of them blonde gals that looks like their brain needs a hotter cam was running on. She said the Feddle Gummint's gonna make bars all get A-bomb finders. How's that gonna work? Then everybody'll have to go in by the back door."

"How much you said a A-bomb finder goes for?"

"This blonde gal said six million dollars."

He thought a moment. "I'm in the wrong business. How do you make a A-bomb finder?"

"Damned if I know, Hant. I guess you get a box and somebody sits in it and peeks out till he sees a radium watch, and then he blows a horn. That's how it works at Lou Bob's."

Hant got a shifty look to him. For a minute he didn't say anything. "Reckon Jiffy Lube would sit in the box when the sheriff was after her?"

I said sure, if you fed her beer through a hole in the box, and that's how Hant got in the A-bomb business. He started buying boxes. Pretty soon there won't be a radium watch in West Virginia, I guess.

21 THE THUMBING YEARS

I Wouldn't Trade Them for a New Corvette.
Probably.

The big roads were safe then, or we thought they were. Many of us, the more adventurous, poured onto the highways, just going, moving, looking. We were devotees of the long-haul thumb, crossing and recrossing the continent, dropping into Mexico, whatever.

A camaraderie held. There were rules. On an onramp it was first come first served, no butting in line and anybody with his thumb out was taken as a friend, or at least friendly. "Hey, man, got any shit?" was a common question. This meant grass, pot, ganja, herb, and good manners was to share.

A theme of the age was that "Dope will get you through times of no money better than money will get you through times of no dope." This makes more sense than might seem today.

It was wild to be alone in the sun and clarity of the southwestern deserts, trucks howling by, a blast of wind and whining of tires, and it was just you and the whole desert stretching in sand and cactus to the horizon. You might end up sleeping in an arroyo and if there was a gas station in sight there might be a bottle of Triple Jack.

The song that caught the era was Born to be Wild, Steppenwolf, and at my local biker bar in Mexico it still produces an electric shiver and a sadness for things gone. Someone once said, "The symphony ain't been wrote that matches the lope of a Harley, *potatopotatopotato.*" Could be.

There were black holes that you could hitch into but not out of, where despite traffic or the lack of it you could spend days without getting a ride. One was in Canada–I swear it was called Wa Wa or something like that–that had a buddy of mine and I contemplating homesteading. On an obscure onramp in California someone had carved into the post of a stop sign, "Day 13. We killed John yesterday and ate him."

Once in Berkeley, on Telegraph Road, Hill, Avenue, or whatever it is, a friend, a depressive Irishman, was in a phone booth calling back East. The connection was bad. "Plattsburgh. No, Platts–no, P as in psilocybin...." She understood him. Such were the times.

One afternoon after crossing the continent from DC my ride dropped me on the Riverside exit in California. I was looking for my friend Jimmy Auld, who later killed himself by swimming out into the Rappahannock River at two a.m. in mid-January. But that's another story. The day was sunny and I felt good after a long haul and in the distance I heard Carmina Burana.

That would be Jimmy. He was a music freak and had a Fisher tube-amp that he managed to carry with him everywhere.

So I reached the house on the main vein through town and there in the living room was Jimmy sitting on one of maybe five pink porcelain toilets, connected to nothing. Just there, in a sort of ring. I asked him why toilets.

"I stole them," he said, clearly thinking this a reasonable explanation. It seemed he had worked in a hardware store.

"Oh," I said. "But why toilets?"

"They watched everything else."

It made as much sense as anything else in those years. It was an age of hunting and gathering.

One thing we all noticed on the road: The less a car cost, the more likely it was to pick you up. Caddies? Forget it. Thing was, people in old cars had probably been down on their luck. They knew what it was. So they pulled over. A crumbling ten-year-old pickup covered in Bondo and pop-rivets would usually stop.

Another thing we noticed was that in the South people were friendlier and more charitable. As you went from DC south, there was a sort of social thermocline at Fredericksburg, a sharp increase in warmth and courtesy. . You could feel that you somehow belonged in Fredericksburg. In the north, you were always just passing through, and usually under suspicion.

I once got dropped off in Boone, North Carolina, almost dead broke. Mountains loomed green and gorgeous and the towns thereabouts had the feel fn having been there since at least the Civil War. I went into a local eatery, Dixie Lee's of something with Dixie in its name I think, to spend my last buck on a coke. The owner could sort of see what was going on and she gave me a burger on the house and offered to let me wash dishes until I found something better. A construction worker, hearing this, put me up on his floor if I needed it. I did.

A lot of kids, late teens, early twenties, were in Brownian motions then, drifting from coast to coast, city to city. Since we seldom had anywhere to stay while in transit, we learned to forage for accommodation. One insight was that if you go ten feet off the sidewalks even in a crowded city, and lie down in tall grass, you no longer exist. In Waverly, New Jersey, hoping for a train south, I spend several nights in a clump of bushes not a yard from a sidewalk and maybe fifty feet from a Puerto Rican bar. Nobody Noticed.

One summer night in one year or another a friend and I–it was Jimmy Auld–had climbed into the Pot Yards–the Potomac

Yards in Virginia just outside of DC–planning to hop a freight to New York. I say climbed: The yards were protected by one of those nine-feet-high chain-link fences with the Y-shaped out-leading barbed wire.

Why these are thought to provide security, I don't know. A wiry stripling jumps as high as he can and grabs the fence. The gaps provide a toe-hold. He then tests the outleaning Y-piece to be sure it will hold his weight, very carefully throws a leg over, and the other, leaving him inside the Y, and reverses the process down the other side. This might take thirty seconds.

The only sounds were the diesel yowl and the shuddering *clangsbangbang* of couples hitting each other.

Anyway, we hid under some bushes at the edge of the yards and watched the yard mules making a train to head north, where we wanted to go. The yard crews didn't really care if you hopped trains, but it was better not to make them decide.

We heard but couldn't see someone approaching. It was an old black guy–both "old" and "black" were obvious from his voice–with a couple of gallon jugs of water. We said hey, what's up, nice night. Once it is clear that no one is threatening anyone, people in such circumstance feel pretty much at home with each other, or close enough.

It turned out that he had nowhere to live and was staying in a shelter of some sort that he had put together out of sight and had to go for drinking water. A hell of a way to end your life. Then as now America was killing large numbers of people in foreign countries and then, as now, I wondered why they couldn't give this old fellow a few C-rations. He gave us some hints as to which trains stopped where. We said goodbye and he walked slowly away with his water. I don't think his joints worked too well. The diesels were still howling as mournfully as ever.

There was then in Austin a sort of outdoor beerhall called the Armadillo World Headquarters where various bands played, such as the Greezy Wheels. Austin was where corn-fed blond guys and gals met Haight Ashbury and engaged in joyous syncretism. The presence of the University of Texas did nothing to inhibit this. The result was a rich country-music scene fueled by forbidden substances. At places with names like the Soap Creek Saloon, with girls danced on the tables for the sheer fun of it while a beer-drinking contest raged about them A deeply conservative Texas was properly horrified.

At the Dillo, as it was called, as in Alice's Restaurant, you could get anything you wanted. The freaks would holler, "Waiter, LSD," and it would come in mugs.

Lone Star Draft

Today the roads are empty. I'm glad they weren't when they weren't.

22 GRAND CANYON

Down and Up Again: Three Maniacs and Four
Days in the Grand Canyon

L
ast September a couple of college buddies and I walked
across the Grand Canyon, from the North Rim to the
South. It was one of those trips we were always going
to make, sometime, but hadn't. Planning had been elaborate.
The Park Service wisely limits foot traffic, requiring permits
that must be gotten far in advance. It's a nuisance, but keeps
Disney out. Rob and I flew into Denver, where Dan lives, and
drove the rest of the way.

The open road was a relief. The flight out had not been pleasant. The country was in the grip of its new institutionalized
fear. The security police were being themselves. I had thought
to bring a book on the Wahabis to read on the flight, but had
imagined a security apparatchik deciding he had found a ter-
rorist. I left it at home.

On the far side of the Rockies the land flattened out and lost
the excessively lived-in appearance that begins to make Colorado look like the East. I realized that I hadn't crossed the
deserts since I had hitchhiked them in the Sixties. Much had
changed since then, and more since I had first seen the big
empty lands while crossing the continent at age six with my
parents. The deserts were still appallingly large despite the
intrusion of the Interstates. Towns, though, were giving way
to the homogenization and franchised conformity that cause
any part of America to look like any other. The West remains

magnificent territory.

The Canyon was the same glowing caldron of reds and dusky purple that I remembered from earlier trips, changing shades and hues with the dying sunlight. It is probably impossible to take a bad picture of the Canyon. At the North Rim we checked into the lodge, ate, and hit the sack, suspecting that four a.m. would come early. It did. We saddled up in chilly darkness, had breakfast, and hoofed it toward the trail head. The last day would be a climb of 5000 vertical feet, so we kept our packs light at about thirty pounds.

Going down, you don't see the Canyon. The trail descends through a narrow side-canyon, a crevice, so that you find yourself traversing vast walls that loom above and fall away to depths that an acrophobe would not want to contemplate. The rock face varies from green to tan to brown, weathered by thousands of years of wind and rain. You walk for hours in a huge shaded silence. The thought inevitably comes that you are in the presence of something above your pay-grade. The Canyon was old when whatever partial molar and fragment of jawbone, thought to be our ancestor, was gnawing bones in the perplexity of too much skull and not enough content. It will be around when we are long gone. I doubt that we will be missed.

In my wandering years I passed through the South Rim, I forget just when or why. Hitchhiking by its nature is anecdotal: You remember people and places, but not how they are connected. At a place on the rim that did not seem much traveled, I climbed down a face that was exposed enough that I probably shouldn't have done it. Falls tend to be long in the Canyon. In the rock face I found a small chamber, hollowed out I thought by hands. It was deep enough to escape both weather and detection, and did not look natural.

I sat in it for some time and surveyed the Canyon, which wasn't doing anything. Since then I have wondered whether anyone else had been there since some Indian, for whatever reason, had sat where I was sitting, and watched for...what?

We continued down. A cold stream ran along the trail much of the way, tumbling and splashing and seeming to enjoy itself mightily. When the urge hit we sat in it, buck nekkid if we chose, until the heat of the trail had dissipated. If life gets better, I'm unaware of it.

The lodge and campground of Phantom Ranch at the bottom were, like everything in the Canyon, well run and full of good people. Long-haul backpackers are extraordinarily convivial and decent. I don't know why. They seem to have a better idea than do most of what is important to them. Those who solo hike the 2000 miles of the Appalachian Trail, as several of these had, tend to be self-contained and able to fend for themselves. We ran into a couple of Chinese nurses from San Francisco and an Australian gal and her boyfriend to pal around with. They confirmed me in my liking for both Chinese and Australians.

We were booked for two nights at Phantom. The next morning Rob and I did a twelve-miler up the Kaibab Trail, across the plateau on the Tonto, and down Bright Angel. The climbout the next day would be a serious day's walking. We wanted our legs to be ready for it. Besides, we were crazy. For hours we went across rolling empty pink country, immense, pocked with blue-gray vegetation like frozen mortar bursts. A shriveled creek provided water and shade for lunch. Except for us and one idiot who had gotten lost–you can die in the desert— the world was deserted.

I decided that if God hadn't created the Canyon, he missed a good chance.

Next day to be on the safe side we began the climb out at first light. Rob and I had a long history of week-long up-and-down hikes through the mountains of the East, with substantially heavier packs, but this was going to be pure, steady, serious as-cent. We wanted to get the jump on it. The store on the South Rim carried a book called something like *Death in the Canyon,* of which there are some. I'm told that most involve out-of-shape people who proceed to cash in because of heart attacks and heat stroke. Still, it is wise to respect the geography.

It was a hump, but not a killer. A major help were Leki poles, now almost universal in the back country. Their virtues are hard to quantify, but they improve balance, avoided twisted ankles, and shift muscular effort to your shoulders. You go faster. As we ascended above the level of the plateau, we found ourselves on endless sunny switchbacks overlooking the whole gaudy basin. The walls of the Canyon have well-marked strata. You measure your progress by which of them you have put below you.

It was a splendid trip. If you have the chance, do it.

23 ROAD STORIES

The Weirdness of it All: Tales from the American Road

Times were strange in 1969. Dan and I had just hitchhiked from Thunder Bay in Canada into the main vein of Berkeley. The early afternoon sun was hot and heat shimmered off parked cars in little squiggles. He had a backpack and I had a duffel bag, containing our lives. We had no idea where we were going. In those days it didn't seem to matter.

Dan was a morose Celt who had graduated from college and the Air Force about the time I had finished the Marines. We weren't hippies exactly, but the brooding dissatisfaction of the age lay heavily on us. We'd talked semi-seriously in dorm rooms of paddling into the Okerfenokee Swamp to build a cabin on a hummock and live on tomatoes and watermelons. Trouble was, girls weren't nearly crazy enough to live on tomatoes in a swamp. Anyway the mosquitoes were known to carry off dogs.

The reef life of the Sixties pattered barefoot through the streets of Berkeley. There were student Marxists who had confused their parents with capitalism and were enraged to the gills, and sunburned patriarchs of twenty just in from desert communes, and mind-burnt acid freaks packaging brain damage as mystical insight. Some Hare Krishnas pranced with tambourines in orange sheets and shower shoes from Dart Drug. Peace, brother, jingle-bang. Oh, and your spare change.

Never forget your spare change.

Dan was in a phone booth calling someone in Plattsburg. The connection was bad. I heard him say to the operator, "Platts... no, *Platts*...no, "p" as in psilocybin...."

She understood. Things were different in 1969.

Odd things stick in your mind on the road. The high point of the trip had come for me when some librarian-looking lady in a drugstore in Hannibal, Missouri had watched Dan leafing through *Playboy.* "I think you need a sexual outlet," she sniffed. It was a racy remark for Hannibal. "I've got an outlet," said Dan. "I need a receptacle." Never cross swords with a depressive Irishman.

The roads were strange too. There were places you could hitchhike into but not out of, like black holes. Nobody understood them. One was a place in Canada, called something like Wa Wa, where fifty freaks stayed beside the road for days and couldn't get a ride. The rumor was that some of them had started families.

That night Dan and I found ourselves at a lonely freeway exit curving into nothing a few miles from some Spanish-sounding town–Los Frenes, El Volante, whatever. Traffic died. Nothing moved. The freeway stretched into the night and the quiet was deathly except for the keening of bugs.

We knew we were doomed. In two hours, no car passed. The exit was set between high grassy banks speckled with dispirited trees. Light came from one of those mercury-vapor lamps that made flesh look green and a week dead. High school students used to avoid them because they made acne turn purple.

It was boring. We read the back of the stop sign, where other practitioners of the long-haul thumb had scrawled their sorrows. Little tick marks counted the rideless hours. Five, seven, thirteen. Somebody had written, "Bob died. We buried him under the lindens." I think it was lindens. Anyway, one of those vegetable-sounding words that mean trees. Somebody had written below, "We killed Chris, and ate him." They probably didn't really.

The hours crawled on like picnic ants. The night grew cooler. We weren't worried. All we had to do was lie down out of sight and go to sleep. A lasting insight of the Sixties was that if you get twenty feet off the nearest sidewalk and lie down out of sight, nobody will know you exist. Little specks of mica glinted from the concrete. I started thinking they might be lost cities in a science fiction novel, beaming lights upward to signal for rescue. I probably needed my head examined. You can get stir crazy in a black hole.

Dan reached into a cranny in his pack I didn't know was there and pulled out a pint of Jim Beam. "The bar is open," he said. Some men rise to greatness in time of need. We retired to some high grass for the rest of the night. Today we'd be too dignified. I knew we'd never get off that ramp. Ever. Dan wanted to get up the next morning and move in, build a cabin of clay and wattles made. Trouble was, we didn't know what a wattle was.

I don't know how long we lay there, telling tales. The Sixties were an age for tales. I remember telling Dan about the time I thumbed into Riverside to see our friend Jimmy, a musically gifted oddball I used to hop freight trains with along the eastern seaboard. Jimmy was nuts.

Anyway, I'd walked up whatever the main street was. Riverside was a generic pseudo-Spanish Levittown like every freeway stop in California. I was carrying a duffel bag, and began to hear crazy Wehrmacht music from a frame house a block ahead. It was Carmina Burana, and loud. You probably could have heard it on the Mexican border.

In the living room Jimmy was sitting on a section of tree stump. He looked exactly like Rasputin. The walls were plastered with detergent boxes in garish colors. (*"Tide! Bold! Dash!"* What it said about advertising's conception of the housewifely libido, I wasn't sure.) Gilded coil springs dangled from the ceiling. There were six pink porcelain toilets, attached to nothing, in a ring in the middle of the floor.

I asked, "What the hell are these?"

"Toilets."

"I got that far. Why toilets?"

"I stole 'em from a hardware store I work at. "

"Ah. But why toilets?"

"They watch everything else."

Somehow it seemed to make sense. It was 1969.

Anyway, Dan and I actually got out the next morning. An orange pickup with an ardent Marxist stopped and we agreed for a couple of hundred miles that that the dictatorship of the proletariat was at hand, as I've since decided it actually was. Watch any daytime talk show. But we didn't die there on the sidewalk.

24 NIGHT TRAIN

Playing with Extinction

August of '70 was waning when Jimmy Auld and I decided to hop a freight train to New York* The idea was
a bad one. My best ideas always are. Good ideas, I have
found, are overrated. We were nineteen, dumber than dead
owls, and didn't know squat about trains or, for that matter,
life. We hadn't been there yet.

We went to the Pot Yards-the Potomac Rail Yards in suburban Alexandria, Virginia, northern terminus for the old Richmond, Fredericksburg, and Potomac, now closed-and looked
through a high chain-link fence. It was getting dark.

I was a skinny country kid with a crazy streak and a paranoid
delusion that I was secretly Jack Kerouac. I may have been
right. Jimmy was a head case. He had been valedictorian at
King George High, where we had been rivals for Alpha Wise-
Ass. He would kill himself eight years later by swimming into
the Rappahannock River at midnight in January. Between he
had a few productive years of transcontinental hitchhiking,
motorcycling across the Western deserts, indulging a gargan-
tuan appetite for drugs, and discovering late in life that he was
homosexual.

I know, I know. But the times were different then.

After dark we went over the fence. The Y of barbed wire at
the top of fences was easy if you knew how. On the other side,
box cars and gondolas loomed against the light pollution of

nearby Washington. The yard smelled of creosote and insulation. We fell prey to an exhilarating sense of being where we weren't supposed to be.

We sat in a patch of shadow and wondered what to do next. It's one thing to want an adventure, another to know how to have it. Fog rolled in from somewhere and put halos around lights. The night cooled in the coming autumn. A yard mule howled and *wheedle-wheedled* in the drifting mist, big diesels surging as it moved cars around. The mass and raw power exalted us. All good, but how did you actually hop a train?

Cinders crunched. An old black man was walking along the tracks with a plastic jug of water. We chatted. I forget his story. He was down on his luck and living in an abandoned building, I think. He didn't know what trains were going north. Ask the yard crew, he said; they'd help us. And they did. People in the low demographics will give you a huss. They know the need.

He said goodbye and walked down the tracks.

Jimmy got up his nerve to ask a yard guy who approached with a flashlight. He pointed to a line of cars and said, "That one. She's going to New York City."

We chose a boxcar with that for whatever reason had cardboard on the floor and a door open just enough to let us slip in. It was stupid. If someone had closed the door we could have died of thirst before anyone found us.

Then, nothing. The yard mule howled, dim figures moved in the night, but the train sat there. Half an hour later, still nothing. We lay on the cardboard to sleep. Finally the beast began to move. You could hear the couplings go tight along the line of cars, bangbang *bang*Bang! then metallic creaking as she started laboriously to roll.

The rest of the night it moved and stopped, being a local, moved and stopped. We woke up briefly from time to time and went back to sleep. I don't know how long we drowsed after it stopped. It didn't matter. On the road you don't have to be anywhere. Come late morning, we hopped out, eager to finagle our way to Manhattan.

We were still in the Pot Yards. A yard engine had been pushing us up and down the yard all night, putting together a train.

Some adventures work better than others.

The next try we made it. This time we picked a gondola with a couple of huge pieces of machinery, generators I thought, chained down. I hoped the chains were healthy. A freight is a huge merciless machine that will squash you like a bug if you get in the wrong place. We realized this. We just didn't know where the wrong places were.

A crazy exaltation comes with rattling through the evening on a pounding, clattering monster as if it belonged to you. It was a big feeling. We hopped around the generators, whooped like wild Indians, and decided to climb from the gon onto the roof of the box car in front of us. It wasn't smart. We weren't either, so it seemed about right. Statistically it wasn't dangerous. The swaying ladder on the box was within reach. With both hands on a rungs it would be hard to fall under the wheels. Well, fairly hard.

Don't try it at home. Some things are best left to idiots.

We were as gods-atop a shaking whanging steel python, hollering like maniacs in the wind blast. Outside the rules lies a freedom most people don't notice. The hurtling thunderbolt was pure muscle yet we had tamed it--we thought. We could smell the passing forest. Isolated houses flashed by and I felt the strings on my face.

Strings, distinct cords hanging from something we had passed under.

From some dim forgotten cranny of my mind there popped up one of those crucial datums you don't know you have. As a kid I'd read everything within reach, without judgment. Somewhere, maybe in some seven-year-old's *Big Book of Trains*, I learned that strings meant you were coming to a tunnel. They were a night warning to train crew.

I shrieked at Jimmy and tackled him. A moment later we indeed went through a tunnel. We'd have hit the concrete at fifty and dripped in globs onto local newspapers.

Now, I may get email from a dozen train crew saying, Fred, you're full of it, there ain't no such strings and there's no tunnel between DC and New York. I never verified my string memory. Jimmy and I hopped some other trains and it is barely possible the tunnel adventure happened on another run. But there were strings, and there was a tunnel.

(Actually I later verified both tunnel and strings.)

Tell your kids to read more.

Some day I'll tell you what happened in the Village and the Waverly yards and sailing back on a flat car through Philadelphia in the Cagle Cape and how you could tell the passing factories by their smell--tires, chocolate-chip cookies, something based on petroleum. Meanwhile it's a pretty good rule in life: When you feel strings, duck.

25 WITH JAWLESS IN DC

Jawless, Batcagle, and Me: Three Guys and Not a Lick of Sense

N ow, about Cagle. He came, fresh meat out of Danang, onto the eye ward at Bethesda Naval Hospital in, it must have been, the summer of '67. He was a handsome, wiry mountain boy out of Tennessee. In a rice paddy he had endeavored to fire a rifle grenade at several of what were then called "gooks," but are now more commonly known as "mathematicians." The grenade exploded on the end of his rifle, and jellied his eyes.

For about three days he lay curled in a ball on his rack, in those blue pajamas they gave us, saying nothing. New blind guys always did that. Then he began to pull out of it. They made them tough in Tennessee.

It turned out Cagle was a natural socialite, connoisseur of poontang, and raconteur extraordinary. He fit right into the life of the ward, which was fairly strange.

There was Jawless, who had taken an AK round in the jaw at Plei Ku, shattering the bone, which had to be removed. While the doctors looked for a replacement jaw, he had an NG tube coming out of his nose so he could eat nasty mush, and he talked like he was gargling Silly Putty.

Rooster was a jarhead whose retinas had begun peeling for unknown reasons at Khe Sahn. And there as McGoo, a tall doofus squid who had done something heroic on a PBR–that's Patrol Boat, River–and gotten a major medal and shot up doing it. He wore thick glasses like glass base-plates for a mortar. Navy guys are weird.

An open-bay ward wasn't a bad place to be. It was certainly better than where we'd been. Washington was nearby, bursting with beer and women. Cagle liked both. We started taking him downtown to go sightseeing. He liked sightseeing. We'd take him down to the Mall in the afternoon and point him at the Washington Monument. Cagle would say, "Oh man. God that's something. My brain-housing unit can barely wrap around it. Out-fucking-standing."

The tourists could tell he was blind as three bats in a leather bag and thought we were terrible to be tormenting him that way. Once we pointed him at a tree, and told him it was the Capitol. He went into raptures about how he recognized all the Senators coming out. The tourists weren't sure what to make of that. Jawless and his tube didn't help them decide.

Anyway, that night we came back through Friendship Heights, the closest the bus came to the hospital, and we were several sheets to the wind, and probably the blankets and pillowcases too. It was dark and rainy. We ducked for shelter into a doorway and discovered a high school couple trying to cuddle there. They really didn't want four shot-up jarheads without jaws and other parts to share their doorway. But it was raining.

The guy kid had one of those red soft-cotton fender covers mechanics use to keep from scratching up your car. He gave it to us so we could use it for an umbrella and go away. We did.

I forget whose idea it was, but somebody noticed that the fender cover looked like a cape. So we got a marker pen and wrote, "Bat Cagle" on it, and Cagle wore it with his blue PJs. He also had a pair of jungle boots without laces that he slopped around in, just for the hell of it. Discipline wasn't too bad on the ward. The doctors realized we needed a little room to re-assemble ourselves. And as Cagle said, "What are they going to do? Send me to Vietnam?"

That would have been the end of it if we hadn't found some-where a garrison cap–the hat with the visor and the cloth cover on top. If you take the cloth off, there's a little white wire pole with what looks like a halo attached. We gave it to Cagle and let him feel it. He sort of liked it. His own halo. He thought maybe he could deceive women with it.

For some time nothing happened. We took Cagle to parties arranged by Senators who didn't give a damn about us but thought giving us parties might get votes. We didn't care. Beer was beer. The Senators always stocked the pond with college girls. Cagle could work the disabled-hero routine to get more poontang than any six guys needed. He had the drawl and the aw-shucks yes-ma'am cute-and-dumb-as-seven-foxes pat-ter and looked like Elvis.

Well, one day they said there was going to be a huge inspection of the ward. The nurses went into a prevent defense, cleaning everything up. For days it went on. They told us we were sup-posed to stand at the end of our racks and come to attention on command. I'm not sure we got into the spirit of the thing.

The big day came. We stood at the end of our racks. The com-manding admiral's entourage swept regally into the ward–the big guy himself, a cloud of friendly low-ranking nurses, and the head of the nursing corps. This was before many hetero-sexual women went into the career military, and the head nurse looked like a front lineman mixed with a pit bull.

So help me, Cagle was there in blue pajamas and the Bat Cape, in the unlaced jungles, with the black visor and his halo on its little pole. And holding his white cane. I guess he didn't care any more.

As they came by, Cagle snapped up the cane a in a precise rifle salute. It was awesome. The admiral took one look at this apparition, said, "At ease," and swept by. He probably had a sense of humor, and anyway what was he going to do? Put a blind Marine in irons? It was the wrong hill to die on.

The young nurses smiled despite themselves, since Cagle really did look like Elvis. The head nurse glared hatred. She was ready to eat a doorknob. She wanted to stop and kill him, but the admiral wasn't in the killing mood and so she had to go with him.

Cagle was our hero. Someday I'll tell you how Jawless got another jaw.

26 DRAG RACING

How I Was a Big Time Drag Racer. Well, Almost

I n high school I was a nationally ranked drag racer, almost, and nearly went to Bakersfield in California, to race against Don Garlits and Swamp Rat II. Garlits was then the king of high-revvin' screaming, blown, nitro-fueled, bored-and-stroked, ported, polished, and wildly over-cammed rocket sleds running on exotic chemicals, big rubber, and the bare fringes of metallurgy.

I might have won. I really might have.

You need to know this.

This was in 1963 in King George County, Virginia. The county was a wooded region of the Southern mentality where nothing mattered to teenage boys except cars, beer and, of course, that. The country boys were muscular and unpolished, accustomed to hard lives. They worked shifts in gas stations, changed their own transmissions, and hunted deer in autumn. They knew cars. Some of them got their cobbled-together old jalopies to do things you wouldn't have believed possible. Such as start.

In those days, drag-racing held the male mind in a greasy but powerful grip. Dragging meant putting two vehicles next to each other on a straight piece of asphalt at least a quarter of a mile long, saying, "Go!" and seeing who got over the finish line first. It appealed to an intense, primitive, almost arthropod competitiveness in young males. There was no point to it, no reason behind it. We figured making sense was an overrated virtue.

I guess I still do.

Anyway, I was then driving a 1953 Chevy the color of sun-baked mud. The engine was an inline six that had perhaps at one time run on all of its cylinders. Now it usually seemed to want to keep three in reserve, perhaps as spares. The suspension made me think of drunken cattle. The tired warrior didn't so much have compression as remember it, as an octogenarian reflects on the ardors of youth. You could tune the engine, as a musician probably could tune a clothesline. It mattered about as much.

Another kid named Butch, dark, saturnine, and sometimes a rival, drove a '53 Ford painted white with barn paint. I forget whether one of the windows was broken or one of them wasn't. The tires usually showed more fabric than a tailor shop. One night Butch and I and some other fools made a high-speed run to Colonial Beach along a winding narrow road, only to have a rear tire sigh and go flat as we pulled into the parking lot of a dance hall. It had worn through.

From time to time we'd run into each other out on the forested roads of Saturday night, maybe in a gas station on Route 301, maybe at the high school, maybe at HoJo's in Fredericksburg, where we drove in endless circles with other kids and ate Mighty Mo's to get a head start on plugging our arteries. We worked on The Look. You know, arm draped casually in the window with a confident but jaded smirk. It was Brando meets Presley in the testosteronal evening, young studs on the prowl. The trick was not to park under a mercury vapor lamp, because it would make your zits turn purple.

We did The Challenge: Stared at each other with cynical assurance, the slightest trace of a sneer disturbing the peach fuzz, sizing each other up. Actually we spent all day together in school, and we were buddies — but that's not how the thing is done. Then we'd tap the gas pedal, *rudden*-udden. The other would push the rpms up a bit, *rudden-udden-udden*. Then the first would really push it, *ruddenuddenuddensceeeeech!* which was no end impressive. Actually, the *sceeech* meant you had a loose fan belt.

You know those nature shows where the male swamp birds flap their wings like crazy and jerk their heads back and forth and gurgle, so the girl swamp birds will love them? The same principle holds with teenage boys. And it works. Men ought to be grateful that women don't have any more sense than swamp birds. If they did, we'd have to date possums

One night Butch and I finally drew down on each other at Winterduck: The shootout. There was in those days a commercial dragstrip called Summerduck. Winterduck, where kids dragged illegally, was a stretch of 206 out of Dahlgren in King George, where it crossed Williams Creek in the woods. One midnight we met there, just the two of us.

Showdown. One of us wouldn't come back. We both knew it.

The night was pitch dark and star-studded. Bugs shrieked in the trees, thinking it would get them laid. An occasional fish jumped *plonk!* in the creek. There was no traffic.

The way you lined up next to each other was by stomping the gas and then stomping the brakes, so the car lurched. This was to give the impression that you had 1,532 horsepower with twelve pounds of overpressure on the blower and beefed-up clutch springs. A really hot car was twitchy, goosey. We knew that much. We'd read it somewhere.

There we were, side by side, cocky, ready to rumble. We gunned the engines against soft automatic transmissions and held the brakes on, trying to get the jump on each other. Butch blew his horn. *Go!* I let go of the brake, as close as I could get to popping the clutch, and waited to be thrown against the seat by blasting acceleration. You know, like a catapult launch from a carrier deck.

Whirrrrr. Ummmmmmm. Sougghh.

When you got down to it, the fitty-three sounded like a vacuum cleaner. I looked anxiously at the trees in the headlights. Was anything happening? Yes, they were beginning to move. I was sure of it. Less and less slowly we went. We hit twenty-five miles an hour . . .thirty. Butch was beside me, lifters ticking like castanets. Thirty-two, thirty-five, headed toward destiny and valve float.

But ...*nooooo!* The barn paint was pulling ahead. It was inexorable. Fate was against me, robbing me of my shot at the big time. Slowly the white blur gained ground and I...

Lost.

That one defeat was all that kept me from national importance. I know I could have taken Garlits and the Swamp Rat. At least I could have if you'd stolen one of his rear wheels, chained the Rat to a fire plug, and filled its cylinders with linoleum cement. And given me a five-minute head start.

27 ROLLING IN THE PLUKE BUCKET

How Space Aliens Greased the Turn

You gotta understand about the Pluke Bucket and me in rural King George County, Virginia, in 1963. (Maybe you didn't know you had to understand this. Well, you do. Life is full of surprises.)

The county was then mostly woods, the high-school boys gangly farm kids who fished and hunted or pumped gas on long lonely summer evenings on Route 301. Towns ran from small to barely existent, and lay far apart. The only way to get anywhere, geographically or romantically, was by car.

By the time a he-child reached fourteen, he could name any car ever made, and some that hadn't been, by looking at three inches of tail fin. Then he hit fifteen, his skin turned to pizza, and he began to look at girls with shocked reappraisal. Whereupon he bought some smoking, oozing, cantankerous rattletrap of a jalopy that sounded like a tubercular's last minutes–and fell in love.

It is a biological fact that a boy can love a car. He learns its every quirk, the whirring of unlubricated speedometer cables, the tick-tick-tick of sticking lifters, the dying sough of the transmission. A car–*his* car–is security in the great dark world after the sun goes down, warmth in winter, status symbol, bar, codpiece, love nest, identity, and heraldic emblem. He may find no greater intimacy.

It was a big feeling to set out at night into those winding wooded roads, alone, skirting adulthood, feeling independent and, however prematurely, manly. My own courser, the Pluke Bucket, was a '53 Chevy with the surging power of a vacuum cleaner, at least a few active cylinders, no compression at all, and handled in a curve like a wet bar of soap. I didn't care. The Bucket was mine. I had for that wheel-borne tragedy the affection someone sensible might have for a faithful dog. ("Pluke" was a local coinage meaning roughly "poontang." "Gittin' any plukin'?" meant, "Have you had the amorous success attributed to French rakes with the cheerleading squad serially?" The truthful answer invariably was "No." It was an answer we didn't much use.)

By age fifteen, a stripling could talk for an hour without saying a thing his mother could understand. Most of what he said consisted of a laundry list of mechanical properties having totemic import for those gripped by car lust.

"*Ba-a-ad* fitty-sedden Merc, dual quads, bored and stroked, 3/4 Isky, phone-flow, magneto ignition, 3.51 rear, Positraction, glass packs. Goose 'at sucker, *Sceeech! Udden udden udden.*"

Decrypted, this meant that the speaker had seen, or hadn't seen and was lying about, a '57 Mercury with modifications that would cause the motor to make loud noises and then probably explode. We didn't have the money to build genuinely fast cars. But we could dream.

The terminology wasn't without meaning, and embodied the male passion for controllable complexity. For example, "phone-flow" meant that the car in question had four gears, mediated by a shifter on the floor boards, as distinct from threena-tree (three on the tree), signifying three gears with the lever on the steering column. Phone-flow was better, especially a narrow-gate short-throw Hurst, especially for power shifting, udden udden, *blap! Sceech!.*

Just as knights recognized each other by colorful hooha on their shields, so we knew each other by our cars. It was talismanic and tribal. Our moms wouldn't have noticed if they had passed a flying fire truck, but we, in that instant of passing on a winding night road, instantly recognized each other–Charles with the fitty-sedden Chev 283, Butch in the fitty-three Ford with the bad lifters, Floyd in the unspeakably glorious '63 Ford 396 Police Interceptor. (He had graduated, and was making big money in a gas station.)

Most of us labored under the delusion that we were racing drivers. I remember having the curious idea that 75 miles an hour was a reasonable driving speed for all occasions. (I know, I know. Teenage boys are dumber than mud walls. If you had taken the aggregate brains of all the boys in King George County, and put them in a garden slug, that slug would have been under-powered.) Reflexes, God, and low traffic kept us alive.

Thing is, hormones don't take no for an answer. One night I was out driving, just driving, putting gas through the engine, feeling that wild male rush to do something stupid and defiant. In a reasonable age, fellows of fifteen would have been dismembering brontosauruses, or banging on each other with funny-looking axes, or putting cities to the sword. Guy stuff. My family didn't have much money. I couldn't afford a sword, or a brontosaurus.

So I started fantasizing that I was Stirling Moss, then a Formula One racing champion. This was late one night on Indian Town Road, a narrow lane shaped like a convulsing python.

The wind poured through the windows like a current of water. Frogs creaked in the swamp and bugs keened in the trees. It's tough being a bug: You screech in a tree all night, trying to get laid, and then freeze to death. It's kind of how teenagers look at life. I came toward a tight downhill unbanked S-turn that would have frightened an Alpine goat. I remember thinking, "Only Stirling and I can take this turn at seventy."

I had overestimated by one.

I remember lying on my back, miraculously unhurt, looking up at the gas pedal. The Pluke Bucket was neatly on her top in the ditch.

Being a practiced teenager, I began rehearsing how to explain it to my father. Space aliens put grease on the turn? Bandits stole the Bucket and rolled her while I pursued on foot? Gravitational anomaly?

Somehow, a week later, I was back on the roads, still dreaming of hot cams and log manifolds, of the smell of gasoline and brake fluid and supercharged big-bores screaming toward high revs, and the quick, sharp speed shift that I couldn't actually do but craved as a protest against the unsatisfactory nature of existence.

It was meaning. I still haven't done better.

28 TALKING
WITH HANT V

Figuring Out Women. Sort of. Almost. Maybe.

The other day I went up the holler to see Uncle Hant. I figured he could teach me to understand women, because he knows everything. Hant lives in a double-wide with a '54 Merc on blocks outside, and a fuel-oil tank painted silver, and a three-legged coon dog named Birdshot. A couple of years back, the old hound stuck a paw under a lawnmower to catch whatever was making all that noise. I guess it worked.

I knew I'd find Hant working the moonshine still he has farther back in the woods. Everybody figures he makes the best shine west of Roanoke. Flatlanders out of Washington just about fight each other to buy it. Sure enough, he was slouched against the cooker, wearing that hat he has that looks like he found it in a cow pasture, and working on the condensing coils.

"Hant," I said, "You know everything. I'm trying to figure out women."

"Get along, boy. The Lord God Almighty hasn't got that far yet."

Hant doesn't actually exist. He's a Convenient Literary Device.

He went back to fiddling with some copper tubing.

"How's that panther sweat selling?" I said to change the subject for a bit. He nearly went out of business a few years back. Then he started putting cocaine in the mash and a little LSD. Sales went up so much he had to double the price to keep from having traffic jams. On Saturdays a line of Volvos backs up almost to Wheeling. They could have bought good bourbon for half as much, but they thought they were getting something special. They were, too.

"I reckon I can live with it. 'Cept two damnfool yuppies drank the stuff on the way home, like I told'em not to, and kilt theirself on a telephone pole."

Yuppies are dumber than inbred possums.

"Guess you feel kinda bad."

He got that smug look he has. "Nope. I guess I'm just a filter in the gene pool."

Hant always was modest.

"I don't know what's got into women," I said. I was determined to get some pearl of wisdom out of him if I had to drag it out with a back hoe. "You know, these days you can't even get in a fight in a pool hall, and smack hell out of somebody with a pool stick, without some woman starts hollering about violence. I don't understand it. Why else would anybody go to a pool hall?"

"I can't imagine," he said, looking sorrowful. "The female mind works in strange ways. They don't like riding drunk on a motorsickle at night with the lights out either."

"That's crazy."

"Cain't git crazier."

You can't teach a woman reason. I used to date this old gal in high school, pretty as a deer gun that's just been blued, and smart too. She couldn't have been nicer if she'd had a passel of angels to show her how. Only problem was she didn't want me to shoot road signs with a twelve-gauge.

I mean, I was that close to perfection.

Hant cocked his head back and looked hard at the condenser coil. He looked like a man who was pretty satisfied with himself.

"I reckon you got it fixed," I said.

"Weren't broke."

"Then why work on it?"

"Marketing. Gotta look authentic. You know, like that old Merc by the trailer. I had to go all the way to Bluefield to get one beat-up enough. A yuppie won't buy shine from anybody that drives a Toyota."

That was Hant. Always figuring the angles.

I said, "Another thing I don't understand is how come women always want commitment. Seems like just about the time you're having a good time together she gets all lit up about it. How come they always want to get married? Not me. I wanna keep *my* trailer."

It's the lord's own truth. First it's commitment, and then it's marriage. Nothing ruins a couple like getting married. You got no reason to behave anymore. Five years later you hate each other and she's got your kids and satellite dish.

Hant must have been satisfied with the coil. He spat a stream of tobacco juice and sat on a stump. Nothing's more authentic than tobacco juice. I saw a camel spit like that on the Discovery Channel. I reckon Hant had better aim, but that camel had him hands down on throw-weight.

"Nothing wrong with commitment, boy. I always thought it was good stuff. About an hour at a time. I wonder if I need more tube."

I was starting to like marketing. "I got an idea...," I said.

"Treat it kind, son. It's in a strange place."

Never give Hant an opening.

"You need a stoneware jug and some Mason jars, *I* think."

He pondered, like he always does when money is on the line.

"I guess you might be right. There's this company in New Jersey, makes'em for the tourist trade. Maybe I'll git some." He pulled a bottle of Jim Beam from behind the cooker and sat on a stump. Hant knows better than to drink that rattlesnake pizen he makes.

"There's gotta be a answer, Hant. I was talking to Bobby McWhorter the other day. Sally's mad at him again. She says he needs to stop keeping his crankshaft in his kitchen sink. Well, where else is he going to put it? The engine block's in the bathtub. I mean, it seems like women just don't know how to think. Bobby's got a race in two weeks."

"Figures. Well, I guess it could be worse."

"How?"

"I don't know."

When a man can't keep his car in his own sink, something's wrong, I guess.

"She says he ought to buy table cloths."

"What's a table cloth?"

I was beginning to realize that maybe Hant didn't know quite everything.

We gave up and got to talking about things that made sense, like bass lures and monster trucks and how to sell more shine to the yups.

"I'm thinking either battery acid or PCP," he said. "Probably won't be a telephone pole left between here and Washington. I never cared for telephone poles anyway."

I gave up and went home. Hant's pretty smart for a literary device, but some things are beyond him.

29 KING GEORGE DAYS

A Youth No Longer Availalbe

I beg the reader's indulgence since this is in a large sense a personal communication more than a column for all. It will resonate with many, or some, so I post it anyway.

I am preparing to fly to Fredericksburg, Virginia, for the—God almighty--fifty-year high-school reunion of King George High School. Perhaps we all do it eventually, unless of course we don't. It is a curious thing, I have learned at previous reunions, to meet after half a century people you last saw when they were seventeen. They seem so little changed.

KG was mostly wooded, on the Potomac River, Dahlgren Naval Proving Ground the biggest employer, with a fair number of kids who got up at four-thirty in the morning to help their fathers with commercial crabbing on the river.

There was nothing special about the class of 1964, or about King George High, except for those of us who were in it. Our yearbook looked like ten thousand others across America, portraits with acne removed in the photo lab, the basketball team exactly like everybody else's, the cheerleaders conventionally glorious, conventional adolescent good-byes in ballpoint pen—but without misspelling or bad grammar.

We, largely rural kids of the small-town South, represented without knowing it a culture, an approach to existence, and a devastating principle: You can't impose decency, honesty, good behavior, or responsibility. They are in the culture, or they are not. If they are, you don't need laws, police, and supervision. If they are not, laws won't much help. And this is why the US is over, at least as the country we knew.

The names in the yearbook are just names: Sonny, Rosie, Butch, Kenny, Joyce, Cecil, Ricky, Kit. Just names. But. But, but, but. With any of these people you could leave your keys in the car—we did—or the front door unlocked—we did. We had one cop in the county, Jay Powell, a state trooper, and he had little to do. The high school did not have metal detectors or police patrolling the halls. We had none of the behavior that now makes these things necessary. It wasn't in the culture. We could have raped, killed, robbed, fathered countless illegitimate children like barnyard animals. We didn't.

It wasn't in the culture.

We were not obsessively law-abiding. It may be that a certain amount of beer, even a substantial amount, was consumed in contravention of the law. I may know somewhat of this, though I can't swear to it.

Well, OK, I can swear to it. The statute of limitations has run. I remember my first encounter—don't we all?—with the demonic grape. One summer night in my fifteenth year I and a carful of country youth went to the Blue Note, a black club somewhere on Highway 301, where clients would for a price would have bought grog for a nursing infant. The night was warm and humid, full of hormones and inexplicit promise, though not much judgement.

You probably remember that teen-age at-large-in-the-world feeling: lithe and loose, never having heard of "tired," razor sharp on a long jump-shot, male, unsupervised, almost grown up, or at least close enough to make it worry. There is nothing better. It never comes again.

I had never drunk before, but wasn't going to admit it, and so simulated the worldliness of a French rake. The others bought beer but I didn't like the taste. I somehow got a bottle of a ghastly purple substance, later determined to be sloe gin. The others were showing off by chugging beers. So I too chugged... oh God. Oh God. Even now it hurts, a half century later. Perish forfend, a hangover so bad that I began to retch if I blinked. I was sure I was going to die. I hoped so.

And yet there was an innocence to it. It was a rite of passage, not a door to iniquity, and while we did ensozzle ourselves, we didn't get into fights or do anything murderous, vicious, or shameful.

It wasn't in the culture.

So with our kinship with guns. The boys had them. They were mostly shotguns for deer hunting, .410s, over-and-unders, twelve gauges, and maybe a .22 Hornet for shooting varmints. If you have a field of soybeans, you don't want whistle pigs eating them.

We were free in those days. I could walk out the main gate of Dahlgren with my Marlin .22 lever-action over my shoulder, and nobody blinked. The country store sold long-rifles (for the frightened epicenes of today, that's ammunition) with no questions asked. There was no reason to ask questions. We didn't shoot each other. Only savages unfit for civilization would do such a thing.

And we weren't. It wasn't in the culture. You don't have to police people to keep them from doing what they aren't going to do anyway.

There were memorable times. One frigid winter night me and this other fool—it was Rusty Reed, no relation as that would have represented too great a concentration of recessive genes —set out to shoot rats at the Colonial Beach dump. We were in my '53 Chevy, which had the aerodynamic lines of a jellybean, but it was mine. To be on Route 301, empty of traffic, windshield gone in frost, unsupervised—it was heaven. No one knew or cared where we were. There was no reason to care.

Rusty had a twelve-gauge double-barrel with a few rounds and a .22 semi-auto rifle. I had my Marlin and a couple of boxes of long-rifles. It was colder than a witch's tit in a brass bra. No moon. We had that glorious sense, silly but not, of setting out into whatever came our way, unsupervised, free. You know, like wild Indians.

The dump was isolated, in man-high frozen brown scrub, a dirt road more hole than road leading to it. I turned off the headlights and began bucking along the road, frozen puddles crackling under the tires. A '53 Chevy driven by a country teenager can go places that would have sent Rommel into a sanitarium.

Rusty wanted to catch the rats off-guard, so he got out with the twelve and sat on the right fender. We reached the dump. Rats squealed and cans clinked on the piled refuse. I turned on the lights.

Blam! Blam! Rusty let fly and fell off the fender with the recoil onto his head. It was absurd. It was wonderful.

And it was wild, I guess. It was assuredly unsupervised. It wasn't irresponsible. That wasn't in the culture.

30 SMITING THE INFIDDLES

And Malt Does More Than Milton Can, to Justify God's Ways to Man

Cyberg, Tennessee—The Reverend McBilly Osfeiser strode to the rostrum of the Full Bible Perfect Word Baptist Church, a frame building reeking of plainness and Protestantism. He was a tall man, with the sharp facial planes and hard visage of a desert patriarch about to kill something. The congregation shrank in their pews. He was a man who brooked no sin, and no sinners, whom he consigned to eternal damnation, and thought they were getting off light. He looked fiercely about, and spoke:

"Brethren, I come before you to preach the word of God, for these be evil times, and the children of Israel, and yea the parents and grandparents, even unto their heirs and assigns, are sore beset by the tribe of Mohammed, and Beelzebub, and Luciferin and Luciferase. In the name of God, we must gird our loins, whatever exactly gird means, and smite the followers of Allah, and suffer them not to live, neither child nor mother with child nor suckling babe. Their lands shall be accursed and nothing there shall prosper, neither tares nor the wild ass; thus saith the Lord God, the God of Israel, the God of love and mercy.

"Today we shall begin our sermon with the story of Samsung

and Delilah, in the book of Hezekiah, chapter fourteen, verses nine through twenty-seven, in the reign of Herod Agrippa. In that time Israel was sore beset by the Malachites and the Catamites, even the Stalactites and Stalagmites, and the Assyrians of King Arepagitica with many chariots threatened the city of Solomon. But Samsung spent three days and three nights fasting and praying, and sacrificed a sheep, and it was good in the eyes of the Lord. In the morning he went forth and slew them all, cutting through them with sling and samothrace as one scything wheat until not a Stalagmite was left standing. saving the city.

"Today, brethren, we of Christ face the same test of our faith. In Afghanistan, as we speak, the Mohammedan Taliban build mighty forces which they will use to conquer all of Christendom and enslave us, having gotten here mysteriously.

"The powers of the darkness are many and patient, and the Mohammedan awaits to make our wives and daughters into harem slaves. It is well said that if we do not slew them there, or perhaps slay them, they will slew us here, or a slew of them will slay a slew of us there, maybe here, or they will...whatever. Remember the second book of Malthusians, when Chaysuss expelled the Gadarene Swine from the woman afflicted with leprosy, "Rebus sic stantibus," he said. "Carthago delenda est," which is the Latin for "Get thee back whence thou camest, and thy towel."

"I urge you, brethren, to support our Christian troops who with magnificent courage are killing the heathen with drones strikes from thousands of feet while sitting in Colorado. To those weak in faith, who say that we are killing innocent women and children, I say unto ye, women are the source of all Taliban and thus must be military targets. If we destroy arms factories, should we not destroy Taliban factories? As the mighty warrior Chay-suss would want, we will smite them, and leave them bleeding and dying, and wailing over their broken children, blinded and crushed and burned, that they might learn to walk in the ways of righteousness.

"And now, brethren, I want to introduce you to one of our own warriors for Christ, Willy Bill Bedford, who is just back from the heathen land of Afghanistan, and wounded—*wounded,* brethren!–smiting the in-fiddle for Chay-suss. Willy Bill, will you come up and testify?"

Willy Bill was a big, chunky kid with a sloping forehead you could have used to bank a turn in a motorcycle race, and about every other tooth was missing so he looked like a piano keyboard. His left arm was in a cast. "Willy Bill," shouted Reverend Osfeiser, "Tell your brothers and sisters in Chay-suss how you been doing the Lord's work."

Willy Bill seemed uncomfortable but he sort of scrunched up his courage and said, "Yeah, well. OK, Reverend. Well, we was out in Litani Province and there was twelve of us in a Humvee with 'bout a thousand rounds each of seven-six-two and a sack full of Bibles an'..."

The reverend roared, "And tell the brethren why you had Bibles, the inerrant perfect word of God, with you!"

"Oh, yeah. We belong to Bible Spreaders, we try to bring Moslems to know Jesus, you know. BS, I mean Bible Spreaders, is real important to us, so we always...."

"You hear that? Bringing souls to God!"

"Well, we came to Awali, that's this village, maybe three hundred sand-nig—Taliban and their kids, all dirty and livin' in mud huts because they don't love Jesus and the kids there beg for something to eat because they don't know that beggin' ain't right. Well, we told them to get away and smacked them around a little because they might be suicide bombers, you know, and you could just tell the grown-ups hated us for our religion and our freedoms and all, and then we heard a rifle go off. Well, they ain't supposed to have rifles. So the lieutenant called in a air strike and a couple of sixteens came in, and whoom, they just smacked the livin' dog-snot out of those fuckers and....."

"Now, Willy Bill, don't be using language like that. Do you think Chay-suss talked that way? It's a sin."

"I'm sorry, Reverend. I won't do it again. I don't want to commit no sin. Anyway, it was a good strike, killed almost everybody although a few was left screamin' and makin' a fuss and women was huggin' kids or what was left, I mean, how much sense does that make? I guess they learned their lesson. So we went through and left Bibles on top of some of the dead ones so whoever found them would come to Jesus and then I fell off the Humvee and broke my arm."

At which the Reverend McBilly Osfeiser shouted, "Hosannah! Praise the Lord! While we have sat here, living a life of ease, Willy Bill, Cyburg's own Willy Bill, has smote the in-fiddles, and saved our precious daughters from being in harems, though perhaps not in back seats, and saved our holy Tennessee, where we are free and snakes have handles and the God of Wrath rules as he did with Noah in the Sinai!"

I need a drink.

31 CULTURE AND CIVILIZED - BEHAVIOR

Ain't Much Difference

Machodoc Creek in King George County was three-quarters of a mile wide. Virginia has a robust conception of creeks. Kids were essentially amphibian. We spent half our lives on the water, with no one watching us. We had heard rumors of life jackets, but couldn't see their purpose. There was no damn-fool federal law saying we had to have a license certifying that we knew how to operate a canoe. Nobody ever drowned. We just weren't real drownable. It would have taken three SEAL teams and a D9 Caterpillar to do it, and even with them the then odds would have been about even.

Sex had occurred to us, but didn't occupy our thoughts except when we were awake. The girls were shapely, neither fat nor emaciated, without such signs of mental disturbance as anorexia and bulimia, which had not been invented. We were not sexually supervised. A large, emptyish county with lots of woods offered many places where a couple could park discreetly at night, and we did. Oh yes. In nearby Fredericksburg there was that old American standby, the drive-in theater, colloquially known as the Finger Bowl. We engaged in much experimentation, some sex, many happy memories, and few pregnancies. No rapes and, among the boys, no disrespect (as distinct from lust) for the girls. It wasn't in the culture.

Again, an innocence. The boys watched their language around the girls, and vice versa. We weren't gentlemanly, having no exposure to that sort of thing, didn't wear spats, but neither were we toilet-mouthed. We just didn't do that

Stray thought: One night I was somewhere with Fred Burrell. Being already a promising wise-acre, I scratched myself indelicately and said, "Damn. My Burrells ache." To which he replied, "My Reed itches." Smart-ass.

King George High School was I suppose typically American for the time. The teachers were not brilliant, but neither were they stupid. Brilliance was not needed. It was then thought that schools existed to impart knowledge. This could be done at the high-school level by following a syllabus and requiring that the students learn the material. It worked, to no one's surprise, since it always had worked. Since the studentry were entirely white—my class, 1964 was the last such class—no reason existed for lowering academic standards.

Discipline was not rigid. It did not need to be. The country kids were more unpolished than rough. There was the class clown—I have no recollection of who that might have been— but clowning stopped well short of real misbehavior. Fights were very few. When one occurred, no one picked up a piece of rebar or kicked the guy who was down. These boys weren't wussies. Viet Nam took a large bite. But there were things we just didn't do.

No one would have thought of disobeying a teacher, much less shoving or threatening one. The result I think would have been instant and permanent expulsion, but it never happened —not because of fear, but because it wasn't in the culture.

The word "motherfucker" was not the chief component of speech, even among groups of boys, and its use in school would have been thought inappropriate to people with opposable thumbs.

We didn't know it, but we were what made America what it was, and isn't.

The Sixties followed hard on our dispersal in 1964, and Viet Nam, in which KG suffered dead and wounded. Butch Jones, my buddy in school and later a SeaBee in Nam, showed up at he the Naval Support Activity hospital in Danang to visit me after I had proved my virtuosity more as a target than a Marine. I think we both thought, "What the *hell* are we doing *here*?" It.

Come graduation, we blew every whichaway, like dandelion puffs, and became all manner of things. "Rural" doesn't mean stupid: There were physicists, engineers, and such like rabble. We were not shiftless, semi-literate, dependent, infantile, narcissistic, vulgar, spoiled, or whining.

It wasn't in the culture.

32 IN SAIGON'S ALLEYS

A Place I Greatly Liked

Dawn comes to the alleys around Tan Son Nhut Field with a faint grey light seeping past the graveyard and up the dusty road toward the banana market. Pots begin to clatter and red charcoal dims in brightening courtyards. A hungry dog sniffs in the ditch. A cyclo, a motor-driven coal scoop equally useful as a conveyance or means of suicide, sputters hungrily down the alley in search of fares. A few women in black pajamas haggle over fresh bananas gleaming like fat yellow and green fingers in the stalls. For a moment all is quiet. Then, suddenly, ochre swarms of children rush out to begin the day's battles, and swarms of motor scooters appear from nowhere. The sinuous, tired cry of a soup-woman floats over the chaos.

Old Mr. Wang opens the shutters and stands beneath the sign that says, "Wang's Grocery" and "House For Rent." He folds his hands across his sagging chest, surveys the alley with dignity appropriate to the biggest paunch in four blocks, and smiles broadly. The day is officially begun.

The thoroughfare of the slums in Truong Minh Ky Street cuts through the rich decaying life of the back streets like a monotonous grey artery. Hungry and vaguely frightening men in work clothes jostle against hard-faced women carrying baskets of produce. Dirty buses roar and fill the air with choking fumes. Toilets flush onto sidewalks, washing orange peels and rotting vegetables into the gutters. From the counters of little pharmacies and sundry shops the Chinese merchants calmly watch the ebb and flow.

As you move away from Truong Minh Ky along side streets, commerce dies. Tangled alleys twist at bewildering angles. High walls and barbed wire shield palatial residences of wealthy Chinese while bony dogs and endless children play at the gates. Whole apartment houses of chattering prostitutes overlook shacks made of ammunition crates and roofed with tin. Everything in Southeast Asia is made of ammunition crates. Children in Saigon think that wood grows with lot numbers for howitzer shells.

The heart of Asia beats among the muddy recesses and noodle stands, in the ever-present smell of fish and charcoal and sewage. Westerners do not come here. They don't like to see rats floating in stagnant pools of green water. And so they never eat rice and fish sauce on the summer rooftops or drink beer and talk away long mornings with the bar girls or see Thao Han playing with her baby. They never see Asia.

By seven o'clock sunlight streams across the outlying rice lands, crosses the river, and deliberately enters the window of Bill Murphy. Bachelors have their routines just as other people. Every morning Bill tries to hide under the pillow when the sun hits his face. Then he curses a little, rises grumpily, brushes his teeth, and spits over the balcony into the empty lot. Vacant lots are intended as urinals in time of need and places to spit. Bill is fond of this particular lot because he likes its pattern of oily puddles and old crankshafts.

Every morning he forgets the crushed cockroaches on the floor, steps on them, and growls under his breath. Each night at eleven they run from under the walls and rush in mindless circles, making papery noises, until whacked with a shower shoe.

"You oozy bastards," he tells them, and twiddles them by the legs to break the congealed juices. They go over the rail into the lot.

He doesn't discard his roaches at night, because he is too drunk. The world is steady if not importunate in its demand for slightly lurid newspaper copy about the East, and the typewriter on the table allows Bill to supply the demand. The secret of writing, Bill believes, is to drink just the right amount of Vietnamese beer. Too much makes the product florid, too little leaves it sparse and dry. With just the right amount of beer, adjectives come with ease and taste, clauses flow in balance and pattern. Unfortunately, the right amount makes it hard to walk with accuracy.

He runs the back of his hand over a stubbly chin and decides that he should shave this week, though not necessarily today. One reason Bill stays in Vietnam is that shaving is optional. The other reasons are women and a lack of alarm clocks. Bill feels that satisfying physiological urges is the end in life. Anything else, he suspects, is going beyond God's intent.

On the cramped landing the Korean family, the only other residents of the second floor, squat around a can of charcoal. Mrs. Li smiles in a glow of gold teeth and waves a limp carp from the six-by-ten room where the Lis and their six children live. "Murphy-san, fish, have. Him boocoo dead, don't you?" Her English is colorful, if not technically correct.

"A fish, undeniably. Mr. Li get a job yet?"

Her face falls. "No, him no job yet."

She brightens. "No sweat. Rice still have, some little."

Mr. Li has been gone since before light, looking for work. There is no work in Saigon. If there were, Mr. Li could be an electrician, truck driver, second mate of an oceangoing tug, or conscienceless infantryman. He is smiling and deferential to everyone.

The Li children would baffle a platoon of sociologists. They are healthy, neat, and sound of character despite abject poverty. More puzzling to an American is that they are civil and love their parents. The older ones are already learning to read, though they have never seen a school.

The small Lis have decided that Bill's pale skin and odd eyes are aberrations to be forgiven. Kim Li Kuan, who at seven is already a dangerously charming woman, smiles up from her rice bowl. Her eyes flatten into sideways black slits. "Murphy-san have candy?"

"Unprincipled imp," says Bill, stepping over her into the bathroom. Life is personal at high density.

In the courtyard, the wizened caretaker squats. A discouraged black beret droops across his cropped head. His face is a ploughed field of wrinkles, big gaping gullies, tiny delicate rivulets, middle-sized crevices. They flow across his face in waves, break around his nose, and reflect from his ears. Some catch in the wattles of his neck. He is three hundred years old, and his mother was an earth sprite.

Every morning when Bill Murphy leaves, the old man croaks under his breath and looks puzzled. He is puzzled because there are always crushed roaches on his doorstep, but Bill Murphy doesn't know that. For a man of three hundred he is fiendishly clever. When Bill counts the rent money into his hand, "Four, five, six" the old man takes them in French, "Three, four five," and Bill invariably pays an extra bill.

His mother isn't really an earth sprite.

In a dim room behind Madame Hai's betel-nut stand, Buddha glitters in chill ceramic complacency at a nude seamstress from Chicago. Why the prostitute who owns him put the god on a girly magazine is a mystery. Perhaps Loan, who could seduce a marble slab, suspects Buddha is not as unreachable as he seems.

On the bed, Loan stirs and opens travel-poster eyes that urge intimacy when she is thinking only of breakfast. Beside her in a forlorn pile are the tools of her trade, glittering high heels, false eyelashes and scanty dress. She looks better without them, but that isn't how the thing is done. She stretches seductively and glances at the jeweled wristwatch given to her by an American contractor. Eleven o'clock.

Graceful and tiny as a cameo elf, she rises and gathers clothes to wash. By two she must be in Kim Ling's club at the dusty edge of Cach Mang Street. Her life passes among dimness and canned beer, in a gaudy cage of drunken helicopter mechanics. She is free as a force-fed hen.

Bill Murphy, who once lived with her, asked why she didn't marry some sucker and spend all his money in America.

"Then nobody take care my mother. She old now, die soon."

Such sentiment surprised Bill, who thought she was a reincarnated lamprey.

"Can get plenty men," she said, understating the case. "Only have one mother."

Bill goggled.

"When I small, my mother do everything for me. Now I do for her. What men do for me?" Extremely little.

Bill, tired of having his pockets picked, moved out.

Before starting her washing she meticulously dusts her cosmetic table, a tacky creation of plastic wood and blue polyethylene roses. It has a mirror and two drawers, one of which works smoothly. It is the most beautiful thing Loan has ever owned. She paid three month's savings for it. Sometimes she gazes at it for an hour. It depressed Bill Murphy to watch her, which is the real reason he moved out.

The noonday sun beats down on Saigon. By the roadside

mangy dogs pant in available shade, wary to avoid a kick. The festering head of one of their friends grins in stale agony from a pool of ditch water. His owners ate him yesterday, but it is too hot for the living to be concerned. Aged mama-sans move more slowly under loads of firewood and vegetables. At the meat market flies hum drowsily around hanging flesh, hardly disturbed by customers' fingers. Even the children seek shelter. A blind beggar couple in their eighties hobble painfully by Loan's gate. The small boy with the alms cup pulls respectfully on the rope which ties them together. The old man tires to help his wife with a ropy blue-veined hand on her shoulder. Both totter with the effort.

Downtown, tourists drink gin and tonic and gaze at martial statues.

On the dark walls of Kim Ling's club a lizard hunts, dragon eyes smoky with fly lust. Kim Ling counts the month's bribe money at the bar. At 35 she is tough, infinitely shrewd, and still pretty.

She riffles the big orange bills with a practiced thumb, dragging a finger to test the texture of the paper. It is a slow day, and the girls won't come until two. The glasses over the bar lack the gleam that colored lights will give them and, without bottles of beer, tables look cracked and stained, tired almost. Kim Ling doesn't notice, being immune to illusion. Illusion is in the minds of foreigners, who believe anything you tell them. Kim Ling deals in substance.

Traffic rushes past on Cach Mang. Kim Ling lights a cigarette and reclines against the bar, her face very tired. Smoke curls to the ceiling, disturbing the lizard.

Twenty years have passed since a swarthy French lieutenant led Kim Ling into a bungalow in the northern village where she was born. In the ensuing exchange, he took her virginity and she got his wallet. The pattern persisted, though now she deals in the innocence or experience of others. The years, while profitable, have been wearying. She continues because there is nothing else for her to do.

The East takes a practical view of sin. Kim Ling gives order and comfort to what otherwise would occur in dark alleys, asking only half a girl's take in return. She nurses her girls when they are sick and dismisses them gently when they are old.

The bills go into Kim Ling's brassiere to await the police chief's agent. She stares at the wall, thinking about nothing. There is nothing to think about.

By midafternoon the life of the alleys imperceptibly begins to wane. In front of Nguyen Thao Thi's ramshackle barbershop, the leather-faced peasant women mechanically swing their picks in the roadbuilding project. The wizened care-taker at Bill Murphy's house empties Bill's trash in the courtyard and examines it piece by piece with senile concentration. In Wang Chi's pool hall, which floods knee-deep in the rainy season, the cue ball cracks against the floor and is pursued by small boys.

Caught in the merry-go-round of a failing economy, people who have little to sell try desperately to sell it to people who can't afford to buy. In the shade of the broken wall by the graveyard, withered women sit in endless patience beside a dozen peanuts or three balls of rice paste. Nobody wants rice paste. Small boys beat tock-tock-tock with pieces of bamboo to advertise the soup their mothers are selling.

At a bomb-bomb stand on Truong Minh Ky a thin white man and an athletic black from Georgia sit over warm beer, a picture of contented lethargy, gazing at the life of the streets. Their careless slouches suggest unfamiliarity with mobs and responsibility. Midas Randall leans back and looks at the sky in sleepy speculation. With a long drag on his cigarette he says to Bill Murphy, "I may put up a hotel downtown. Some friends of mine and me. Something to do on the side, until I get back on my feet. Big money in it."

"Suppose?"

"You know it ain't the money. As much money as I've had, I don't like to bother with it anymore."

His pained expression indicates the burden of money. "Yep."

"Of course, it all depends on the Greek shipping interests."

"Reckon?"

Midas shrugs with the air of one to whom high finance is crystal. The lapel of his coat, stolen from the coat rack of a tourist restaurant, is stained with six weeks of breakfast. Hs own clothes were left behind when he deserted from the American navy seven years before.

"We got the debenture collateral and our management associates — between you and me, now — they're gonna drop the TWA contract and work with us. That's how big it is. But it's the fealty assiduities, you know."

Bill stares at his beer with furrowed eyebrows, struggling with the fealty assiduities.

"Yeah...yeah, assiduities are rough these days. Damn those assiduities."

Men who have been badly used by the world must manufacture their self-respect. Most of the American derelicts on Truong Minh Ky have made and lost millions and been familiars of royalty. Many speak several languages though not, of course, any which anyone else is liable to speak. The iron-clad rule is that you never question the other man. You let him be a magnate down on his luck, and he lets you be a CIA agent on a secret mission of unspeakable importance. It is a generous system and saves a lot of effort.

Midas hits the table in a theatrical outburst of sorrow.

"Dammit, Bill, this region has so much potential! It hurts when the big interests ain't interested. But they just won't listen...." His eyes are tragic.

"Yeah, the big interests are like that," says Bill, paying for the beers, and wondering how a liar as good as Midas could have failed to make good.

In late afternoon the sun gleams blood red on the rusting tin roofs of the alleys. High overhead the clouds glow pink and gauzy in the deepening sunset of Asia. Beyond the city green rice fields grow suddenly dark in the red light. The alleys dim. Activity slows. The lights come on in Wang's Grocery and House For Rent as Mama-san Wang begins the evening shift. Bill Murphy crosses the dusty way to buy his nightly three quarts of beer.

Beneath rows of dried fish and cans of condensed milk, beside brown sacks of rice, Mama-san Wang sits with patient calm. At Bill's entrance the wrinkles of her plump face flow in a ritual smile of welcome. The foreigner has three bottles, so he must want three beers. With slowness partly of age and partly of character she rummages in the leaky galvanized icebox that keeps the drinks lukewarm.

Beneath the fish sauce a thin pretty girl sits on a case of Hong Kong crackers with her baby. Her name is Mae Li and she is always serious and a little sad. At Bill's entrance the baby gurgles and crows excitedly with much waving of small arms. No dolt, he remembers that the large stranger will sometimes give a fellow chocolate or other good things from the glass case by Mama-san Wang. The trick is to get his attention.

"Gitchy-goo, kid," says Bill awkwardly, unused to children. With an experimental finger he pokes at the squirming child. He suspects there must be other things one may say to a baby. His mother speaks the only grammatical English in the alleys, learned from her American husband before he decided he wasn't really married to her and went back to California. She plans to marry Bill though he, an obtuse male, suspects nothing.

"He is a very fine baby-san, is he not? He satisfies me very well."

"Nice little fella," says Bill peering curiously. "Reckon he'd like some chocolate?"

"Oh, yes, I do think so."

Bill removes his finger from the sticky grasp and supplies the chocolate, which is wetly eaten. He wishes Mae Li weren't trying to marry him. Being Western, he doesn't realize that it isn't very important to her. Life will go on in any event. It always has.

Mama-san Wang hands him the brown bottles with their green-eyed tigers and gives him his change.

"Night, mom. Night, Mae Li. You too, kid."

Mama-san Wang smiles, wondering whether foreigners mean anything when they speak. Bill Murphy crosses the alley and doesn't count his change until he is out of sight, which is the furthest any sane man will trust a Saigon shopkeeper.

Sunset wanes to darker tones. The air cools. Wind rustles in the trees and there is a hint of rain. In the courtyard below Bill Murphy's balcony, a slender girl walks through the darkness to the peak-roofed shrine beneath the flower tree. By day it is a mass of green and gold dragons, by night a dark outline obscuring the moon rising in the still-cloudless west. A faint smell of incense floats into the night as she lights joss ticks. The glowing points trace cherry arcs as she bows again and again.

From the distance comes the lingering thump of artillery, a movement of air more than a sound. The nightly fighting is beginning in the countryside. A young girl bowing to Buddha while the guns roar in dark forests — thirty years of Vietnam.

33 CHUCKIE MANSON, THOR, AND THE ARK

Average Day in California

In the year of the Great Radioactive Goat-Curd Craze and Flood-that-Wasn't, Matamoscas was just another sleepy California town in the high desert near Barstow. The only geographical feature of note anywhere near was a low mesa called Las Pulgas, about three miles out of town where the Ark was.

About a year before, a peyote-enhanced guru named Mahmud al Gravid, who looked like Charles Manson but probably wasn't, had descended on the town with his followers. Gravid had the deeply spiritual look that comes of minor brain damage and exposure to Los Angeles. His followers were scrofulous late-adolescents with love beads. Being teenagers, they thought the world had been invented yesterday and they were the only ones who knew anything about it, especially as regarded matters spiritual. They said they were in Matamoscas to find themselves. It was a good place to look, because that was where they were.

Anyway, Gravid had received from on high a notification that a Great Flood would soon wash away the world, beginning for

157

reasons not immediately obvious with Matamoscas. Gravid and his lemmings were to prepare by building an Ark on Las Pulgas, made of cubits. They weren't sure what cubits were, but figured they would find them in the desert. It didn't hold together Biblically. They didn't know it, so it didn't matter.

Anyway, they built an Ark that would have foundered in a heavy dew and awaited the flood.

For California the idea wasn't peculiar enough to stand out from the background, so the locals mostly drove around in pickups and drank beer in the town's only bar and ignored the seers out on the mountain. Given the way the Coast was pulling down the aquifers, they weren't really worried about a flood. They would have started one if they had known how.

Then Otto Swedenborg, a huge square-shouldered Scowegian meatball out of Minnesota, had roared in on a Harley hog with a little trailer in tow. He looked like Thor and had eyes the color of swimming pools. The trailer contained pickle jars of Radioactive Goat-Curd, he said, which would cure anything, and make one's aura resonate with the inner force of being. He had discovered it while raising goats in land containing uranium ore. Ten bucks.

The locals needed radioactive goat curd like they needed a third elbow, so they sent him to the mountain. They figured nuts rolled uphill, and there was no other hill around.

Gravid apparently saw Swedenborg as a threat to his position as alpha-guru. In the ensuing tension one of the followers said the hell with it and went back to L.A., where her father was big with CBS. A camera truck duly showed up at Las Pulgas. The whole kit and caboodle were on national television that night, auras resonating. Swedenborg got thirty seconds to expound the virtues of his goatish pudding.

The results were astonishing and unexpected. Goat curd took hold of the Californian imagination. First a trickle and then a flood of seekers of enlightenment began to show up in Matamoscas. They were a cross-section of the state: vegetarians, Hare Krishnas, sun-worshipers, fruit-juice drinkers, Ethical Culturists, and a residue of the Orgone Box movement. There were coked-up aspiring movie stars who had believed the desert was a large beach, and Valley Girls who thought the whole idea was groovy to the max. Matamoscas was overrun.

Having manufactured the event, television also covered it. A reporter asked a slack-jawed blonde beachboy, who seemed to have the IQ of a shinplaster, how he felt about the new spiritual order.

"Well, I, like, you know, I think it's really true."

"What's true?"

"I'm not sure."

Swedenborg did land-office business in radioactive goat-curd. In fact, he ran out the first day, and resorted to selling jars of mayonnaise from the local grocery, after taking the labels off. The price went up like taxes in a Democratic administration. When asked how to use the curd to greatest inner advantage, he said to let it age for a week, and then rub it liberally over the entire body. The customer presumably ended up looking like a frankfurter in search of a roll.

There was talk of building a theme park in Matamoscas based on goat curd, as well as a hotel with a golf course, and a factory to turn out soy-based curd-substitute. Several hotel chains expressed interest. Investors were sought to buy a reactor. Swedenborg was offered a high position that didn't require that he be able to do anything. Matamoscas was On Its Way.

Then ABC, concerned about its slide in the ratings, reported that in the cliffs along Route 101-A, out of San Francisco, a rock formation had been found that was an unmistakable likeness of Che Guevara. It glowed in the dark and wept tears of proletarian solidarity, said a professor of psychiatry from Berkeley. He had discovered the likeness while processing his issues among the rocks with the help of some really dynamite mescaline. You could just feel the essence of Che trying to communicate some message of importance to all mankind.

Next morning, Matamoscas was empty. The spiritual freight train had moved on. Swedenborg left with his remaining jars of mayonnaise. Gravid and his followers vanished. The locals went back to driving around in pickups and drinking beer at the bar. The Ark is still there.

None of this happened. But it's all true.

34 MERCENARIES AND POTTED PLANTS

With Colonel Kangaroo at a Soldeir of Fortune Convention

This first appeared in the Washington Post magazine.

T he firing range lay in spectacular desert hills rising to a huge sky over Las Vegas, a blue immensity bounded by worn red stumps of rock like shattered molars. Startling pink strata cut through darker layers the color of clotted blood. Scrub vegetation struggled on the dry earth, forming such a wasteland that it was hard to focus on a couple of hundred people in military fatigues and antisocial T-shirts.

"S Troop on the road! Move'm out!" bellowed a man to no one in particular, indicating his community with fighting men everywhere.

The spectators, a convention of drugstore commandos pretending to be mercenary soldiers, sat in wheeled grandstands brought in from nearby Las Vegas. The men tended to fat, with the swarthy complexions of bulldozer operators and, sometimes, tattoos fading with the years. Everywhere was the aggressive T-shirt, loud with threat and bravado. "Happiness Is a Confirmed Kill," said one. "There Are Few Social Problems That Can't Be Solved By The Proper Application Of High Explosives," offered another. A favorite was "Kill Them All And Let God Sort Them Out."

Officials, some wearing side arms, stalked about while the *chungchungchung* of a heavy fifty-caliber. In front of the stands stood a long table covered with pistols that use 9mm ammunition (more fashionably called nine mike-mike); silencers; a laser-aimed, silenced, fully automatic .22; submachine guns; machine guns (the distinction is that subguns fire pistol ammunition, while machine guns fire rifle ammo). Further out stood paper targets depicting hooded terrorists, generic targets for generic hostility, and permanent metal targets for pistols.

The announcer, in camouflage garb (cammies to those who know) and blue reflecting sunglasses, chatted with the crowd a bit and said, with the assurance of one who knows he is saying the right thing to the right people, "Today....we hope to prove...once again...that bullets speak louder than words."

Applause. "Amen, brother." Shoot them suckers. Any suckers.

Every year about 600 of these milk-wagon mercenaries forgather at the Sahara Hotel in Las Vegas for an annual convention held by *Soldier of Fortune* magazine, by reputation a dread manual of mercenaries. Though some genuine adventurers appear here, most of the attendees are gun buffs, Marines, Rangers, veterans and grocery clerks with weak egos. Each pays $100 for four days, exclusive of accommodations, to stalk around in camouflage suits, raise the price of brewery stocks, watch obscure guns being fired, and pretend for a brief interval that life isn't as boring as it in fact seems to be.

Soldier of Fortune itself, circulation more than 150,000, was founded on $10,000 in 1975 by Robert K. Brown, an old rogue formerly of the Special Forces, formerly of...well, formerly of many groups and exploits, most of them not so much un-savory as irrational. More of Bob later.

The magazine bills itself as the *Journal of Professional Adventurers*, by implication of mercenaries, and sells a sort of warlike swagger and ominous significance, for which there is a bull market. The articles deal in genuine reportage from penny-ante wars, and in hard-eyed hokum about sniping techniques and the strangling of sentries. Some of the classified ads seem aimed at recruiting mercenaries and gunmen.

At the firing range, a wind-burned blond woman in a T-shirt ("D&B Sniper Rifles, The Next Best Thing to Being There") watched two small children in camouflage. She applauded, as did the children, upon hearing that bullets speak louder than words. The patter may have been bloodthirsty, but it was purely atmospheric. The combined police records of this crew would be a boring collection of speeding tickets.

The announcer explained that for the next few hours the reps of gun manufacturers would model on the runways, so to speak, the latest in fall gun fashions from the collections of the better designers.

Next to professional golf, there is nothing so tedious as a fire power demonstration. Blap-clang-clang, blap-clang, baba-babaclangalang. The noise is not loud in the vastness, and nothing of interest happens. Blap-clang. The etiquette at these things is that when an automatic weapon is fired, one listens in silence, as though contemplating an ad-lib from a jazz combo, and then applauds furiously, the degree of fury depending on the length of the burst.

The sun was fierce, and after some idiot swung a loaded Uzi over his head on its sling, so that it pointed at the crowd in its arc, I decamped to meditate behind a concrete pole. Guns should not be used as, or by, yo-yos.

Reporters trickled in. Guns lying on the table pointed at the press, I noticed. Blap-clang, blap-clang. Oh, God, another gun, and it's going to say blapclang.

Finally, a fellow walked out with, why, just an innocent brief-case! Hey, what was he, some kind of lawyer or something? Then, blapblapblapblap! It fired! It was a disguised subgun, *whooooeee*! Just the thing when those international terror-ists try to grab you right there in Turtle Junction, Nebraska. The audience was charmed. What could be more useful? The fellow reloaded and did it again to repeated applause.

There seemed nothing more productive to do than wander around and sample the Zeitgeist. For a moment I watched a fellow with a T-shirt ("Southeast Asian War Games, Sec-ond Place") trying a pair of binoculars. "These have a hell of an optical presence," he said knowledgeably. The clicking chatter of a silenced subgun came from the range. "Vietnam, Ours Was a Noble Cause," read a T-shirt. Another of the by-standers, evidently a cop, told of beating up a suspect with sap gloves, a nifty item of apparel having lead sewn into the knuckles. Doubtless the manufacturer sells them only for de-fense against terrorists, or perhaps for playing Liszt. "They don't leave a mark," the cop said. "Not at all." A T-shirt strolled by, "To Err Is Human, to Forgive Divine, Neither of Which is Marine Corps Policy."

The culmination of the firepower demonstration was the fir-ing of about a dozen machine guns simultaneously, including a .50-caliber, a wicked thing suitable for dawning airplanes. All these guns are legal to own if you have the right license. Far downrange against dry brown hills stood an abandoned bus wired by one of the staff to explode. "Just imagine," shouted the announcer, "that out there in that field is an attacking horde of Contras accompanied by a CBS crew, and we're going to get them."

Huh? Wait. I could see puzzlement spread over the faces of the reporters. Aren't the Contras the good guys? Then, what....? The announcer knew perfectly well who the Contras were, having spent a lot of time in Central America. But his distaste for the press was so great that he momentarily forgot who the real enemy was. Much of the audience didn't notice.

The guns opened, *brrt, whirrrp, chungchungchung,* and the bus exploded in a flash of C4 and gasoline. *Wowee,* death to transit.

The bar back at the hotel was dark, packed with cammy-clad hardware clerks enjoying the camaraderie of men who have been through hell, but probably not through a war. The number of Vietnam vets at these martial clambakes is falling. The vets are getting older, acquiring obligations, families, habits and judgment. From time to time someone shouted, "Incoming!" or "Dinks in the wire!"

"Sweet gun," somebody said. "You can take out a point man at 600 meters."

The conventioneers, not quite resigned to lives of quiet respiration, were ardent for some desperate glory. Surely, they hoped, there must be more to life than stocking spark plugs at the local NAPA outlet. The solution was the T-shirt: "Join the Air Force, Go to Exciting Countries, Meet Interesting People, and Kill Them."

"Check six! Check six!" said someone urgently. To a pilot this means look straight behind, which is where he doesn't want an enemy airplane to be. It is a very military thing to say. The threatening aircraft in this case was a cocktail waitress.

"Whooo-eee!"

Colonel Robert Brown himself wandered in, tight-coupled and fit in his early fifties, white of hair, greeting old friends. He has a shrapnel-pocked face and a conspiratorial tone hinting of many secrets, some of which he knows, and a hard glint in his eyes that, if you didn't know he was play-acting, might persuade you that he was a dangerous man indeed. This is nonsense. One of Brown's many travails is that he is not sure whether he is a mercenary or an over-grown kid imitating a mercenary. He suspects, though.

Bob is everybody's friend but few are Bob's friends, a distinction he does not encourage people to make. "Hey, Fred, you old deleted, how the deleted are you? Wife? Kids okay?" Checking his six, he whispered, "We gotta have a drink later." He said it in the tone in which one would say, "The place is wired to blow, get out fast."

Every Disneyland needs a terry-cloth mouse with big ears to set the tone for the clientele. *Soldier of Fortune* is no exception, so Brown trails behind him a retinue of spooks, Huns, and blade artists who seem to be peering deep into your carotids.

I once worked for *Soldier of Fortune* for a year, hoping to write a book about it (without success: "This is great stuff, Fred," said the publishers, "but we know you're making it up." I wasn't.). On staff, one sees how wonderfully screwy the whole enterprise is. There aren't any mercenaries to speak of today. Every weedy little country with vague boundaries and a vaguer colonel has an army that, no matter how ragtag, is still too powerful to be overthrown by a few neurotic brigands. Mercs don't make much money, there being an oversupply of bored ex-soldiers. Brown, who has a memory like a sieve, couldn't be a mercenary if he tried, being insufficiently organized to get to the airport without the help of a large staff.

From a marketing standpoint, however, the magazine was a stroke of genius, appealing to some dark and sodden instinct thriving on grave mold and histrionics.

Upon starting *Soldier of Fortune*, Brown displayed a flair for... precisely what isn't easy to say, but he certainly had a flair for it. The cover of the first issue was a moody moonlit shot of a bush-hatted merc sitting with his rifle behind barbed wire, and inside the magazine was a photo, now famous in certain circles, of an African who had been shot an inch above the eyes with a 12-gauge shotgun. It was a trifle grotesque, but the greatest attention-getter since Larry Flint discovered gyne-cology. Never mind that the issue appeared to have been put together by the inmates of a vocational-training school for lunatics.

The eccentric colonel and his magazine immediately won the riveted, horrified attention of the national media, which began carrying on like school girls who have discovered a snake. In the presence of cameras, Brown invariably adopted the expression of a man who spends his evenings pulling the legs off spiders. His voice, a sardonic abrasive gargle, seemed at home saying shocking things like, "I'd rather be killing Communists," with an even more shocking sincerity.

The networks quickly detected fascism in *Soldier of Fortune*, a diagnosis correct perhaps of many of the readers but not at all of the staff--well, most of the staff--who are either amused liberals or grown-up kids playing in a paramilitary sand box. Brown improved his reputation by parading around with every known sort of exotic weapon, running ads apparently intended to recruit mercenaries, and spitting tobacco juice like an unruly camel. To make matters worse, multiple mur-derers and pinchbeck mercenaries over the years have tended to be subscribers. For example, Daniel Gearhart, the would-be mercenary from Kensington, Md., who was executed in An-gola in 1976, got his job through an ad in *Soldier of Fortune.*

Believing the magazine to be dangerous, the media responded by making it successful. They savaged it. Unfortunately, the magazine appeals to people who detest the media, so that, commercially speaking, a denunciation by Phil Donahue was invaluable. Brown worked the media like a hand-crank, got his denunciations, got rich, and spent the money sneaking into Laos, Burma and Afghanistan for kicks. The magazine's pages were filled with photographs of Brown waving an AK-47 on camelback somewhere outside of Kandahar, or Uncle Bob (with his staff) grinning from the camps of the Lao resistance. His writers regularly filed from deep within every war zone from the Spanish Sahara to Central America.

The old rogue holds his conventions chiefly to bask in the splendid good fortune of being Bob. He is a self-made man with an artist's pride in his work, surrounding himself with admirers who swagger around in fatigues, talk just like soldiers, and generally maintain the requisite illusions.

Going up the escalator of the Sahara Hotel from the casino, I came to what was perhaps appropriately called the Space Room, filled with the exhibits for the *Soldier of Fortune* convention. Almost 9,000 people, not including conventioneers, paid $4 to see them. Once inside, I spent a few minutes chatting with the magazine's female staff, acquaintances from years back. The women are by a long margin the most competent of the staff, although the men have a small edge in military experience. Both the men and women, by the way, are nice people, although for commercial reasons they try to suppress this information.

Someone gave me a brochure from "School Division, Shadow Protectorate International," which offered to educate the earnest student in such things as "Sentry Removal--Hasty and Deliberate," or "Expediential Death--The Quick Kill" (the latter being particularly attractive, I suppose, to the harried executive who barely has time for lunch).

Inching through the green mass, I found a bulletin board hyping a sort of endurance course in which one navigates across country collecting "heads" consisting of sandbags. The notice said: "Do you want to become a member of the most elite group going today? Would you like to earn the coveted Headhunter patch and thereby command the awe and respect of other conventioneers?" No, actually.

The hall was packed with cammied people moving among booths offering such useful things as ammunition and fighting knives; demolition manuals ("Improvised Explosives–How to

Make Your Own"); T-shirts of crafted pugnacity, some having a lyrical and poetic nature ("Eat Lead, You Lousy Red" and "Kill a Commy for Mommy"); Army field manuals ("The Effects of Nuclear Weapons," and "Tank, Combat, Full-Tracked, 105mm Gun, M1, 2350-061-2445 General Abrams"); and curiosities ("Spando-Flage-Deadly Deception" and "World's Largest Manufacturer of Blowguns and Mold-Injected Darts"). There were stickers for your door ("Is There Life After Death? Trespass Here and Find Out" and "Never Mind the Dog--Beware of Owner"), for your bumper ("Poland Has Gun Control"), for study by your psychiatrist ("The Only Way They'll Get My Gun Is to Pry It from My Cold Dead Fingers").

Just inside the door was the booth of Heckler & Koch, a German gun manufacturer. A heavyset fellow in the booth's machine-gun emplacement grinned--he looked like a biker--and rolled up his sleeve. He said, "The right to bare arms."

A group called the Female Commandos, in cammy Jan-of-the-Jungle clothes, sold photos of themselves reclining languorously on tree branches.

An announcement revealed that a young couple intended to plight their troth, through good times and bad, in sickness and in health, in front of the Heckler & Koch booth. Las Vegas is noted for quicky-wedding chapels, but few of them contain machine gun emplacements. At the appointed time the bride appeared, a pretty blond Army sergeant, accompanied by her to-be, both dressed in cammies. They stood in front of the sandbags, under the logo, "In a World of Compromise, Some Men Don't." She held a bouquet. A large, approving, and green audience surrounded them. The pair seemed very much in love and were clearly having a hell of a good time. The bystanders spontaneously formed a bridal arch of crossed assault rifles, these being available in various calibers and rates of fire from surrounding booths. The newly joined negotiated the arch, and Brown made a short speech wishing them well with a minimum of suggestive allusions.

The crowd in the Space Room had a strong tendency to swagger, which didn't bother me at all because sensible people love to show off. Nor did the heavy-duty masculinity. Washington's tastes in codpieces run to Maseratis, press cards, uplift bras and good tables at trendy restaurants, but they are just another form of Smith & Wesson. And glorification of war is understandable in those who haven't seen one.

But the romanticizing of death did bother me. Too many people here were dwelling on the grotesque and murderous, on the peculiar satisfactions of killing a guard with piano wire. There was a T-shirt showing a rat gnawing a skull, that read: "Rats Get Fat While Good Men Die." Another, showing a skeleton in cammies pointing an AK straight at you, read: "I was Killing...When Killing Wasn't Cool." Twice I heard someone recount the story of the peacenik woman who approached a soldier just back from Vietnam and said, "How *can* you shoot women and children?" "Easy," he said. "Lead 'em a little, and don't jerk the trigger."

The final banquet, presumably the high point of the convention, was held on a parking lot. Night having come, the cammied figures became vague shapes lit by signs advertising tasteless shows. At a long row of raised tables, brightly lighted, sat Brown and his friend John Donovan, a 300-pound all-muscle former Special Forces captain who works as an industrial demolitions expert. Behind them was a huge American flag, flanked by the *Soldier of Fortune* banner, a white field with red beret and crossed stilettos over the legend "Death to Tyrants." The tyrants seemed incidental, but perhaps a flag saying simply "Death" would have been excessively candid.

I gnawed cold ribs, idly wondering whether the cow had been garroted, and watched the crowd. Many were just having a good time. A few believed themselves to be at a convention of mercenaries. Finally, Donovan stood and told the Marine color guard to do whatever it is that color guards do. Everybody rose with a great surge and rustle and wondered whether to salute, slouch in resentment at the imposition, or recite the pledge of allegiance. A retired colonel said a benediction of sorts without evoking much response.

The speeches began, tedious as those at any convention but interesting for the reaction of the audience. In particular, an Afghan spoke, struggling with English. I wondered where he thought he was. The crowd roared approval of the Afghan cause, applauding the hopes of the brave freedom fighters for victory over godless communism.

I repressed the suspicion that many of the roarers weren't quite sure just where Afghanistan might be, and were not in fact deeply concerned over its form of misgovernment. Those who hate communism most seem to be those who can't spell it, or have lived under it.

Donovan, who has a voice like a train coming through a tunnel, rose to lead the congregation in "America the Beautiful." Unfortunately, he apparently couldn't remember the words, falling silent for long periods and waving his hands in the manner of Lawrence Welk pretending to conduct an orchestra. The audience soughed on like the wind through the trees.

I left, barbecued-out, reflecting that theirs had indeed been a noble cause, in which they killed them all that God might do the sorting. Rats no doubt fattened while good men died, but one must expect some casualties while killing Commies for mommy.

The next day I ended up having a drink with Brown in the bar by the pool. When Brown drops his twin roles of mercenary chieftain and anti-Communist Robin Hood, both useful to him in different ways, he is a bright and engaging fellow with a fine sense of humor and not a trace of the morose murderousness of some of his followers. Some readers may find this rude of him: A mercenary ought to have the grace to be decently awful.

The damage Brown does in the world results from inattention to consequences, from regarding wars as tree houses to be played in by his bandido gang, from a narcissism that is simultaneously without a trace of meanness yet not much interested in who gets hurt. His outlook is essentially tribal: He cares about a small group of close friends, and will go to great lengths to help them, but outlanders don't concern him. Now, he is being sued because a professional hit man allegedly used *Soldier of Fortune* to place ads for his services.

Brown's friends drifted by, chatted, laughed, remembered old times. They were not drugstore commandos. An attractive thirtyish woman with an accent and wide experience in Africa chuckled about the difficulty of judging altitude while free-falling through clouds. This led a fellow to tell of skydiving into the frigid air at 35,000 feet (with oxygen) and how miserably hot he got a lower altitudes. "It was really quite awful. I was throwing gloves and things right and left." A young man who had spent nearly a year inside Afghanistan told of flying just outside the perimeter of the Soviet airfield at Bagram and listening to the tires squeal as the MiGs touched down.

A heated discussion arose on the virtues of the A1 Skyraider fighter-bomber for close air support. A man who had been supported by them in the CIA's war in Laos expressed approval. Then came discussion of means of evacuating wounded mujahedin from Paktia.

An intense young fellow, a born warrior, said, "You worry too much about the wounded. That's a fixation of Western democracies. In places like Afghanistan, you accept casualties. They don't matter, unless they get to the point of jeopardizing the mission." Nods of agreement came from along the bar.

Monday morning in the casino of the Sahara Hotel: The early shift of gamblers hypnotically cranked quarters into the blinking machines. The casino was largely deserted. Several gamblers sat around a sort of slot-machine terrarium in which plastic horses jiggled along in slots. They yelled encouragement at their polyethylene nags while hooves electronically pounded. A remaining green-camouflaged conventioneer walked by, the Last Soldier, on his way to catch a plane. His T-shirt, thank God, said nothing.

35 MARRIAGE

To Marry or Not? That's Easy

W ere a young man to ask me, "To marry perchance, or remain forever single?" I would, given the hostile circumstances today of law and love, urge caution. "Marriage is a commitment of several years of your life, plus child support," I would say. "Do not make it rashly."

The question is simply, "Why marry?" As a young man full of dangerous steroids, your answer will probably be, "Ah, because her hair is like corn silk under an August moon; her lips are as rubies and her teeth, pearls; and her smile would make a dead man cry." This amounts to, "I'm horny," with elaborations. It is as it ought to be. The race continues because maidens are glorious, and striplings both desperate and unwise.

Note, incidentally, that by the time October rolls around, corn silk is shriveled and brown.

Why marry, indeed? In times past, marriage occasionally made sense. Life on a farm required two people, a woman to work herself ragged in the cabin while the man carried heavy lumpish things and shot Indians. Later, come suburbia, the man did something tedious in an office and the woman did two hours of housework and stayed bored for six. It worked, tolerably. In the Fifties, nobody expected much of life. It generally met their expectations.

And there was sex, though not enough of it — the scarcity being the propellant behind matrimony. Back then, before the miracle of feminism, women had not yet commoditized themselves. A lad had to pop the question before he got laid regular. Women controlled the carnal economy and, in a world that was going to be boring anyway, that was probably a good thing. At least kids had parents.

Times change. Some advice to young fellows setting forth:

First, forget that her lips are sweet as honeydew melon (though not, of course, green). It doesn't last. One of nature's more disagreeable tricks is that while men are far uglier than women, they age better. Remember this. It is useful to reflect in moments of unguided passion that, beneath the skin, we are all wet bags of unpleasant organs.

Soon you will be a balding sofa ornament and she will look like a fireplug with cellulite. Once the packaging deteriorates, there had better be something to get you through the next thirty years. Usually there isn't.

Prospects have improved for the single of both genders. Sex is nowadays always available. If you don't marry Moon Pie, which would be wise, you may get another chance when she comes back on the market with the first wave of divorcees. It's never now-or-never. Getting older doesn't diminish your opportunities. As you gain experience, you will recognize the tides, the eddies, the whirlpools of coupling — the urgency of the biological clock, the lunacy of menopause. Men by comparison embody a wonderful clod-like simplicity.

As you ponder snuggling forever with Moon Pie, compare the lives of your bachelor and your married friends. The bachelors come and go as the mood strikes them, order their apartments with squalid abandon, drive Miatas or Harleys if they choose, and live in such pleasant dissolution as is consonant with continued employment. The married guy lives in a vast echoing mortgage beyond his means, drives sensible cars he doesn't like, and loses his old friends because he isn't allowed to hang out with them.

Self-help books to the contrary, marriage does not rest on compromises, but on concessions. You will make all of them. Perhaps it doesn't have to be this way. But it is this way.

Moon Pie has only one reason for marriage: to get her legal hooks into you. She doesn't think of it in these terms, yet, and she has no evil intentions. She just wants a nice quiet home in the remote suburbs where she can live uneventfully, raise progeny, and keep her eye on you.

If you think surveillance isn't part of the contract, try going out late with your old buddies. Marriage is an institution founded on mistrust. If she thought you would stick around if not compelled, she wouldn't need marriage. She wants monogamy, at least for you and, with some frequency, for herself. She knows viscerally that you would prefer the amorous insouciance of an oversexed alley cat. You know it consciously. Marriage exists to control the male, until recently a good idea. Now, however, she can support herself, and doesn't need protection. She doesn't need you, or you, her.

She will, however, want to have children. Women do. At which point, God help you.

Given the schools, drugs, latch-keyism consequent first to working parents and then to divorce, and the cultural pressure on children to be slatterns and dope-dealers, reproduction is a gamble. You may not even particularly like the children, or they, you. Nobody talks about this, but how many people do you know who hardly talk to their grown children?

And you've just tied yourself into twenty years of raising them.

The moment Junior enters wherever it is that we are, Moon Pie will have you screwed to the wall. She won't think of it this way, yet. She'll be delighted with the cooing bundle of joy, his little fingers, his little toes, etc. But divorce usually comes. The chances are two to one that she will file: Women are more eager than men to enter marriage, and more eager to leave it — with the kids, the house, and the child support. It won't be amicable, not after seven years. You will be astonished at how ruthless she will be, how well she knows the law, and how utterly hostile to divorcing fathers the law is.

You don't understand how bad the divorce courts are. You probably don't know what "imputed income" is. You think that "joint custody" means "joint custody." Think again. Quite possibly you will have to support her while she moves with your kids to Fukuoka with an Air Force colonel she met in a meat bar.

In short, marriage often means turning twenty-five years of your life into smoking wreckage. Yes, happy marriages exist (I personally know of one) and there are the somnolent marriages of habitual contentment or, perhaps, of quiet resignation. But the odds aren't good.

Permit me an heretical thought. In an age when neither sex economically needs the other, in which women do not need protection from wild bears and marauding savages, not in the suburbs anyway, perhaps marriage doesn't make sense, at least for men. The divorce courts remove all doubt. A young fellow might do well to stay single, keep his DNA to himself, pick such flowers as he might find along the way, and live his life as he likes.

36 A DARWIN LETTER

To a Reader in Self Defense

Over the years I have written columns about the growing doubts among scientists and mathematicians over aspects of Darwinian evolution. The fury aroused among the faithful has been intense and often personal, the doubts being called "ridiculous" but with no explanation of why they are ridiculous. These assertions are frequently, but not always, made by people who couldn't tell toluene from the Taj Mahal. The following, for what if anything it is worth, is a response I wrote to an internet acquaintance whom I will call Derek.

xxxxxxxxxxxxxxxxxxxxxxxxxxxxxxxxxxxxxxxxxxx

Derek,

Since you have attacked me harshly and even insultingly for my doubts about what might be called doctrinaire evolutionism's official story, perhaps you will permit me to defend myself.

I note that your castigation of me has been devoid of substance, being partly ad hominem ("Fred, you are just a retired reporter...."), partly crowd-sourced appeal to authority ("Ninety-nine point nine percent of biologists agree...."), and partly rank-pulling ("I hold the following imposing degrees

from Berkeley, an imposing university....")–none of these degrees, I note, being related to evolution.

Should not a conversation on evolution deal with evolution
rather than the personal virtues and defects of those convers-
ing? And I am not clear just how you know regarding which
matters I have, as you say, "absolutely no knowledge," but
there are many of these and I presume you have your sources.

But to the matter at hand:

Perhaps I err, but I do not believe that science can best be
advanced by refusing to examine it. Had this approach been
followed in the past, we would still believe in epicycles and
the spontaneous generation of mice (as we now believe in
the spontaneous generation of all life). The angry dismissal of
questions seems to have less in common with science than
with religious fanaticism, the more distant shores of Marx-
ism, and conspiracy theories. I will add that in decades of
journalism I have noticed that the intensity of outrage at the
questioning of a belief varies inversely with confidence in the
belief. It is not necessary to defend the invulnerable.

It is not true that virtually all biologists accept orthodox
evolutionism. The ideas you deride in my writing are of
course chiefly not mine. They are those of the substantial and
growing number of highly qualified specialists who question
Darwin. Many of them hold doctorates in the evolutionary
sciences from such places as CalTech and Cambridge and have
done decades of research at these or similar institutions. Many
have written books. From previous correspondence I gather
that it is not your practice to read things that you might dis-
agree with (I apologize preemptively if I am wrong) but I can
give suggestions if you will make an exception. Perhaps ob-
tusely, I adhere to my prejudice that it is unseemly to dismiss
as ridiculous books that one has not read and ideas that one
has not encountered.

That doubts arise regarding Darwin is not surprising since the theory when propounded was more a philosophical idea than a scientific principle, and based on almost nothing, which is how much was known of the relevant cell biology. The 161 years since the publication of *The Origin* is an awful long time for a scientific theory to go unquestioned. In that period physics suffered (among other astonishments) the Michaelson Morley experiment, special relativity, general relativity, the wave-particle duality, the EPR paradox, and quantization of light. In astronomy, the red shift, the 4K background, pulsars, black holes and all sorts of other things. Biology became a field that would have been unrecognizable in 1859. Why should evolution, uniquely among the sciences, enjoy an almost religious aura of infallibility?

I plead not guilty to the arrogance you charge me with. Most of what I have written on evolution consists of questions. A question is an admission of ignorance. How is that arrogant? Permit me an example:

Evolution proceeds by incremental, viable steps from earlier forms. (Is this not so? Am I misstating?) Today's cells employ three nucleotides per codon, providing 64 permutations to code for 20 aminos, control codons, and some redundancy. (Is this not so?)

My question: from what simpler, viable system can this have evolved? From two nucleotides per codon, allowing coding for sixteen aminos with no control codons?

If no transition from two to three can be adduced, then how did the current system come about?

This is a clear and simple question about a simple and universally well understood coding system, probably taught in high-school biology. If you think the question stupid, tell me why it is stupid. Otherwise, please answer it clearly, or have a specialist of your acquaintance do so, whereupon I will stop asking. But if you do not answer, I will ask why it is not a clear case of irreducible complexity.

I offer the foregoing example because it is unambiguous and does not lend itself to evasion. But a great many other questions, quite fascinating, exist regarding the Ediacaran biota, the Cambrian phyla, the Chengjiang Maotianshan shales, intraflagellar transport, the various protein fractions of sequence space, DGRNs, multiple simultaneous mutations, and the countless examples of what seems clearly to be irreducible complexity from Behe's famous bacterial flagellum on.

You say that I am not an evolutionary biologist. I am not. I know no one who is. And as we have had pounded into our heads, A little knowledge is a dangerous thing, drink deep or taste not the Pierian spring. On this basis only PhDs would be permitted to write and only on their subjects, not a particularly practical arrangement. You write on many subjects in which you have no formal expertise. We all do. But of course the warning is most wisely made against those going beyond the limits of their knowledge.

For example, while I am not a trained classicist, and you are, in a column I could name (though I am not sure why I would) the members of the Second Triumvirate or the competitors for the throne after the death of Nero, without going beyond the bounds of my competence. These are simple and uncontested facts within the purview of anyone who reads. By contrast, if I waded into the deep waters of classical controversy, such as whether Claudius really was pulled from hiding by Praetorians and made emperor against his will, or whether this story was concocted to keep him from seeming an usurper in a city still unhappy with the demise of the Republic, I would be going far beyond my competence. So I don't do it. In short, the foundations of most fields are accessible to anyone bothering to open a book. A deep understanding is not.

So with technical subjects. If I were to write (God knows why) that vector cross products, being determinants, are not commutative, or that rotaxanes have been considered as bistable devices for computation, or that pH is the negative logarithm of the hydronium ion concentration, or mention the difference between Shannon information and specified information, or say that thrashing is what happens when the domain of a loop crosses a page-frame boundary, or other such basic stuff, I could do so with confidence though I am not a

mathematician, chemist, information theoretician, or professional programmer. But I do not pretend to be any of these. Most of the things mentioned above are the stuff of introductory undergraduate courses.

The same reasoning holds for the evolutionary sciences. For example, I certainly make no claim to authority in biochemistry. The little I know comes mostly from having read a single book, *University Biochemistry*, which is at the *Dick and Jane* level for a biochemist, presumably an undergraduate text. I do not doubt that you, being of a technical background, know vastly more than I do.

Yet the difficulty of the basics of deep subjects can be overestimated. For example, the first-grade level of biochemistry is just Tinker Toys and Legos, no more mysterious than the workings of an internal-combustion engine: DNA, the RNAs, peptide and phosphodiester bonds, purines and pyrimidines, ribosomes, codons and anticodons, methylation of histones, sugar code, ion channels, all are simple ideas made apparently difficult by technoglop names. The genetic code, which sounds terribly arcane, is far easier to understand than, say, high-school French

In conclusion, there really are many cracks in the official story and many intriguing questions regarding what arguably may be our most fascinating and intellectually important subject we know: Where did we come from, how, and why? Perhaps investigation and thought would be more illuminating than vituperation and personal attack.

Happy surfing,

Fred

37 HORNETS

Indispensable ThoughtThereupon

I've been thinking about hornets. "Why?" you may ask. Because I'm bored with the little voices and can't find my Haldol. Anyway, I claim that hornets show that the human race collectively isn't nearly as smart as it thinks it is. Especially about hornets.

The worrisome thing is that hornets know too much. A hornet has practically no brain, probably a few milligrams or some equally depressing amount. But consider what the dangerous little spike can do.

A hornet can fly, with precisely controlled speed and angle to the ground. It can also hover precisely. This is not easy. Controlling the speed and angle of wings, or whatever the beast controls in (as we say) real time, is not a freshman's project in programming. Boeing couldn't do it.

A hornet can walk over broken ground, effortlessly negotiating obstacles; it can do this hanging upside down. It is no simple thing to control six jointed legs. If you think otherwise, talk to a robotics engineer. A hornet can fly up to a tree branch, adjust its angle in the air, and transition from flight to walking. Easily.

A hornet can see. How well it can see and what it can see, I don't know. I have never been a hornet. Hornets that hunt things can certainly see well enough to find whatever it is that they hunt. This requires integrating the output of the multitudinous ommatidia that constitute its compound eyes into a useful image. Try to figure out how it does it.

Further, it can understand what it is seeing. I'm not sure what I mean by "understand." Probably I mean the same thing you do when you look at something and know what it is. This is a quite different problem from forming an image. It is easy to get a computer to take a picture, much harder to get it to "know" what is in the picture.

How does a hornet with virtually no brain do it?

Today the language and modes of thought of computing dominate the biological sciences. One speaks of behavior as being genetically "programmed" or "hard-wired," and of a brain's "processing power," of "integrating" information in "real time." We are perhaps not always aware that we do this. When you think in terms of a particular scheme, you can begin seeing it where it isn't, begin projecting it onto the world.

When I think of how the control of a hornet's legs must work (except of course that it doesn't have to work the way I believe it must), I think in terms of sensors of angle and force, of procedures to calculate this and that. Do hornets do it this way? Maybe not. Scientists as much as other people struggle to escape their preconceptions or, more usually, don't struggle. Many don't seem to know that they have preconceptions.

A hornet's aggregate behavior is not trivial. It can navigate almost infallibly. In a former rural home in Virginia, I watched them set off across a bean field of a hundred and fifty yards, apparently going to the woods on the other side. They came back. In the jungles of South America, dim under thick canopies, with dense undergrowth, I have seen nests hanging. The insects fly though the growth without getting lost.

Hornets know how to build nests—what to chew, how to find it, when to chew it, and how to paste it together to make (depending on the variety of hornet) a smooth hanging grey gourd full of elaborate cells. This begins to be an awful lot of behavior contained in virtually no brain. (Stray thought: What is the unit of behavior per neuron?)

Hornets know how to mate. Mating with a hornet is not to be undertaken casually, and I do not recommend it to the reader without professional instruction. However, hornets seem to do it. In the default computer-think of the sciences ("default," I say automatically) the explanation might be as follows: The hornet's pheromone receptors send a medium-priority interrupt to the central nervous system which then branches to its mating procedure. Click, click, click, like mechanized tinker toys.

I wonder. I do not know whether hornets mate while flying, as ants do, but it must be beastly difficult to copulate and fly at the same time. Think in terms of airline pilots and you will see what I mean. In terms of computing, mating is an extraordinarily tricky problem. Both bugs have to "want" to do it, recognize each other, know how to align various body parts without error, and produce the needed physiological responses at the right moment.

I know how I would try to write the program to do these things. I do not know how I would make it work. Especially in bare milligrams of brain. Something curious is going on here, methinks, something that we don't understand.

Yet further, hornets know how to protect themselves and their nests. (I have stepped on one barefoot. I can assure you that they know how to protect themselves.) This, like so much of their behavior, is not as simple as it might seem. Stinging in itself may be a reflexive spasm, though hornets that paralyze their prey with stings have to know exactly where to sting. (How do they know?) You generally do not want to miss with a tarantula. Their overall defensive behavior is a tad more complex.

They have to decide that they are being threatened. How? I could come up with some function, probably silly or at least inadequate, of apparent size, nearness to nest, velocity, and so on. ("Function." Back to computers.) That's a lot of calculation in no brain. In any event, being able to simulate a process in a computer doesn't mean that the computer is doing it the same way the hornet is. Computers today clock at several gigahertz. A hornet's barely-brain runs on slow mushy diffusion of chemicals across wet synapses. They are doing something very different.

Further, disturbed hornets look to be angry. They give every indication of being aggressive. Now, it is possible that I am anthropomorphizing. It is also possible that I am not. A thing that appears to be angry may in fact be angry.

Unless I fall into solipsism, I have to assume that if you begin screaming and throwing things at me, you are angry. On equally good evidence, I assume that when my dog behaves playfully or affectionately, she is so. I am not sure why I have to believe that an apparently infuriated hornet isn't.

Now, add up all hornetary behavior, including a lot we haven't touched on—communication between hornets, caring for the young, and so on—and ask how much more complex, if at all, is the behavior of whales, who have brains you could sleep in.

Hornets? I think the little monsters know, within the limits of their world, exactly what they are doing. I am not so sanguine about humans

38 CALIFORNIA DREAMING

How Los Angeles, Well, Almost Was

T he Great Custom Lawnmower craze of 1972 caught California unawares. The state is not easily astonished. Still, Mikey Deeter managed it.

Mikey lived in Riverside, one of those pseudo-Spanish Levit-town's that dangle like beads from the freeways. He was seventeen. He had long blonde hair, a great tan, and the vacant expression one associates with surfers. His total vocabulary came in at perhaps 127 words, mostly automotive.

It was deceptive. As the world would learn, there was method in his blandness.

One afternoon in August Mikey sat in his backyard. He was pondering the unfairness of life, a phenomenon that always takes the young by surprise. All his friends in high school had cars: Deuce coupes and '40 Fords, chopped and channeled, with gleaming hopped-up engines and tuck-and-roll Nauga-hyde interiors and improbable paint jobs. Cars had practical implications. Mikey suspected his buddies were doing the cheerleaders because of their hot mo-sheens. Mikey couldn't afford a car, even a Plymouth. He pondered suicide.

Then a glint came into his eyes. Maybe…just maybe….

No. It would never work.

But...it just might. Anyway, it was worth a try. He went to the garage and retrieved a deteriorating lawnmower.

All afternoon, and for many consecutive afternoons, he labored over the tired machine. He detail-stripped the beast — took it apart to the bolts, gunked the engine, sanded the body to bare metal. He sent the motor and blade to Big Daddy Sparkle's style shop to be triple-chromed. Next he painted the body with twenty-seven coats of hand-rubbed Kandy Kolor Lava Mist metal-flake lacquer the color of molten plums. When he finished you could look deep into it, and the little swirls seemed to move. The neighbors thought he was crazy.

Finally he built-in an eight-track stereo that played *Little Old Lady From Pasadena,* added ape-hanger handlebars covered in plastic chinchilla fur and, for ecological awareness, installed a plastic recirculating waterfall he found in a flower store. When he was through the thing glittered with little points of ruby light and the engine shot diamonds. It was wonderful, indescribable, and perfectly useless. He put it into his friend Bungie's pickup truck and they drove it to a Kustom Car show in Los Angeles.

Now, Kustom Cars as understood in California have little to do with cars, and nothing to do with transportation. They are a form of automotive sculpture, having vast supercharged engines that won't start because the gas tank has been removed to make room for a refrigerator. Sometimes they won't even roll: The wheels, dismounted so the car will sit rakishly lower, rest beside it on satin cushions.

Mikey and Bungie pushed the mower through crowds of aficionados to the Free-Style division and found the presiding official. This worthy was beaded and pony-tailed and had grease under his fingernails. His T-shirt said Duke's Speed Shop. He eyed the mower doubtfully.

"It's a Class-A nontraditional off-road experimental," said Mikey with more confidence than he felt.

He turned the throttle and it played *Little Old Lady.* The official, though puzzled, was charmed. Then Mikey turned on the recirculating waterfall. The official peered intently and said, "Far-r-r-r out!"

"But, I think, you know, it has to be a vehicle," he said.

Mikey countered, "I could stand on it and roll down a hill."

It got in.

To everyone's amazement, it also took First in Class. It was so…different. Further, it was the only entry. Crowds gathered where the mower lay on a cloud of peach-colored glass wool, waterfall trickling.

"It's like, you know, sculpture art," Mikey told a bored reporter from the *L.A. Times.* "Like stuff in museums." The reporter returned to the newsroom, where he mentioned the mower as he might an outbreak of plague. He had been in Los Angeles too long.

Luck had it that the art critic for the *Times* was on deadline with nothing to write about. He knocked out a piece about how the mower "represented a cross-pollination between the technical underpinnings of modern industrial society and the yearning for a new and meaningful esthetic by the young." He baptized the new movement Kinetic Bauhaus. Then he got drunk to salve his conscience.

The effect was galvanic. Up and down the coast, young males raced to garages. They sandblasted, welded, and painted, surfing on the wave of the new art form. Though few appeared to be repositories of high intelligence, or any intelligence, they were in fact technically adept and imaginative, the kind of young men who had made America into whatever it was. They believed instinctively in the Californian principle that if a thing isn't worth doing at all, it is worth doing to wild excess.

Mowerdom flourished. Shows proliferated. Magazines appeared: *Kustom Grassblaster* and *MegaMulcher.* They carried articles like, "440-C Blades vs. Polycarbonate Laminates: Which Is Better?" and "Nitro-Fueled Unlimiteds Take On The Elephant Grass of Northern Thailand."

These were halcyon days for Mikey. He was a guru, in demand on the radio. He explained The Movement, which was now generally recognized as representing a fundamental new direction in artistic expression, and perhaps a basic alteration of Western consciousness.

"It's a new thing and all. If you go to an old art museum, the paintings are, you know, like flat. They just *hang* there. That's the trouble with old art. It doesn't *do* anything"

However, ominous clouds were brewing. What with being a spiritual leader, appearing on talk shows, and clearing up a backlog of cheerleaders, Mikey was sliding imperceptibly down the slack side of the wave. Already his mower was regarded with antiquarian interest, like the Wright Brothers' airplane.

Others pulled ahead. A post-doc in biochem at Berkeley mounted the engine from a Harley Sportster on a mower modified with dune-buggy wheels. For ecological piety it had the now-mandatory recirculating waterfall, in a cage with a gaudy macaw that shrieked obscenities in Spanish. It would have won the Nationals had not the macaw taken to coughing horribly. The vet determined that nothing was wrong with it. It was just trying to imitate a Sportster engine. By them, unfortunately, the Nationals were over.

Mikey didn't have the money to compete. The death blow came when a wealthy proctologist from Anaheim, with extensive holdings in the stock market, announced that he was going to mount a surplus helicopter upside down on wheels, trumping even the Harley with its confused bird.

It was terrible. Mikey's own movement had left him behind.

So did the cheerleaders.

Shortly he was again sitting in his backyard, pondering the unfairness of life.

39 HANT VI

The Sage of Busthead Gives a Backwoods Explanation of Economics

Saturday morning I walked down the holler, along the old rail line, with a fresh jug of Beam to see what Hant was up to. I wanted to ask him about dodge ball and jumping jacks and violence and all. Hant knows everything. Well, nearly about.

Summer was just starting to get up a good head of steam and the sun was pouring down the holler like it had something in mind and bugs was shrieking and buzzing the way they do, trying to get laid. If I was a bug, it's what I'd do. Considering what bugs looks like, I don't see how they ever do it. Anyways the mountains was green and peaceful like. The tracks was mostly weeds since the coal mines went bust. Pretty much most of West Virginia is that way.

Hant works a moonshine still that's hid off in the woods. He sells to yuppies out of Washington, the Yankee Capital, that wants a Authentic Mountain Experience. Most of them survive it. I won't drink that panther sweat he makes. It ain't *much* worse than battery acid and don't really kill more than a few yups every year, maybe thirty or forty, but I always carry me some Beam.

Hant was standing over by his pile of authentic mountain stone jugs he gets bulk lot from Taiwan and pouring a bottle into the mash. He's getting on in years now and kinda stiff, and when he sits down it takes a while. He's got a jaw like someone in the family went into the bushes with a front-end loader, and this flat slouch hat that made you think he found it behind a cow.

"What you putting in that mash this time?" I said.

He's always putting some new devilment into that bust-head he makes. It's to give the yups a little extra kick. He tried stove polish and bug spray and I don't know what all. LSD did the trick but the yups ran into so many electric poles that we didn't have light for a week.

"This here's Joe's Cuervo. It's Tea-kwiller that them Meskins drink. I reckon Joe is who makes it. Tastes like floor-wax remover. It's most likely why Meskins don't have teeth."

He was eyeing the Beam. He may make rat-killer for the yup trade, but he's got better sense than to drink it himself.

"Gimme that," I said, taking the bottle back while there was still time. "I saw Willy Bill McNutter down by Lou's Rib Pit and he said he heard on the radio out of Wheeling that some kid stepped on a jumping jack and poked a hole in his foot. Now the Feddle Gummint says jacks gonna be illegal and if they catch you with one you go to jail. How much damn sense does that make?"

He looked puzzled. Hant knows everything, but sometimes a few things kinda slip his mind.

"Hell," he said, "a jumpin' jack ain't nothin' but a set of orthogonal identity vectors with little tiny balls on the ends."

"Now don't you go talking like that, Hant. You're gettin' out of character."

He looked unhappy. "I know. I'm a low-down sinner and no good to nobody. I wanted to go to CalTech to learn me some math, but they told me I couldn't because I don't exist. It ain't easy being a Literary Apparition. Gimme nuther hit of that Beam."

He sucked down about three gurgles and looked powerful content. He may be a apparition but he can sure put away other folk's whiskey.

"Well, jacks is agin the law now. So's dodge ball. Gummint says it's violent and dangerous. And you can't shoot cats outa car windows any more either."

"What's dodge ball?" he said, kind of edgy. He don't like to admit he doesn't know a particular thing.

"It's when one kid stands in front of a wall and the others try to smack the bejesus out of him with a big rubber ball."

He got this pole-axed look on his face. "What's wrong with that? We used to do it with rocks. Country's going to the devil, I guess."

I knew what he was thinking. There's only two things to do in a car at night, and if you can't shoot cats, you're down to one. Them gummint varmints is always meddling where they got no business. I'd put a bounty on'em.

I could see I wasn't gonna find out much about jumping jacks.

Hant went over to a big stump and got a can of rust-cutter and poured it into the mash. Like I say, he's always trying to pep up his shine for the yups. He can tell how well it worked by reading the obituaries the next day.

"I figger this will balance out the Tea-kwiller," he said, looking satisfied. "Jiffy Lube still hiding?"

Jiffy Lube is my girlfriend when she's not trying to kill me with a pool stick or run me over with her car. Her real name is Jennifer Imidazole Fergweiler, but we call her Jif. She's a good girl, just kind of excitable.

"Yeah. Sheriff says she can come back soon's that last guy she smacked comes of of the coma. She says she might start a revolution. What's the world coming to when you can't smack a rascal with a hunk of rebar, she wants to know."

I sat on a log and nursed pretty hard at the Beam before Hant killed it. Hant's old three-legged coon hound, Birdshot, came over so I'd scratch his ears. He used to be four-legged until he put his paw under a lawnmower to see what was making all the noise. It don't pay to wonder too much.

Hant got this solemn look on his face like he does when he thinks he's about to say something important.

"We got too much gummint," he said. "They tell me I can't shoot revenooers no more. If I don't do it, who's going to? I'll bet they didn't think of *that* in Washington. How's a body going to make a living if he can't shoot revenooers?" He looked tragic.

I said I had to go and he asked me to bring him another jug of Joe's Cuervo next time I Came. I went off to look for Jiffy Lube. If a feller can't step on jumping jacks, or play dodge ball, or shoot cats or revenooers, there ain'tt much else left to do.

40 IN A MOONIE HIVE

TheWorship of Ammunition, Seen During An Interlude with Moon's Curious Church

Having recently watched documentaries of various dismal cults, notably Buddhafields and Scientology, I bethought myself of Moon's Church, owner of the *Washington Times,* and my brief association with it ages ago. Thinking that it might be of sociological or psychiatric interest, I post the following. *Early Seventies. Unpublished.*

The tall scrawny freak with the red hair converted in the spring of 1972, several months before Jerry wandered, roaring, onto the scene. I had recently graduated from both Vietnam and college and, not knowing what else to do, was living with a collection of hippies at Stafford Court House, Virginia. The other freaks were the usual unemployed prophets, fruit-juice drinkers, tarot-card readers and desert patriarchs in from communes in New Mexico. Most were sane without being extreme about it. A few were psychic train-wrecks trying to reassemble themselves, and mind-burnt druggies who had learned to package brain damage as mystical insight.

The Sixties were waning fast. The freak years had been fun for those who could handle them, but by now everybody sensed that the ride was over. Kids looked sourly at the future, judged that the market for aged hippies was limited, and wanted out.

They weren't sure how to get there.

Seeking the escape hatch, the crowd at Stafford started changing religions the way other people changed their socks. For a while the preferred faith was acid. Everybody stared for hours at patterns in the upholstery, garnering wisdom. Then Buddhism held a corner on truth for a week, but faded. Hinduism had its brief moment. A bearded seer from somewhere out West once peered into my eyes with bovine serenity and said, "Hinduism. You know it's true, man." His cow-like assurance was like a current of water, carrying me along so that I thought, "Yeah, hadn't thought of it, it is true, isn't it?"

Finally the skinny red-head thumbed to Washington with his girlfriend, who had been a Moslem the week before, and returned full of confused faith in someone called Sun Moon. At first we assumed that anyone named Sun Moon must be an itinerant witch doctor from one of the desert tribes, perhaps a protégé of Carlos Castaneda. We soon heard that Moon was a Korean guru with holdings in an ammunition factory.

"I think I really believe it," the red-head told me regarding the epiphany of the weekend. "It's really, like, you know, true. I know it is."

"What's true?"

"I'm not sure yet."

He wanted to believe that something was true. He didn't much care what, and anyway he could find out later. Within two weeks several others from Stafford had joined Moon's church. They were formally committed to the worship of a Korean arms manufacturer. The idea was curious, even for the times.

The Sixties were treasure years for the connoisseur of oddities: bikers, SDSers, hopheads, hallucinating paranoiacs, anything you wanted. Moon's church, however, seemed a genuinely new kink in the social rope. For the next several months the lunar faithful (I tried desperately not to call them Loonies) was a hobby, sideshow, and source of free meals. Seen from the inside, from the level of the sidewalks of a giddy age, they didn't bear much resemblance to later accounts in the newspapers. They didn't bear much resemblance to anything.

Soon the Stafford believers thumbed up to the Moonie hives at 1611 Upshur Street, NW. I went along, wondering what to expect. The Moonies were not the only new product on the faith market. There was the New American Church, which worshipped the better grades of dope, and the Hare Krishnas, who seemed to worship attention and Georgetown, and something called Maharaj Ji, such a tender golden-brown butter ball that one's instinct was to baste him. The Moonies were the first faith to crack the defense sector however. A faith based on ammunition was categorically worth seeing.

The Moonies had rented several adjacent row houses on Upshur and, as I soon learned, held picnics to attract proselytes, of which there seemed to be a bumper crop. We arrived looking like refried death and discovered a swarm of kids in suits, ties, stockings, pretty dresses, and a state of unearthly cleanliness. An attractive girl in an up-market blue dress hailed us with a bright smile. She was pretty, deliberately pretty, which was startling in an age of funk.

"Hi! I'm Linda Marchant. I'm so glad you could come. Won't you join us?"

I thought to myself, "Soap." Even today people think "soap" when they meet Moonies. But the outgoing friendliness was undeniably nice, very nice. They could turn it on and off like water, but it was nice. It appealed powerfully to the lonely and confused who, however they talked of Thoreauvian independence, were getting older and suspected they had missed an important boat. This assertive gregariousness, grown devious and systematized, later become known in Moon-talk as "love-bombing."

Under spreading trees in the back yard, girls rushed about with bowls of salad. They all looked like Heidi. The guys looked like stockbrokers. Several other freaks stood around, kind of embarrassed but kind of...you know...digging it.

We all sat. After a brief prayer to a god as yet unspecified, whose chief quality seemed to be syllabic extension ("Faa-aa-a-a-ther....") there were a few words about the sacred mission of the United States. Characteristically the Moonies told us very little about themselves. They preferred that a recruit find out what he was committed to only after he was committed to it, an idea acceptable to a surprising number of people. The peculiar gift of the Moonies was to pursue sincerity, frankness, and a revival of ethical values by means of deception, manipulation, and a disregard of ethics.

A heavily freckled kid next to me, explaining that he was in real life in the Coast Guard, said, "We ought to put naval mortars on the roofs. For protection." Good idea. "Protection from whom?"

"Communists. They want to break up the church. These people need military advice."

He kept looking up at the eaves.

Shortly thereafter, in hopes of working the fertile recruiting grounds of the University of Maryland, the Moonies established a splinter cell in Hyattsville in a decaying frame house that is now a parking lot. Like most political cells, it should have been padded. They began rehabilitating the house furiously in shifts. About that time I was angling for a job as a part-time special-education-and-computer-science teacher at Suitland Senior High, and hoped that maybe some of the Stafford converts might arrange to let me stay at the new hive for a week while I found an apartment. They couldn't unless I converted, which was too much rent. For a week I lived in the back of my 1957 Chevy, the Blue Bomb, which had a mattress running from the back seat into the trunk. By day I helped the

Moonies rebuild their house. The stability of the set-up was uncertain. Instead of killing the termites, I noticed, the Moonies caulked up their holes.

At a Moonie recruiting session one night in an apartment in College Park Towers, I met Jerry, a short club-footed Nazi who liked blacks and Jews. Actually he wasn't a Nazi, but said he was, which is stranger than being one. The Moonies were hawking the Divine Principle, as they called their theology, to a gaggle of freshmen. These latter were all agog, what with being at a real college for the first time, and hearing about a genuine exotic oriental religion and all. They had never heard of anything so advanced, not even in Wheeling.

At the time Principle involved something called the Base of Four Positions, which looked on the blackboard like a baseball diamond with God on second, Adam and Eve on first and third, and humanity at home plate. The idea was that Satan, currently in the guide of communism, had long ago gained control of the earth, and God kept sending people to try to redeem it. Abraham, Moses, and Jesus had all tried and failed. ("Oh Lord, whyfor hast thou forsaken me?" was considered corroborative.) Moon by implication was the next redemptive Marine to storm ashore on the cosmic beach.

People drifted and munched on potato chips. I was bored to the point of twitching but didn't want to go back to the Chevy. The door opened and a deep bass voice growled, possibly not intending to be audible, "Hello. I'm looking for a bunch of maniacs...wait. I think I'm here."

Jerry was about five feet six inches tall and nearly as wide, with bushy black hair, a tangled beard, and a big orthopedic shoe. A fierce angry energy radiated from him. We shook hands—he had the delicate fingers of a pianist--and he growled, sotto voce, "You don't look like one of these. Are you?"

"God no."

"Let's go somewhere and talk."

We escaped to the balcony. Jerry then spoke roughly as follows, always in staccato bursts. "Yeah, I'm getting a Ph.D. in political science...god, it's nonsense...quantification of political behavior. I can make it work but who cares? These crazies, ain't they something? It's the decline of Rome all over, the Weimar Republic gone bad...four thousand years of progress for nothing...everything is downhill, *heehee*. This little Nazi is sick of it...If there any hope, it lies with the proles."

Jerry called himself a Nazi, but purely as a rhetorical device. He lacked the ideology, the mean streak, any obsession with race, in fact any of the traits necessary to Nazism, and had in most respects the politics of an angry Democratic populist. He said he had been a real rostrum-pounding right-winger in school up north, but reality had grown on him.

"Right wing politics in nonsense. So's left-wing politics. The center doesn't have politics...Took me a long time to see that...God, it's awful." He was mad at everything in general, perhaps because of a difficult life and a crippled leg, or perhaps because of excessive observation. He was too rational to be mad at anything in particular.

Anyway, Jerry was drawn to the Moonies by their psychiatric interest, by his lack of anywhere else to live, and by Caroline Libertini of the Hyattsville nest. Lib was a basic broad-hipped Italian earth-mother with bronzed skin and high cheekbones that looked almost Indian. She radiated the Italian womanly virtues, genuine in her case, like an antenna: Warmth, security, friendliness, concern, and a funny sense that you were part of her family. The lonely and shell-shocked fell in love with her, absolutely inaccessible though she was, whereupon the Moonies tried to convert them. I don't think it was conscious tactics, but it worked.

Soon Jerry was following her around like a growling congenial puppy. Then he moved into the Moonies' tiny unfinished basement on the tacit understanding that he might convert any day now, which he had not the slightest intention of doing. It was strange to see him stomping around the kitchen making spaghetti or acting as a towel rack for Lib, a troll among Snow White's dwarves. Beneath the fuming, he was sociable, and they were pleasant by ideology.

The Moonies didn't know what to make of Jerry. They themselves were given to indirection, manipulation, diplomacy, and a certain understatement of the truth. Jerry had the finesse of the Wehrmacht. Upon listening to a circuitously phrased obliquity intended to get him to do something, Jerry would amiably say, "Dumbest goddam idea I ever heard. What idiot thought of that?"

"Hey, Reed, gimme a hand moving my hate. Gotta lot of hate to move," Jerry said to me one day.

By this he meant a large collection of screwy far-right books. He also referred to mail as hate: "Gotta go check my hate-box." Soon we were laboring up and down the stairs to his bare cubby hole with some of the strangest literature known to man: Six-volume sets about the communist influence behind the fluoridation of water, and disintegrating works by obscure syndicalists. I felt trapped in a comic book: In the basement of a weird Christian cult somewhere in the nation's capital, a right-wing troll and his accomplice, a crazed hippie anthropologist, discuss the destruction of America's brains by toothpaste...." Jerry banged away with hammer and scrap wood. He didn't believe in his books any longer, but he collected them as a connoisseur.

"Need some more hate shelves."

"Jerry, this stuff is nuts."

"Yeah, bonkers. Real loony-tune stuff. Let me show you something really wild...."

We became friends, in part because of a common fascination with the curiosities inhabiting the ground floor. We discussed them endlessly in the beer dens of the University. Jerry would sit bristling with horror and foretell the collapse of society.

"It's all over. You see, don't you? Cults are the sign of collapse. The Orphic mysteries all over. Except they're sexless. Like monks. I'm going to go to Canada and live. Tell them I went to Mexico, will you?"

Sexless they were. Despite all the mass gimme-eight-hundred-volunteers weddings, mostly in the future then, they were as hostile to sensuality as the early Christians. The few married couples had pledged four years of abstinence to Fa-a-a-ther. I forget why they thought he wanted it. Dating outside the church was discouraged. So was dating inside the church.

"Oh, twaddle," I said, "It's just...well, auto-therapy."

"It's brainwashing. Just like a North Korean POW camp. You see how much sleep they get? None. They don't sleep. It's destroying their biochemistry."

"Moon doesn't make them crazy, Jerry. He just collects them. I think."

Actually I had to admit that Jerry might be right. No sleep, constant frantic activity, the unvarying presence of the group, rigorous discipline, lots of ritual. Maybe it did gum up the old metabolism.

The Moonies were a peculiar phenomenon: Extremists of the center, militant middle-wingers. Yet theirs was a cultural, not a political, centrism. They were kids who had grown up in the optimistic brick-box suburbs of 1953 when the economy was booming and it really seemed possible that all of humanity, after thousands of generations of struggle and evolution, might finally get a washing machine. On countless Saturday mornings the Moonies had watched Superman jump out of the window in a howl of wind while the announcer intoned approvingly of "Truth, Justice, and the American Way," which were then thought to be synonymous. Two Buicks and glossy teeth were ingrained in their psyches.

Then somehow they had fallen into the fetor and anomie of the Sixties. For them the age was not a time of thumbing through glowing green mountains and having adventures. They were the casualties. They had waked in too many sour crashpads, engaged in too much thoughtless sex, done too many drugs. Moon's church was the way back. It was the faith of clean shirts and fanatical normalcy. Thus they managed to be those strangest of creature, zealots of moderation.

I was still living in the Blue Bomb when Jerry saw his first prayer session. The Moonies knelt in the living room as the spirit moved them, put their foreheads on the floor, and gasped, "Fa-a-a-a-a-a-a-a-a...ther!" with a little explosion on the last syllable. Then a tumult of prayer would burst from the penitent, mostly apologizing to Fa-a-a-*ther* for the pain caused by errant humanity. Then they looked at Jerry and me to see whether inspiration might have taken hold of us. Invariably it hadn't. The first time Jerry looked at me in candid dismay. "This isn't happening, is it?" he whispered.

"Why?"

"It can't be happening. That's obvious."

"Oh."

"It's the end of civilization."

Later, Jerry learned to grin an aw-shucks-fellers, maybe-next-time grin. The Moonies waited, figuring he had to crack sooner or later.

Washington had now discovered the Moonies and contemplated them with a pleasant sense of alarm. The war in Vietnam had grown boring. Here was a new lunacy to titillate the jaded palate of the Potomac Byzantium. With luck, the Moonies might do something horrid and interesting.

Liberals, easily puzzled by unfamiliar categories, decided the Moonies were fascists. Almost everyone assumed that they had some hidden agenda, the reason being that they had no obvious agenda. Generally ignored was another possibility, that they had no agenda at all, a suspicion supported by the eerie pointlessness of everything they did. All zealots are narcissistic tragedians, wrestling with destiny beneath their inner Klieg lights, and not especially interested in practical results. This is a truth that few in Washington could afford to concede so they figured the Moonies had to be up to something.

Actually they seemed to be engaged in the passionate, urgent, frantic pursuit of nothing in particular. Nothing they ever did had an effect. Their propaganda persuaded no one, and wasn't well calculated to persuade. If Moonery was a conspiracy, it was a conspiracy without a purpose.

One day in late fall they came running into the house from a local shopping mall, faces red with cold, an ecstasy of self-sacrifice lighting them like bulbs.

"We've been having a Rally for God! It was great!"

"Yeah! People were spitting on us!"

They constantly invented new religious tics. For a while they made a fetish of standing for a second of silent prayer before entering any door. Then there was Holy Salt which they sprinkled around at times of solemnity. I've seen sumo wrestlers do the same thing.

One evening in winter I dropped by to see Jerry in his cubby hole and found the whole cell bundling up.

"Hi! We're going to Holy Ground. Want to come?"

Holy Ground, it seemed, was a patch of earth on the Mall which Moon, for mysterious reasons, had declared sacred. Stranger things have happened, though probably not much stranger.

"Sure, why not?"

Off we went down Michigan Avenue. They were bubbling and

happy, infused with the usual sense of warmth and illusory direction. They knew Fa-a-a-at-*ther* was with them, pulling them through life like a rope, and they left a broad wake of enthusiasm. At the Monument they piled out, well-groomed and middle-class and home at last from the alien ideologies of scag and Lenin. They rushed to a spot apparently located by triangulation, stood in a circle, and looked reverently at the sod. It had grass on it.

The church was starting to get a bad name, not so much because of anything it really did as because it stole children—or so the parents preferred to put it. With few exceptions the Moonies were so warped by a wretched home life that they became susceptible to Moon—but this was not the wisest thing to tell parents whose kids were buzzing and clicking.

And there was the practice of Divine Deception, which is exactly what it sounds like. Some of it was airport technique ("Hi! I'm taking a survey....") but through the years a lot of kids would go to what they thought were summer camps, only to find out later that they were at the robot factory. Angry apostates told tales of psychological ruthlessness that wobbly proto-Moonie egos couldn't take. The Moonies responded that anyone who wanted to could leave. Unfortunately many of those sufficiently off balance to be Moonies in the first place were not good at independent action.

The Moonies earned their worst reputation among those groups who produced the most Moonies. Jews seemed especially hard hit, perhaps because they were especially vulnerable. The Jewish Moonies, all from secular families, had the usual Moonie problems of unloving homes. They also had the additional burden of not being Jewish enough to feel rooted in it, but too Jewish to be entirely at home in the surrounding society, and not about to convert to Christianity to assuage their spiritual yearnings. So they ducked the question by joining Moon.

Kids from military families also showed in up numbers. Having authoritarian fathers possessed of a certain combative simple-mindedness and not much affection, and having gone through the terrible insecurity of moving and losing their friends every two years, they needed something warm and fuzzy to hold onto. A fair number of Catholics showed up, feeling at home in a heavily ritualized faith. So did kids from Protestant families in which a great show is made of Christianity for the purpose of browbeating the child and out-holying the neighbors. The parents were furious, twenty years too late.

For a while Jerry resisted my view that the Moonies were dynamic idlers, but the evidence kept coming in. For example, they held what everyone called a Nuremberg rally on the Monument grounds. It was wonderful. Scaffolding went up. Technicians in white jump-suits scurried about, assembling great banks of phenomenally large loudspeakers and a big platform for dignitaries. An enormous speaker's platform went up. The reverend Moon's face in cyanotic blue began to peer from posters on every fence in the city. Sound buses drove crazily through the streets. Suddenly in front of Woodies would come an unintelligible blare of loudspeakers. A bus would turn the corner, plastered with blue Moons. As it drove past bellowing nothing understandable, which echoed from buildings (*"Arblewargmonumentwunhwarbworworworld"*), scrubbed faces peered out with the characteristic crazed expression, hands waving mechanically. "Join us, join us!" The impression was of a mechanical asylum worked by a spring.

On the day of the rally the big speakers roared, perfectly intelligible from anywhere on the grounds. The technicians had not been amateurs. The grounds began to fill as an efficient Moonie organization bussed people in from Philadelphia. A hootenanny outfit began singing to pull in more audience. The chestnut smell of dope wafted about in clouds. The scale, the volume of sound, were Orwellian. The moment demanded a howling demagogue to bay hatred at the cosmos. This was it, everybody figured with a little frisson. The Moonies were going to demand that Nixon be made Reich chancellor. Instead, the political speech was brief, a hiccup in the hootenanny, and said America was a great country and the world depended on us, and now have a nice day and back to the music. That...was...all. I walked through the crowd, mostly hippies and inner-city blacks, and asked what the rally was for. Hey, man, I don't know, wanna toke?

I didn't know either. Neither, I think, did the Moonies.

One night Jerry and I were sitting in my largely bare apartment, drinking beer and trying to figure out Moon's Barbie Dolls. He started talking about himself, and I suddenly realized why he knew so much about nickel-and-dime politics. He was a celebrity of sorts. A few years back on the strength of his then-impeccable conservative credentials, Jerry had gotten a job with Liberty Lobby, which exists in the airy region where the right wing runs out of feathers and empty space begins. Discovering a lot of virulent anti-Semitism in the Lobby's files, he had decided that Liberty Lobby was nuts, stolen the files, and given them to Drew Pearson.* There was a certain brutal directness in Jerry's approach to things. The resulting expose had somewhat tarnished his reputation in the circles of the loon Right, and left him unsympathetic to cults, political or otherwise.

Who did he like, I asked? Well, just sort of folk, he said. Especially the under-folk, such as blacks, and those who had otherwise suffered discrimination-you know, Italians, Jews, Poles, Indians, and so on.

God, I thought. I'm living with a liberal Nazi.

The ferment rose again at Upshur Street. The Moonies were gearing up to smash world communism. The trouble was that, being mostly kids, they identified communism with the student Left, the only Left they knew. Consequently they attached great importance to the Trotskyite left-deviationist schismatics of the International Bracero Labor Party's Maoist-revanchist wing, consisting of two half-literate sociology majors who were about to graduate and become management interns. The central hive on Upshur Street seethed with excitement. They began having workshops on the techniques of political action. Jerry and I showed up for one of these.

We got a chilly welcome. Friendliness to the Moonies was a political technique only, their real interest being their spiritual scar tissue. They got real cold real fast.

"Are you expected?" asked a prim girl who reminded me of a motel manager. All Moonies reminded me of motel managers. I'm not sure what brought on the freeze, but I think too many hippies had learned that you could, as at the Salvation Army, get a free meal if you listened to the prayers.

"We're from Hyattsville," I said, thinking it would be adequate explanation.

"Who do you wish to see?"

"Barry Cohen," I told her, Barry being head of the Hyattsville cell.

"One moment. I'll check with Mr. Cohen."

Mister Cohen? Another administrative lunge. First names were too informal for a movement that saw itself as a spiritual IBM. The frost princess finally let us in. The basement was full of folding chairs. A fellow with a flip-chart was lecturing approximately as follows:

"To be effective we have to know the enemy and how to counter his techniques. The communists and their allies use street theater, for example, a powerful technique. What do you do when you see three SDSers dressed as Vietnamese peasants with American soldiers beating them? We have to learn to speak effectively, how to handle hecklers. And remember, it won't be easy or pleasant. We will be abused, even beaten up.

Possibly some of us will even lose our lives...."

Hard and lonely work, I thought, but somebody's gotta do it.

"Martyrs looking for a stake," growled Jerry. "It's the end, I tell you. This stuff is spreading." Jerry's problem was that he took the collapse of civilization personally.

To demonstrate counterhecklerism, the instructor appointed some Moonies to simulate the SDS and launched into a speech on American values, a big Moonie theme.

"And save...."

"Fascist pig! Fascist pig!" shouted the heckler-appointees, warming to the role. The speaker, demonstrating correct countermeasures, waited in lofty silence and continued with heightened feeling.

Jerry was chortling with delight. "Aw right! Belt out that hate! Let's hear some good hate!" The Moonies weren't sure what to make of this, not understanding that his was the technical appraisal of a student of maniacs.

"Hate! Hate! Hate!" shouted Jerry encouragingly.

"Stop giggling, dammit," I said, "or they'll turn on us."

The Moonies thought they were combating communism, but really they were just scraping up fill dirt for the inner emptiness. None of it mattered at all.

Nothing lasts, not even the end of civilization. One day Jerry got seriously fed up with political science and decided to go to Florida and live by tuning cars. Exposure to a political-science department will make any sensible person want to work with engines. My teaching job ran out. For that matter, the Hyattsville hive was showing sings of falling apart: Only the hardy can stay with a cult for long.

One last time Jerry and I sat in the apartment with a case of beer, trying to understand Moon's giddy sideshow, lobbing the empty bottles across the room into a cardboard box.

"It's the age of the cult, amigo," he said. "They're starting the slide into the mist. The whole show's gone bonkers...If there's any hope, it lies with the proles."

The next day he disappeared southward. I never heard from him again. I packed the Blue Bomb for a drive to California, planning to go on to Taiwan and learn Chinese. For several years I heard nothing from the Moonies. Then in maybe 1979 I bumped into Diane Something-or-other in Dupont Circle, a nice kid from the Upshur Nest. She wore a turban and spoke of her devotion, to Islam, which had given meaning to her life. Her eyes were unhappy and she was looking a bit old for that sort of thing. Moonies? Oh, she had passed that stage. We said we should have lunch soon and, by tacit agreement, didn't.

*Drew Pearson was a noted political columnist.

41 CANOEING, ODDLY

*The Canoe as Camel: Paddling Where the
Water Wasn't*

The time Frank Green and I paddled the canoe through the dry hills of King George County in search of water would, I suppose, discourage naval historians. Fact is, we'd have had a better chance of finding water in the Sahara in mid-August of a drought year. I will say, however, that the adventure got us covered with some the finest ticks bred on the Southern seaboard, which is the best tics country on this or any other continent.

We were fifteen and didn't have a brain in our combined heads. Frank was from a family that made its living by getting up at four a.m. and pulling crab pots on the Potomac, because people in Washington wanted to eat crabs. He eventually became an electrical engineer. King George was wooded hills and fields full of deer and whistle pigs and reasonably poor people who actually worked for a living. I was just me.

I had bought the canoe a few months before with paper-route money. Frank and I had proceeded to do with it every wrongheaded thing we could come up with. We had capsized it in the Potomac and gotten it full of jellyfish. We had loaded it to the gills with Pepsi and paddled the Rappahannock from Fredericksburg to Port Royal. We put girls in it —three of them once, which was more that it would hold, so one of them was always falling out and we had to tow her home, as she couldn't get back in without tipping us over.

At this point there was nothing left to do. The flavor went out of life. We were thrown back on our usual pursuits of reckless driving, purloined beer, and wild, fruitless dreams of lechery.

Then Frank asked why we didn't explore Peppermill Creek. On Route 206 a few miles out of metropolitan Owens, a conurbation of population maybe thirty, the road drops sharply into an outsized ravine and crosses a rivulet running through the woods. As a body of water it is, if not navigable, at least wet.

The hill itself will live forever in local lore. Kids liked to lie about losing the cops on it at 130 miles an hour, generally in unmuffled wrecks that could have made 90 if you had pushed them out of an airplane.

Friends dropped canoe and us at the reedy marge of the alleged stream. It was one impoverished waterway—about three inches deep on the average. Salamanders lived in it, along with brown scum and the occasional water snake. We found a channel deep enough to float the canoe, but not straight enough: If the stern was afloat, the bow was on solid ground.

We picked up our vessel and carried it fifty yards down the middle of the stream. Here the channel straightened out. Both ends of the boat would float at once — but not with us in it. Our weight pressed it firmly into the mud.

You begin to get the flavor of the voyage.

The United States is a great country, and certainly a marvel to the world, because its citizens don't ask whether a thing is reasonable, or even possible, before doing it. We were as American as you could get.

I heaved on the bow painter, which is technical for a piece of rope stuck to the front. Frank shoved mightily on the back. Twigs scratched us. Deer flies bit us. We sweated and swore with fervor and artistry. At intervals we sat in the canoe and drank Pepsis. Clouds drifted past above the thicket and birds made bird noises and dragonflies sat on the paddles and watched us. Life was mighty satisfactory, we said.

It was not travelsome, however. We heaved and hoved and huffed through the undergrowth, a yard at a time. We were establishing that you can go anywhere with a canoe, but not necessarily in a canoe. The rivulet did not behave as in all honor it should have, deepening with distance from its source. Instead it spread out into an almost-marsh of soggy earth, thickly covered with swamp grass. For practical purposes, we were in a canoe on a prairie.

We drank more Pepsis and pondered. Common sense suggested surrender. We couldn't have picked common sense out of a lineup if it had waved at us. We were determined not to accede to reason, mass, topography, or the sheer intransigence of life. Boyhood doesn't work that way. We didn't, anyway.

With great perseverance but little intelligence — and, by now, with a spirit of sheer vengeful stubbornness — we began poling the canoe across the field, rather like demented gondoliers. Exactly like them, in fact.

You can propel a light canoe across slick grass by putting the paddle in the ground in front of you, but at a backward angle, and pulling down on it fiercely, as if chinning yourself. Which sometimes happened: Either the canoe moved, or we found ourselves, so to speak, up the paddle without a creek. It was a new concept in wrong-headedness. Once the canoe slipped out from under me, and I was left hanging on my paddle, and had to walk back.

We expected the creek to resume, but it didn't. Once I actually climbed a tree looking for water, while Frank sat in the canoe. The Pepsis dwindled in number. We started to get tired, a rare state for a country boy. We rested and looked at the swamp grass glowing pale green as the sunlight began to come at it from a lower angle and the shadows of things got longer.

Finally we gave up. We seemed to be heading west and the next body of water might be the Mississippi. We consulted the sun to determine the time. No, we were unlikely to reach California by dinnertime.

We carried the canoe out through a nearby cow pasture and got just covered with ticks. They came to latch onto the cows, and brought all their sisters and granduncles and in-laws, and covered everything, like a speckled rug. I had never seen such robust ticks, or so much dry land.

42 THREE FEATHERS AND TENTH GRADE ENGLISH

A Rural Memoir

I peaked early. It happened in tenth-grade English in King
George High, in rural King George County, Virginia, in
1962. The teacher had asked us to write the beginning
of a short story, which she would read aloud to the class for
criticism. I wrote about an Indian fur-trapper named Three
Feathers in Quebec who at the local trading post bought traps
made by Bob Ferguson, an English Canadian. But it seemed
that competition had come in the form of a French-Canad-
ian named Jock Lerouu, which I thought sounded French, who
made stronger traps. Mrs. Souder duly read my effort to the as-
sembled studentry:

"Do you want Bob's traps?" the store owner asked Three
Feathers.

"Three Feathers no want Bob's traps. Three Feathers want
twelve Jock's traps...."

Like I say, life has since been mere, dull, and pedestrian, without savor. You can't go up from the top.

The county was forested, abutting on the Potomac River, with
muddy Machodoc Creek, catfish rich—in that part of Virginia,

three-quarters of a mile wide is a creek—emptying into the river. At sixteen we sailed along winding wooded roads at night in ailing jalopies at least several of whose parts functioned at any given time. We had guns, fishing poles, deer and, blessedly, almost no adult supervision. We parked endlessly in the deep woods with the nicest girls on this or any other planet, and...again...no supervision! Adults assumed we had sense enough not to kill ourselves. Rather to our surprise, we did have it.

If we wanted to paddle half a mile into the Potomac in a canoe and jump overboard to swim, we did. Sunlight. Brown water. Sparkling waves slapping against aluminum hull. Nobody knew where we were, or cared. No life guards. No Coast-Guard approved "floatation device." We didn't need one. It would have taken a major federal program to drown us.

We had less sense that a blue-tail fly in a moonshine jar, but it didn't seem to hurt us any. Steve Hunt and I once made a ramshackle raft by putting four inner tubes under the corners of a sort of platform knocked together from packing crates. Unfortunately one inner tube had a robust leak. We set from bravely from the boat dock at Dahlgren Naval Proving Ground on the Potomac, where we lived, Steve paddling, me working the bicycle pump....

The rural South was car country. We thought cars, breathed cars, drove cars, or at any rate drove wheel-born ruins resembling cars. They were necessary in a county where anywhere you might want to be was miles from where you were. A car was a heraldic emblem, codpiece, bar, salon, identify and, far more in hope than in practice, love nest. Flashing past each other in the night, we recognized each by the merest glimpse of tail fin. And we talked cars, endlessly.

"Saddy night, saw Bobby in that fitty-sedden Chev he got, *ba-a-a-a-ad* mo-sheen, oh man, 283, log manifold, three-quarter Isky, magneto ignition, solids, lake pipes an' cut-outs, phone flow, ported and polished, bored out like buckets, Sun tach, udden udden udden *sceeeeeeeeech*."

Decrypted, this meant that we had seen, or hadn't and were lying about, a 1957 Chevrolet so hopped up as to go fast and noisily, briefly, before throwing a con rod through the oil pan. "Phone flow" is four-on-the-floor, a totemic form of gear shift, hopefully involving a Hurst narrow-gate shifter. It was good juju.

King George shared the gun culture of the South. All the boys had shotguns and rifles. I'd estimate we could have over-powered the average Central American army. The first day of deer season was a school holiday since the teachers knew the boys and Becky B. weren't coming anyway. Guns were thought a natural part of life. No one cared. You walked around with them.

I remember a frigid winter night when my friend Rusty and I went to shoot rats at the dump near Colonial Beach. He had his twelve gauge, I my prized Marlin lever-action .22. We drove my '53 Chevy, and ooched down the dirt road through woods to the dump, lights off so as not to alarm the rats, Rusty sitting on the right fender. Ice in frozen puddles crackled under the tires. We could hear rats squealing and knocking tin cans down the garbaged slopes. I switched on the lights, Rusty snap-shot Blam! Blam! And fell of the fender onto his head with the recoil.

Becky and Rusty eventually married. It actually made sense, but they did it anyway.

Gun culture, yes, but nobody shot anyone, or thought about it. The boys were hardy and muscled from chopping cord wood and "lifting hay," heaving bales into trucks collecting them in the field. They were not delicates. You could get smacked in the mouth if you chose to start a fight, but nobody would have kicked an opponent in the head or picked up a length of rebar or ganged up. It wasn't how we were.

We lacked many of the appurtenances of modernity. Anorexia and bulimia, for example, of which we had never heard. The girls were entirely sane and didn't know what Prozac was, since it wasn't yet. The boys often did have attention-deficit disorder—we called it "boredom," and cured it by finding something interesting to do. Hyperactivity disorder? When you play three hours of fast-break pick-up basket ball after school, plus phys, ed., and spend most of your life in the water or on it, or on a bike, you don't have time to be hyperactive.

They say global warming doesn't exist, but it was sure colder then, and twenty high school kids would drive to Payne's Hill or various ponds to sled and ice skate, no adults, life guards, surveillance cameras, nothing, just snow and ice and stars, and we'd hoot and holler and slide until most had gone home and you were alone in the night with the ice creaking *glooonk*, and the wind coming up, and it was a different world.

The only drugs we knew about came mostly from Anheuser Busch. We often got them from a country store I shall not name, as it may still exist, but would have sold beer to a nursing babe. We were not a particularly drunken lot, usually. at one swig in pursuit of a manhood barely visible on a remote horizon.

And now, somehow, we are sixty-five. How did that happen?

43 ETERNITY AND PICKLE TOPS

A Jorney into the Improbable

On that far-off night in August of 1962, the moon floated huge and yellow over dark Virginia forests that stretched away and away to the glittering broad Potomac River. Chip Thompson and I trudged along the shoulder of US Route 301 from the Circle toward Dahlgren. We were sixteen. The county—King George County in the Tidewater—was mostly woods and creeks, less populated than now, simpler. Three-Oh-One was still two-lane, the main drag from Maine to Florida. Before us it ran like a determined snake up and down the hills to the Potomac River Bridge into Maryland.

Chip was a country boy with no sense or particular prospects but we both had the wildness of our years on us and sometimes adventured together. He was broad-shouldered and buzz-cut and had a rural economy of expression that Twain would have recognized. "Come on, Ricky," he would say (I was then called Ricky), "You're slower'n dead lice." Or, "Damn, my granny's slow, but she's dead."

I guess it was two a.m. Traffic had long since died except for the big semi rigs on the interstate hauls. The Circle, really a wide spot with a few stores, had shut down. Chip and I had gotten there in my '53 Chevy, a rounded and matronly barge, and in need of rings, where she had mysteriously quit.

We decided to walk the ten miles or so home to where 206 intersected the highway. He lived up the hill past Owens, I to the right toward the navy base. The distance was no problem. We were both basketball tough and spent our days on or in the creeks. The pull of the dark countryside was on us. In the spring of life the night appeals powerfully to young bucks, being a time of freedom and vague portent of you didn't know what, which was the appeal. It was a big feeling to be alone in the world, rocking in the windblast of the trucks and the singing of the tires.

We hoofed it, gravel crunching underfoot in the silence.

In those days, boys early got cars of sorts. The county was a place of distances. The nearest real town was Fredericksburg, 27 miles from my home, the Circle ten, Colonial Beach 17. The country kids lived in farms and side-roads betwixt and between. We lived in our cars too, and loved them. On a Saturday night we might drive to Freddyburg to cruise Hojo's, back to Colonial Beach just to keep moving, down to Gus's Esso to see who was working the graveyard shift. If you had a date you parked in one of various isolated spots known to all, and did much less than you let on later. Otherwise you drove endlessly through the night for the sheer independence of it, for the feeling of being alone and left alone.

We knew the roads and we knew each other's cars. We reveled in the odd comradeship of winding along the wooded narrow curves of 218 and having headlights come out of the night and it was Charlie Peyton's '57 Chev, *baaaad* 283, and disappear into the evening. With a two-second glimpse of grill or tail we could tell you the year, make, most probable and biggest engine, and prospects in a drag race.

But the Pluke Bucket—for so my tired Chevy was called—had expired.

On and on Chip and I walked in the silence. Bugs hollered in the trees, but bugs don't count as noise. Our talk was mostly of girls and cars, yet once he said, "Ain't it great, Ricky? Bein' so *free* and all?" It was. The night brooded around us, full of hunting things and lives that had nothing to do with us. We started into the hills that rise and fall before the river. Soon we could hear the eighteen-wheelers as they reached bottom, double-clutching into low gears for the up-haul, then the roaring and thudding of diesel stacks. It was a grownup sound in a grownup world which we were on the verge on entering.

Cresting a hill, we looked down the dropping highway to the valley of the next. The road at the bottom was shining. In the brilliant moonlight, yes, the cooling asphalt lay speckled with a gleaming that made no sense, like drops of mercury or glowing dew. We had never seen anything like it. Nor would again.

Consumed by curiosity, we finally reached the outliers of the strange luminescence. I looked down and saw...a pickle-jar top, such as you find on jars of pickles in stores. Thousands of them lay on the dark asphalt, shining in the moonlight.

Understanding came. Back in the other direction, past the Circle, was what we called the Pickle Factory. It was a bottling operation for Mount Rose Pickles, where the stronger county boys sometimes worked. Apparently a delivery truck carrying jar tops had jackknifed in the road and flipped. The truck was gone, but the pickle tops were everywhere.

It had never occurred to us that pickle tops had to come from somewhere and that whole trucks full of them might exist. In some distant state people spent their lives making pickle tops just as inhabitants of the county fished and crabbed. Here was the industrial belly of the pickle business.

For ten minutes we kicked at pickle tops, scraped them with out feet, picked them up and threw them saucerishly into the woods. No trucks came. We were alone with a thousand pickle tops glowing eerily at the moon with bugs keening in the black foliage. I think we both knew that here was a moment never to be repeated, something that maybe had never happened to anyone before.

Then we kept on down the highway. Dawn lay ahead and I wanted to be in through my window to avoid explanations. In those days you could still see the stars. They gave a sense of mystery to the great universe arching over the dark land. We could hear water trickling in low boggy spots toward Machodoc Creek and there was nobody else in the world. Just us.

44 THE COLOR OF EDUCATION

Race and the Racism Racket: Doing Well While Sounding Good

This first appeared in Harper's Magazine *and caused such a stink that, according to Lew Lapham, the editor, it got him fired.*

Should anyone in authority say anything sensible about racial policy, an event unlikely to occur before the next Ice Age, he would have to say that when it is not merely futile it often injures the people it is supposed to help; that it succeeds in antagonizing whites without benefiting blacks; that it has become more of an ideological battleground than a practical program; and, finally, that it is a fraud, serving principally to benefit groups that grow fat from racial programs. He might be tempted to add that civilized man has never seen such a monumental stream of unembarrassed twaddle.

An obvious observation, which hardly anyone seems to make, is that blacks suffer less from racism than from poor education. Harvard does not reject black applicants because it dislikes blacks but because they are badly prepared. Blacks do not fail the federal entrance examination because it is rigged to exclude them but because they don't know the answers. Equality of opportunity without equality of education is a cruel joke: giving an illiterate the right to apply to Yale isn't giving him much.

The intelligent policy is to educate black children, something that the public schools of Washington manage, at great expense, not to do. In fact the prevailing (if unspoken) view seems to be that black children cannot be educated, an idea whose only defect is that it is wrong: the Catholic schools of Washington have been educating black children for years. The Catholic system has 12,170 students in the District, of whom 7,884, or 65 percent, are black.

On the Science Research Associates (SRA) exam, a standardized test of academic achievement, the average reading ability of eighth graders in Washington's Catholic schools in 1979-80 was at the 52nd percentile, compared to the national norm, and at the 72nd percentile, compared to big-city norms-that is, above average. In arithmetic, the percentiles were 60 and 75-above average. In science, they were 53 and 66 — again, above average. In none of the subjects tested, which included composition, "language arts," and social studies, were scores as low as the 50th percentile.

Most people argue, incorrectly, that the overall scores are being pulled up by the scores of white students; it is remarkable how few people will accept that black children make good grades because they are bright and well taught. But it happens that Mackin Catholic High School, on California Street, N.W., is 94 percent black, and students there average at grade level or higher when tested in reading; they score similarly in other subjects. Our Lady of Perpetual Help Elementary School, in Anacostia, one of the poorest neighborhoods in the city, has only two white students. The students in the seventh grade read at the 40th percentile, or, to put it another way, rank 10 percent below the national norm. Ninth grade students in the public schools in Anacostia rank 26 percent below. St. Anthony's, in northeast Washington, near Catholic University, is about 90 percent black. On a composite SRA score, its eighth graders rank at the 67th percentile against the national norm, and at the 76th percentile against big-city norms. When there are virtually no whites at a school, whites cannot be responsible for the scores.

Skeptics suspect that Catholic schools get good scores by accepting only promising students. There is a little truth in this, but not much. Catholic schools in Washington do not accept hopelessly bad students or students who have other problems, such as serious police records, which would cripple them academically or cause them to disrupt classes. Some schools are more lenient than others about admissions standards, but most accept students who score below average. They do not gather up the geniuses and neglect the rest.

Why do the Catholics get better results? One reason is that the students have parents who care enough to put them in superior schools. Another reason is that Catholic schools have superior staffs, with teachers generally required to have at least a B.A. in their subjects. Also involved is academic rigor-- students are often assigned two-and-a-half hours of homework — and discipline. One disruptive student can reduce a class to chaos. Catholic schools, not being subject to educational bureaucracies and political pressures, can prevent disruption, resorting, if need be, to expulsion.

In my estimation, the Catholic schools also profit by their respect for the students — a belief in their potential, accompanied by a recognition that they are, after all, children. At St. Anthony's I talked to the eighth-grade English teacher, Lorraine Ferris. Ferris seems to be half scholar and half drill instructor, about right for junior high, and strikes me as being about as good as teachers get. She knows English from the gerunds up, which puts her ahead of most college English departments. "The important thing," she says, "is to make children believe in themselves, but you can't do it by coddling them. I won't accept a 95 from a student who should make a 98. It's important to them to see that they can compete. And the idea that black children can't do the work is baloney. I see red every time I hear it."

If black children can be educated, the question arises: Why aren't they? The usual answer is that racism and conservatism are responsible, and much ink is spilled in exorcising these evils. But racists and conservatives have almost nothing to do with educational policy in Washington. Until recently, we've had a Democratic president and Congress; we have a liberal National Education Association, a black city government, a black school board, a black electorate. They, not conservatives or racists, bear responsibility for conditions in the schools.

One may argue that in general the chief hindrances to progress for poor blacks are misguided racial policies and the attitudes of those who make them. It is important to realize that things were different twenty years ago. In the Fifties and Sixties, the civil rights movement was producing results--[1]dismantling the prevailing apartheid, for example. Unfortunately the movement somehow became bureaucratized, then became self-serving, and finally became the problem. Today the obstacle to racial progress is not Bill Buckley; it is Ted Kennedy. It isn't the KKK; it is the NEA.

Race has become an industry. CETA, EEOC, OMBE, and other forbidding acronyms with huge payrolls exist by presiding over the status quo. Various freelance acronyms, such as NAACP, SCLC, ACLU, and PUSH, derive their importance from appearing to galvanize the governmental acronyms. Politicians and influential subcommittees thrive by conspicuously giving their attention to racial matters. The Democratic party retains blacks as a largely docile voting bloc by maintaining the flow of money for racial programs. Billions of dollars, countless jobs, and the political balance ride on keeping things as they are.

The underlying difficulty is that when enough people are employed to solve a problem, means become ends. It becomes more important to continue solving the problem, which provides jobs, than to have solved the problem, which would result in dismissals.

Not all racial functionaries cynically exploit racial division, but many do. People are remarkably adept at aligning their principles with their pocketbooks. Racial bureaucrats will always manage to persuade themselves that their particular programs are of paramount importance in the struggle against oppression. Further, their principal interest being their own interest, they will oppose the elimination of unsuccessful programs to prevent the discovery that nothing very bad would happen if they were abolished.

They have all but silenced opposition with their insistence that He who is against me is against blacks. This argument, repeated often enough, results in something close to censorship, so that it is currently almost impossible to discuss racial programs on their merits-i.e., on whether they work. Whether, for example, the welfare system needs revision isn't considered.

The national media and the major dailies do their best to enforce the ban on open discussion. They simply won't publish serious criticism. Relative freedom from criticism encourages a preference for moralism in place of practicality. The tendency is to see racial questions as a conflict between abstract Good and abstract Evil, in which the most important thing is to display admirable intentions, usually to the exclusion of doing anything useful.

There is a further tendency among racial functionaries to do penance for sins they haven't committed, such as tolerating slavery. Penance is fun, but marvelously useless.

When people are more concerned with seeming good than with doing good, symbols become irresistible. Racial policy abounds in symbols that express concern, cost a lot, and miss the point. There is, for example, the Martin Luther King Memorial Library-oversized, under-used, short on books, with a grandiose lobby that has enough wasted space for several simultaneous games of basketball. The District, however, doesn't suffer from a shortage of books but from a shortage of people who can read them.

The University of the District of Columbia, actually a school for remedial reading, is similarly a symbol. Ninety percent of its freshmen read below the ninth-grade level. Although a new university in the District is not necessarily a bad idea, a fraudulent university whose students are hardly beyond the level of junior high school is unquestionably a bad idea. The sensible policy would be to improve the schools so that the city's children would be qualified to attend a university, and then to build a university or, for that matter, several universities. But establishing a bogus university is quick and easy; teaching a city to read is slow and difficult, and produces votes a decade later.

It is fascinating that the racial establishment systematically blocks the adoption of the educational policies that would most benefit black children. For example, when Vincent Reed, superintendent of schools in the District, urged the wholly admirable idea of a special school for children with the intelligence and energy to do advanced work, the proposal was defeated.

Such schools exist in cities across the country and have worked well. Readers unfamiliar with the workings of the socially concerned mind may not immediately see why bright children should not be educated to their own level. The reason, said those who defeated the idea, is that it would be elitist. Elitism is regarded as a dreadful thing by the wealthier members of the racial establishment, who send their children to Harvard to avoid it.

Preventing elitism by rendering children illiterate is a dubious favor to them and to the nation. The social effect, of course, is to delay the emergence of black leaders and therefore to retard the progress of the race. South Africa achieves the same result by the same denial of education but is morally superior in making fewer pretenses about its intentions.

The racial establishment also discourages the imposition of discipline in the schools, without which teaching is impossible. The problem is horrendous in some of Washington's schools. The students need protection against marauders from outside, and the staff need protection against physical assault by students. Teachers tell of being attacked by students with knives, of being afraid to go to certain parts of the school. Vincent Reed recently voiced his concern over security. "When I have kids being shot in schools by outside intruders and teachers being mauled by outside intruders--last year we had a young girl ten years old taken out of the building and raped--I don't have time for rhetoric."

Others have time for rhetoric. Ron Dellums, a black representative from California, asked at a Congressional hearing whether the presence of policemen in the schools would inhibit discussion of ideas. (Maybe. So, presumably, do knives, guns, drugs, and rapes.) It is a commonplace argument among educationists that discipline is regimentation and a means of racial repression. Illiteracy is a far better means of repression, and disorder is a sure road to illiteracy.

The racial establishment also ensures that black students have poor teachers. One might expect racial politicians to insist on providing the best obtainable teachers for black children who, being behind, desperately need them. It would not be an unreasonable demand. Given the rate of white-collar unemployment, highly educated teachers can be gotten by whistling.

Unfortunately the racial establishment, never particularly energized about the quest for academic quality, is especially unenthusiastic about finding good teachers. There are several reasons, one being that many in the race business belong to the various species of pseudointellectual riffraff that multiplied during the Sixties--psychologists, sociologists, educationists, feminists, the whole touchy-feely smorgasbord of group-gropers, anxiety-studiers, and fruit-juice drinkers who believe that the purpose of education is emotional adjustment. They seem not to have reflected that an excellent source of maladjustment is to be an unemployed semiliterate without the foggiest understanding of the surrounding world.

Educationists, who have a well-developed sense of self-preservation, understandably do not favor higher standards for teachers. Hiring good teachers means firing bad ones. Any serious attempt to get rid of deadwood means bucking the powerful teachers' unions, which, as a variety of tests have shown, would be gutted by any insistence on competence. Moreover, dismissal of incompetent teachers would mean a heavily disproportionate dismissal of black teachers. The bald, statistically verifiable truth is that the teachers' colleges, probably on ideological grounds, have produced an incredible proportion of incompetent black teachers. Evidence of this appears periodically, as, for example, in the results of a competency test given to applicants for teaching positions in Pinellas County, Florida (which includes St. Petersburg and Clearwater), cited in *Time*, June 16, 1980. To pass this grueling examination, an applicant had to be able to read at the tenth-grade level and do arithmetic at the eighth-grade level. Though they all held B.A.'s, 25 percent of the whites and 79 percent of the blacks failed. Similar statistics exist for other places.

Another major reason for the slow progress of blacks is a prejudice, palpable in racial policy though unprovable, that blacks are incapable of competing with whites. Racial functionaries will deny this with fervor; yet if they believed blacks could compete, they would advocate preparing them for competition. Instead the emphasis is on protecting them from it. The usual attitude toward blacks resembles the patronizing affection of missionary for a colony of bushmen: these benighted people are worthy in the eyes of God but obviously can't take care of themselves, so we will do it. Whenever blacks fail to meet a standard the response is to lower the standard, abolish it, or blur it--not to educate blacks to meet the standard. The apotheosis of this sort of thinking was the lunatic notion that black children should be taught in the gibberish of the streets because it "communicates," the implication being that English was too difficult for them. Nobody thought English too difficult for the Vietnamese.

Paternalism has practical consequences. The unrelenting condescension supports blacks' view of themselves as worthless. (If anyone doubts that poor blacks do indeed regard themselves as worthless, I suggest he spend some time with them.) People who think they cannot succeed do not try.

Finally, the absolute unwillingness of the racial industry to police itself--to make sure that money accomplishes the intended results--has made racial programs a synonym for corruption, waste, mismanagement, nepotism, and undeserved preference. It is hard to find a racial program that is not grotesquely abused. The District's annual effort to provide summer jobs is typical. The jobs don't exist, nobody tells the youths where the jobs are thought to be, no work is done if the jobs are discovered, and the youths don't get paychecks even if they happen to do the work. Last year the same thing happened, and next year, one wearily expects, it will happen again. The pattern repeats everywhere. CETA, for example, might better be called the Comprehensive Graft and Scandal Act. Some programs lapse into frank absurdity. Under "affirmative action," group after group musters the clout to get on the deprived-species list until, on a quick calculation, 65 percent of the population qualify as mistreated minorities.

Corruption and mismanagement inevitably lead to resentment among whites whose money is being wasted. This resentment is currently called "white backlash," which has a comfortingly vicious sound and implies that it is someone else's fault. (In the race business, everything is someone else's fault.) Antagonizing half the country by shoddy performance is abysmally stupid politics, especially given that the nation would probably have few objections to sensible programs that worked. I find it hard to believe that many people would object to giving a black child a good education at a reasonable price.

45 BAD SKIN AND PROOF OF GOD

That Adolescents Survive Probably Proves that God Exists

Y ou need to know about how in 1962 I was a half-wild county kid of sixteen in the wooded expanse of King George County, Virginia, and drove a derelict '53 Chevy that shouldn't even have started but in fact went places that would have terrified Rommel's panzers at their brazenest. (You may think you don't need to know this. Well, you do. It's like, you know, real history, and American.)

Now, that Chevy was so old and tired and worn out that its continued motion seemed a high order of miracle. It had six cylinders but ran on three, perhaps saving the others for emergencies. The closest it came to compression was a sort of ancestral memory, and the tires showed more fabric than rubber. But it was built like a tank. It had to be. Kids then were hard on cars.

It is a little-known fact that a rural boy of sixteen can bond with a car—can come to love it. His mo-sheen (the correct word, as in "*baaad* mo-sheen," which paradoxically means "good mo-sheen" and carries implications of nonexistent speed and virility) represents dependability in a hostile world, at least if it usually starts. It is codpiece, heraldic emblem, home away from home, bar, love nest, salon, even at times transportation. When parked on a frigid January night in the wild woods, it is warmth, safety, and escape if need be. It is independence and manhood, or at least the southern fringes thereof.

The county was mostly woods and fields with towns far apart —King George, Colonial Beach, and Dahlgren Naval Weapons Laboratory on the Potomac, where I lived. Cars consequently were our life. On Saturday nights we drove interminably through the dark forests, just driving, moving, rapt with the night and freedom, without the sense God give a crabapple. The times were different. We'd park for hours with our girlfriends in empty fields glowing with moonlight. We actually liked our girlfriends because we knew we probably weren't going to get laid anyway, so we might as well do it with someone who was good company. It didn't seem to hurt us.

We learned things only known to teenagers. Don't park under a mercury-vapor light because it makes zits turn purple and green. Sheldon's Country Store would sell beer to an eleven-year-old. Don't chug a bottle of Wild Irish Rose to impress your friends. It will, but it isn't worth it. Your father is probably smarter than you think he is: If you disconnect the speedometer cable, he'll count the bugs on the windshield and know you didn't really go to the movie three blocks away.

Truth is, the Pluke Bucket—my tired Detroit dragon—was not of high consequence. The best cars had phone-flow. This refers to a gear shift of four speeds, located on the transmission hump. ("Four on the floor" to the uninitiated.) Below in the scale came threenatry–three on the tree–meaning a shifter of three speeds on the steering column. The Pluke Bucket had an automatic transmission, which was prestigious as a venereal disease in a convent. But she was mine.

Our dream car was a fitty-sedden Chev 283, bored-and-stroked, ported and polished, with two four-barrel carbs ("dual quads"), magneto ignition, solid lifters, Isky three-quarter cam, milled heads, Hearst narrow-gate phone-flow, 3.51 Positraction rear end and tuck-and-roll Naugahyde. But this was like saying that Ursula Andress was a hot date. Wasn't going to happen. Not to us.

A great advantage of knowing about cars was that you could talk for forty-five minutes without saying a thing that your mother could understand. Apart from technical argot, we said things like, *Baaad*-ass fitty-eight Ford, cam lope *wubbwubba*, udden-udden, popped it, *sceech*....tachin' two grand..." with gestures indicating power-shifting and the like.

Lots of times we got into sort of half-trouble, which is about right for teenagers. Harry Burrell was a farmer noted for being irascible. He lived on the hills overlooking Route 301 and came out with a shotgun after anyone who drove along the dirt road that crossed his fields. I remember that he held his pants up with a piece of rope. He was that stingy.

Anyway one dark night after the spring rains my girlfriend Rosie and I wanted adventure. There was a crusty farmer we'll call Harry Jones who tied his pants on with a piece of rope to avoid paying for a belt and he hated it when teenagers raced along his farm road at night. So we did it often. We were just scared enough of him for it to be appealing.

One night my girlfriend and I roared in the Pluke Bucket along his road, blowing the horn. It was like poking a hornet's nest with a stick, though I guess dumber. If Harry had shot us, we probably would have deserved it, but that was true of most things that the boys did. Anyway, sure enough, the lights came on in Harry's place and he came after us on his tractor—so help me—just about the time we came to a stretch of serious mud. Our tired chariot began spinning out and fishtailing back and forth toward the ditch.

We began to be scared. Harry wouldn't really shoot us (we thought) but we might wish he had. He was rough. However, the Bucket and I had been in worse places and I knew how to surf in mud. In deeper places the trick was to speed up, bump, whrrrr, and spin through without quite breaking the axle. We speculated that it would work better if the tires had tread on them, but this was an alien concept.

But Harry had a tractor. We hadn't thought of that.

We came to where the road, which is an optimistic designation, dropped down the side of a hill to a narrow creek and then went back up. The tractor was gaining. Not good. We shot down the declivity, crossed the creek on momentum, and then...stopped, tires spinning helplessly on the upslope. Things were deteriorating.

Americans are capable people, though without judgement. I leaped out to push, and Rosie took the wheel. Picture it: Cold mud over my shoes, raw exhaust blowing hot over me, tires spraying mud, and tractor lights appearing at the crest of the hill. Darkness. Wetness. Our bodies would never be found. I made a superhuman effort, seeing no plausible alternative. The Bucket moved a little, and a little more.

Rosie was a country girl, and understood mud. She knew that if she stopped to pick me up, the Bucket wouldn't go forward again, but spin out. She slowed, I ran. I leaped in the door and we went up hill, not very fast but faster than a tractor.

That's why Americans got to the Moon and occasionally win wars. They never ask whether a thing makes sense until after they've done it, and then you can't take it away from them. I mean, can you imagine a Frenchman in a Lamborghini escaping Harry Jones? Nah.

This originally appeared in shorter form in *The American Conservative*

46 LOW-BUDGET RACING IN THE SOUTH

It Was a Trip While It Lasted

This first appeared in Southern *magazine, which was shortly bought by the* New York Times *and shut down, a victim of Yankee hostility to Southerness.*

Road Atlanta--near Gainesville, 40 miles north of Atlanta--more than three miles of twisting, hilly, sports-car track. Team 20 has been on the road eight hours from Farmville, Virginia: two vans with Triumph race cars on trailers, tool boxes and welding rigs stacked everywhere, radar detectors in the windshield, CB radios smoking. Team 20 is at home on the big roads as much as truckers are. From Farmville on, they have plugged into the net of cop-watchers that extends from the beginning of every interstate to its end. The voices seem to come from nowhere in particular, the accents changing as the traffic blends and separates.

"Smokey the bear southbound at mile 25."

A state trooper.

"Yeah, just got him on radar."

"Another taking pictures by the underpass. mile 46."

"Hey, roller-skate, guess what's pulling up behind you."

Law and order is one thing, but what those state troopers do is meddling. Tony DeMuth, one of Team 20's drivers, is in the lead van with a cup of stale coffee on the console and sausage biscuits from Starvin' Marvin's drying beside him. Tony, an accountant for Universal Leaf, is 40 and looks like a close-coupled Hunter Thompson with hairline going north for the summer. Behind comes Fletcher Williams, sharp-faced, in his mid-40s, graying, slightly paunchy, the winningest driver on the team. Fletcher's wife, Sandy, chief wrench and engine builder, sleeps in the back. Racing days start early.

We drop down a steep hill in the vans, and there, spread beneath a Georgia sun that will slowly roast the unwary brain, is the wide tapestry of sports car racing, colorful as a medieval fair: big, purple Vette on jack stands, open-wheeled Formula Fords like water spiders on wheels, flashing red Super Vs, guys rolling a white IMSA Porsche off its trailer, big Goodyear semi-trailer selling tires, tall red tool boxes, generators, everybody in jeans, a decal on a bumper proclaiming, "He Who Dies with the Most Toys Wins, and another, "He Who Dies with the Most Toys is Still Dead."

Stacks of racing slicks, rain tires, welding tanks, barbecues, children, big trucks marked Panther Engineering, Ichiban Toyota--"Number One Toyota."

The Japanese cars are eating racing alive, fast tube-frames with factory backing. A T-shirt declares inarguably, "Hog's Breath is Better Than No Breath." Motor homes--now a part of any outdoor celebration in the South—squat everywhere in low, lumpish profusion: Honeys, big Winnebagos, Southwinds with sleek, spaceship lines, a few slide-ins on pickup trucks.

Some of these gypsy wagons are pricey, from $10,000 for a used El Dorado to $50,000 for a new 34-footer, which is only upper-middle-class in campers; you can drop $200,000 if you want.

Motor homes civilize three days of foully hot racing, sleeping six in comfort with a gas stove, a refrigerator, a blessed air conditioner, safety for the kids, and privacy for the family.

Team 20 putt-putts down to the lower paddock with Tony yelling, '*Whatchaknow*, there's Varble! Hey, Fletcher, Joe's here! Man, gonna be some hard racing Sunday. 1 will be damned, there is Mona. Hey, sweetheart, how's it going? "

Some of these folks have been racing together for decades. It is hotter than a. skillet at a church breakfast, and people are drawing chalk lines around their pit areas, air conditioners humming' on motor homes, and here and there a race car *whoppawhumpawhap* chokes into asthmatic, cold-block life, and lurches off a trailer. Red Porsches, dark green Camaros, electric-blue Batmobiles from every boy's early imaginings.

We are truly, definitely, at the races.

THREE DAYS BEFORE, Tony had been in his garage in the woods outside of Farmville. There in the scrub flats of south-central Virginia, he lives in a small trailer with a large garage, which accurately reflects his priorities. He keeps his car in the kitchen: camshaft in the sink, bearing inserts next to the instant coffee, cylinder block by the dog food, and a piston, a gaping tear in one side, upside down on the table as an ashtray. Some races don't go as well as others.

As Tony grows older, it becomes possible to see patches of kitchen through the overlying car, but in his youth there was only car.

A purist, he drinks nothing but good bourbon and water. For the hopelessly barbaric who want a mixer, he keeps a bottle of cheap stuff under the sink with the Drano.

"A bourbon like substance," he calls it.

Tony is a college graduate, the son of a dentist in Farmville, but he slips easily into the "ain'ts" and "me and him was talking" of a rural boyhood. His trailer looks as if he cohabits with a tornado--books, tools, dogs, and fuel pumps everywhere.

Sitting on the couch requires shoving aside six issues of *Road & Track* and rearranging Amber, Tony's overweight golden retriever. Amber has no obvious function in the scheme of things, but she has a sweet disposition. Viciousness takes effort, which she avoids.

Racing is one of those hobbies to which the rest of life somehow becomes an appendage. Grabbing a couple of beers, we headed for the garage, where Tony plunged into the job of grinding valves. It is possible to work on a car without having a beer on the fender, but it isn't proper.

Low-budget racers spend a lot of time working on their cars, not always with satisfactory results. Racing is hard on cars, so only expensive equipment will stand up to it with anything resembling reliability. Things break.

Years ago, when I first encountered Team 20 in the paddock of Summit Point Raceway in West Virginia, the adversity of the mechanical had asserted itself. Tony had been ready to garotte his race car. This was in Team 20's early days, and each race meant a lot. On that day, Tony had been eager and set to trot: engine tuned and ready and almost legal--and the miserable thing wouldn't start. A hazard, one of many, of low-budget racing.

Tony was outraged, ready to dismember existence in its entirety if only he had known where to grab it. Around him, drivers chatted by their trailers and campers, happily remembering past races. Children played and dogs romped.

But Tony gazed at his TR-250 with dark thoughts of murder. Not a sign of life. Vapor lock? Ignition short? The innate resistance of life to motion through it? Who knew? Tony scowled. Even then, he had a capacity for disgust approaching the paranormal.

"I'm gonna take that damn machine and burn it, " he said.

"Don't believe me? Where's some gas?"

Fletcher had looked on phlegmatically. All Fletcher cared about was winning, which meant putting up with obstreperous buckets when necessary and running them hard when they worked. A broken car, his or Tony's, was just a broken car.

But that was back then. Now, in the cool gloom of the garage, it was different. At least Tony could hope it was. This engine he was working on, recently built by Sandy with loving care, hand-crafted and sweet to the ear, a thing of precise tolerances and sudden torque. It was the best he'd ever had.

It would work. It had to.

"Fletcher and I are different," Tony said, examining head bolts as he talked. "Me, I race for fun, and I don't make any bones about it. ·When I quit enjoying it, I'll get out of racing. This is my way of relaxing. I put in·10 to 12 hours a day at my Job, and I want to do something I like in my time off. Maybe it seems like a strange way to relax, but that's what it is, for me, anyway. Fletcher's obsessed by it. He's gotta win or be pissed off for a week. He's got to win. In some places, like one tricky turn in Charlotte, I let up on the gas. I just won't do it. He keeps it to the floor. He wins more than I do, and he's a hell of a driver. But racing is my hobby, not my life."

A fearsome drone interrupted him. He stopped to eye a huge hornet—a mean, striped thing with an ominously drooping hind end like a pointed thumb--that had come to investigate the coolness of the garage. Philosophy is fine, but those things are aerial agony. There was a nest of them nearby.

"I'm gonna have to speak to those things some night with a can of gasoline," Tony said, and then, "You got to understand what 'low-budget' racing means. It don't mean cheap. What it means is, you can barely afford it on a salary, cheap enough you can still do it, but expensive enough that it hurts. Oh, how it hurts, when you blow an engine. Going to Atlanta's gonna cost me, *hmmmm,* probably $500. That's just the trip, not counting what I have in tools and cars."

Racing, popular in the South, falls into categories determined by its sanctioning bodies. At the top are the professional classes—IMSA, the International Motor Sports Association, whose Camels GTP Series (for Grand Touring Prototype) is the pinnacle for sports cars, with one of these machines alone costing up to $400,000; Championship Auto Racing Teens (CART), whose lndy cars require in the neighborhood of $3 million to $4 million for a season of racing, clearly out of reach of weekend drivers; and the National Association of Stock car Racing (NASCAR), in which precision trained teams hurl big American cars around oval tracks at up to 215 miles per hour, while NASCAR also sanctions the kinds of amateur stock car racing that you can see all over the country on Saturday nights.

Big-league stock car competition can cost a team $1 million a year. NASCAR folk tend to be blue-collar--as do those involved with the National Hot Rod Association (NHRA), sponsor of drag racing in which $125,000 wheeled machines not really bearing much resemblance to cars reach 270 miles per hour over a quarter mile.

But the latest comer to a region more at home with bourbon than white wine is sports car racing, which is more sophisticated, with a European flavor. For this type of racing, the main sponsoring body for amateur competition is the Sports Car Club of America (SCCA), and a reasonably competitive car in Team 20's class costs in the neighborhood of $20,000 to $40,000. The rules are set to discourage really expensive cars. For example, the engines have to be basically the engine the car had when it came from the dealer.

Yet SCCA racing isn't amateurish in the usual sense of the word. A lot of work goes into these cars, a lot of knowledge, and a lot of modifications for performance. Tony's car glitters with Aeroquip, Oberg oil filter, expansion tank for the radi-

ator, high-voltage ignition, reworked heads, and various eso-
terica that mean little outside of racing. He has a full roll cage,
a Halon fire-extinguisher system, an Accusump to keep the oil
pressure up, and a cellular steel fuel tank to prevent fire.

The crews tend to be from the practical walks of life, country
boys who do their own plumbing, welding, machine work.
wiring, concrete, and carpentry. Otherwise they are likely to
be engineers and physicists, also practical sorts.

Team 20 stays with Triumphs, though lighter cars are made.
Low budget means they can't afford the phenomenal expense
needed to maintain a serious racing car. It also means most of
their time and liquidity somehow end up in the car.

For example, Tony bought a television camera and built a
mount just behind the driver's seat on Fletcher's car. The video
of the races is clear, exciting stuff, but that isn't why Tony did
it. The team wanted to see what the oil pressure gauge read
in the hard turns. As it happened, the pressure dropped as oil
sloshed away from the intake pipe. So they dropped the pan,
welded in baffles, and finally went to Accusumps, pressurized
containers that force oil into the system when pressure falls.
The oil pressure stays up now.

"I guess racing is dangerous, sort of anyway, but I don't dwell
on it," Tony said, moving from grinding valves in his garage to
barbecuing ribs in his yard.

Tony's yard is about what you would expect: no grass, just
second-growth woods, and patches of red dirt speckled with
mica, and anywhere from five to a dozen cars strewn about.
Team 20 is like a river, narrowing here, speeding up there, but
always flowing through the years, and the used-up cars generally end up in Tony's backyard.

The name "Team 20," incidentally, came from Fletcher, who
once looked at a successful Triumph racing team called Group
44. He said, "We figured if we did half that well, we'd be doing
O.K. So we're Team 20."

"Guys get killed sometimes," said Tony, turning the ribs. "Brain fade is probably the main reason. Racing requires so much concentration---and I mean intense concentration--that it's real easy to get into something you can't get out of. I know a place on one track where I have time to look down at my gauges for a second instead of looking in the mirror to see what's coming up behind. If I don't look then, I may not have a chance again until the next lap. If you take a chance and look when you shouldn't, you and another car can get more intimate than you want to be.

"Team 20 is real careful. Anybody who isn't had better find another sport. I don't mean we won't stick our noses in when we see an opportunity on the track. We will. But I can't say I'm scared out there. I know I have to be careful.

"Now, airplanes, they scare me. I do not like to fly at all."

Fear can be a curiously selective thing. A man who races at 140 miles per hour, a speed reached by Team 20, gets white knuckles in a commercial airliner, and a stunt pilot panics while scuba diving.

But if it's not some macho game of facing down fear, what is it that sends these guys to tracks around the South, spending money they don't always have in order to go in circles at what, by professional standards, are modest speeds? The answer depends on who you ask and how seriously you take their response. Life gets kind of slow in the hot little towns of Virginia and the Carolinas. There's not much to do out in the pine flats. Not much that's exciting, anyway.

Team 20 perhaps does not know that things are slow in Farmville—except for Sandy, who does know. These are, on the whole, deeply local people who have not encountered the careerist urges and driven lives of people in the big cities. In small towns like Farmville, careers are rarely outlets for combativeness and the competitive instincts. A job is just a job. Tony works hard for Universal Leaf, spending long weeks on the tobacco markets in Rocky Mount and South Hill, Virginia. But it's just a job. In Farmville, you have to make your excitement.

And--a cliché because it is true—there is something in these parts that makes or speed and violence. Come a warm summer evening, with the air still and honeyed and fields turning smoky and indistinct in the distance, and a lot of guys hereabouts think about pushing the pedal down and hearing the motor scream. On summer weekends, the South rattles and howls with dirt-track racing, stock cars, drag racers, and sports cars, all tuned beyond reason and going fast.

For decades, racing has started with drag racing, and it certainly did for many drivers in Tony's general age group—late 30s, early 40s. When it came time to shave, boys just naturally gravitated toward grease and clattering old junkers, and midnight drags on moonlit roads. Aside from girls and a little beer, they thought and talked about nothing but bad-ass 283 Chevies tweaked till they shrieked. All that mattered in existence was magneto ignition, Isky three-quarter race cams, a pair of Carter AFBs, maybe a C&W stroker and milled heads, solids--all the totemic modifications few could afford but craved till their teeth ached.

Southern males of the mid-60s, Tony's generation, knew what these things were and how they worked, just like thousands of kids in dozens of states who endlessly circled Burger Chefs in the sprawling camaraderie of a teenage Saturday night. And they went by themselves onto winding back roads and wound those old mills tight, knowing every click in the rising clatter, watching trees picking up speed in the headlights, feeling the wind rushing like water, sliding like damn fools around curves, and generally yelling something fierce at existence.

Well, you get older, but you never quite lose it.

ROAD ATLANTA The public address system blares, "All Group-

Three drivers should be on the starting grid. All Group-Three .... " Cars begin to lurch past. jerking and slowing, jerking and slowing. A race car isn't fit for polite company. In first gear, at enough RPMs to keep it running, it will go too fast for the paddock. The drivers goose them and clutch them, goose them and clutch them.

A yowling airplane roar comes from the track, the noise used in WWII movies to indicate a dive-bomber. Practice laps. A driver definitely wants to know the track's dips and peculiarities, which way the turns go, before trying it seriously. Team 20, in a group other than Group Three, is still lying beneath the cars with grease up to their elbows.

Sandy, 37, is the most complex of the three--dark, sardonic, somehow abstracted from things and watching from a distance. She is dedicated to racing. and to Fletcher, but she is dedicated to racing, and Fletcher, because she has decided to be. Fletcher can't help it. Sandy doesn't have a lot of illusions about people or things. She is tough enough not to be dominated by Fletcher, yet she is genuinely unhappy at seeing a wounded possum crawling all bloody from a highway. At the same time, she is low key and oddly deferential.

I ask how long she has been in racing.

"Since 1980, when I met Fletcher. Anybody who knows Fletcher for more than half an hour works on his car. I like racing, and I guess I'm not cut out to be a spectator. I have to participate.... Yuck!"

She is taking apart Fletcher's car's spare rear end, which proves to be full of sand and crud. Before now, she has just not had time to disassemble it. Something else was always more pressing: another hazard of low-budget racing. Like most of Team 20's major parts, this rear end came from a junkyard. Some of the cars these parts come from haven't been built since the late 60s.

"God, this is awful," says Sandy. "I don't operate this way, I really don't."

I said, "These cars seem to break a lot. Why?"

"Old. Poor quality to begin with. We overstress them. They weren't made for this."

Succinct, no illusions. The spare rear end will have to do if it is needed.

Fletcher comes off a lap into the hot pits complaining that the rear end sounds wrong. He doesn't know what happened to Tony, who seems to have disappeared.

Sandy jacks the car up and begins unbolting the differential. Three teeth broken on the pinion gear. Old, poor quality to begin with. She starts putting in the spare rear end.

A half hour later, the tow truck brings Tony in on a nylon strap.

"She started running rough," he says. "Lost oil pressure."

Old, poor quality to begin with. She starts pressure."

A narrow strip of oil forms on the asphalt as the car moves.

"Don't look too good, huh?" says Tony.

They put it up on jack stands. It couldn't be a thrown rod. Just *couldn't* be. All that sweat and work and money, that beautiful engine. It couldn't be a rod.

The pan drops. Tony shoves it out from under the car and it rattles, not a good sign.

He reaches in and pulls out half a rod, a blackened bearing insert, two bolts torn in two, half a rocker arm, a fragment of piston, everything but a partridge in a pear tree, and all of it bad.

"It's a rod," Fletcher says.

"Damn. I don't know," says Tony, dispiritedly examining the shards. "I just don't know. I was babying it. I can't figure it."

Anything could have caused it, an invisible internal fracture in a rod, for example. Sandy doesn't look at the panful of innards.

"I've seen them before," she says, not dignifying the horrible by paying it undue attention. She has worked like a dog on that engine and can't be happy. but it doesn't show.

Fletcher tells Tony he is sorry it happened, and means it.

"It's not fair," comments a bystander.

"Nobody said it was going to be fair," says Sandy laconically.

The heat is terrible. That night, as the stifling warmth relents a little and the air becomes savory with the smoke of 50 barbecues, Sandy sits in the van and talks about why people race. She has taken an SCCA driver's school and driven in a regional-- i.e., lower-level--race. As she warms to the subject, she grows animated and positively sparkles.

"It's exciting, a different world out there," she says. "You come fast around that turn and down the straight and all you can think is, *Make it go faster*. And then you pop over the hill and go sailing down the slope and around one curve and around another, and it s like a roller coaster, except you're in charge. That's what racing is like: getting to drive the roller coaster."

Neither Fletcher nor Tony could have said that. Yet her description is deliberate: a repetition, she tells me, of a presentation on racing she once gave at a Dale Carnegie course she took, heaven knows why. There is nothing of Carnegie in Sandy. Nor in Fletcher.

"Can't do much with these old dinosaurs, not when you gotta race against tube-frame Mazdas," Fletcher says, as Team 20 works on the cars into the night, the gasoline pageantry of Road Atlanta swirling around them. "But I can still win. At least I can beat 90 percent of the drivers, just because I've got more experience. I know how my car handles, and I can take'em in the tums. On the straights, they just blast by me. I don't have the power. "

Fletcher is not modest. He is not aggressively cocky, not ungracious, not unpleasant to be around; but just under the surface he has a large ego with sharp teeth.

If he didn't have it, he wouldn't win. Ego, more than talent, produces victory on the track--not conceit, but a single-minded unwillingness to lose. As someone once said, all things are possible for him who refuses to listen to reason.

Sandy uses the oven to heat up a ring gear so it will fit.

"I've got the killer instinct, I guess," says Fletcher. "And, let's face it, racing is mostly ego."

But if he really wants to win, why does he keep racing Triumphs?

"Money. I've got too much invested to start over. Besides, I just like racing these old things. I get a kick out of being able to win in something that isn't supposed to win. it's a challenge."

Does he ever think about having a really competitive car?

"Always. Always. I think about selling the Triumph and getting something better. Thing is, you can never sell your toys for what you've put in them."

He figures he has $20,000 invested in his Triumph, twice what he could sell it for, and a newer, tube-frame car would cost $40,000.

Fletcher might do quite well in a better car. But sooner or later, he would also bump into his limitations--find that there is always somebody better

Team 20 is fortunate because its aspirations match its abilities.

Somebody dropping by offers condolences on the ravaged engine of Tony's car.

"Hell, it sounded good to me. What happened?"

"Dunno, brother."

"New engine, wasn't it?"

"Yep."

"You just have to take what comes," Sandy says philosophically.

The race the next day will show how right she is.

FLETCHER STARTS the day's racing in style, swooping onto the Road Atlanta track with the engine singing--but then pulls into the pits on the pace lap. Later, as Team 20 sits watching the videotapes of the race in Tony's trailer in Farmville two nights after the debacle, what happened becomes abundantly clear. On the last turn before the back straightaway. Fletcher lost every bit of his oil pressure but didn't notice and kept on driving. How that engine held together without oil for most of a lap will be an eternal mystery. On the straightaway. he looked at the gauge and cut the engine, tried to pullover, couldn't get through the pack, and had to fire it up to keep from causing a crash.

The tape shows Sandy running to the car with a tool box, Fletcher explaining the loss of oil, Sandy pulling the hood off. and saying, not quite phlegmatically. "it's hopeless."

The oil line had blown off. The night before the race. they had rerouted the line to bypass the Oberg and had stretched it too tight.

"Guess we got careless," Fletcher, never one to make excuses, would say later. Dark, laconic resignation from Sandy, anger at himself from Fletcher. Both are used to such disaster: Sandy says that they blow an engine about every three races. Usually, though. they complete more than one lap before the engine goes.

Eight hundred miles of driving. a couple of thousand dollars, one beautiful engine wrecked. a rear end ruined, countless man-hours in garages and machine shops, probable damage to Fletcher's engine, nine quarts of oil on the track. and not one lap of racing completed.

This was the first time they had lost both cars without even getting into the race. Yet Team 20 doesn't crush easily. There will be other races, and they will win some of them.

Tony, kicking back in his trailer, says, "You take what comes. If you can't take the heat, get out of the kitchen."

To be a weekend racer, you've first got to love cars the way Tony does.

Sitting in Tony's trailer, the team clicks in another tape, this one of Charlotte Motor Speedway earlier in the year. Even on tape. heat shimmers off polished hoods in little waves. Drivers strap themselves in with heavy webbing, slip on helmets[FR1] and Nomex fire-proof gloves, gaze tense and focused through green visors. Wives check hood latches and tire pressure.

This stuff lives deep in the hormones. The scene differs only in mechanical particulars from a field of medieval knights strapping on armor and checking stirrups for a tournament. Guinevere didn't build engines, but you can't have everything. Even jousting has come to an accommodation with modernity.

On the tape, the official holds up her hand: time to go racing. Motors cough into life, unmuffled, fierce. running rough and sullen. Tuned to the edge of hysteria, cammed for full throttle and high RPMs, they don't know how to idle. Drivers goose them, more from nerves than need. *Whoppobbawhoppobba-whaaap!whaap!* Engine after engine blats into rhythmic explosion, the sound felt in the tissues of the lungs, strong and exhilarating.

The tape shows Fletcher going full bore down the straights toward the next turn, standing on the brakes at the last possible second, down-shifting into third at 100 miles per hour, taking the curve at the edge of traction, flooring her out. then doing it again. Occasionally his hand leaves the wheel to point to one side or the other, telling cars in a higher class which side to pass him on. As a matter of courtesy, you don't block faster traffic.

The car vibrates, engine howls. a tum flashes toward the car and twists to the straight. then the hill drops precipitously down. This is where Tony says he lets off but Fletcher keeps his foot to the floor for every last drop of caterwauling speed. 140 m.p.h. and climbing....

"He won't quit trying", says Sandy. with a mixture of pride and amusement. "

Tony chimes in, "I might figure I had third place and ease off. make sure I don't blow the engine. Not Fletcher. He figures maybe it'll hold together and just keeps on getting it.··"

"I don't go racing to be in second place," Fletcher says.

This may be wise in a quest for national standing. and it may not, but Fletcher piles up a respectable record of seconds and thirds in a car that really shouldn't do it. Not bad for an aging green brontosaurus. When the race is over, Tony turns off the video and starts feeding Amber. Work comes early.

"You know," he says. 'I'm thinking about getting Carillo rods, if I can get the money together. I'm getting sick of engines going south on me."

Carrillo rods, specially made and almost infinitely strong, go for $140 each. Tony's car needs six. A package of eight runs $1,130. The outlay is considerable for a man who has just spent $500 for nothing in Atlanta and has to come up with a new engine fast.

"Buncha money." Fletcher says. as he and Sandy walk out into the night. "Maybe, though. Come on over tomorrow night. and we'll get started on an engine for your car. We can find something."

47 LAOS

Fooling Around in Laos: Nice Country, Needs
Money

The Mekong flows brown and ugly past the beer stalls and restaurants across the street from the Lane Xian hotel, a slightly decomposing pile but comfortable enough. The country is green, perhaps not hopelessly backward but nearly so, and rattles with motor scooters. The people are small and brown. When female, they are often quite pretty. Westerners are not uncommon: A pretty fair current of backpacking tourists comes through, often en route to Luang Prabang. Laos is the sort of place writers invariably call "sleepy," so I won't.

It is a backwater, and was during the years of the war in Vietnam. Today it contains preserved traces of those receding times, like fossilized tracks of forgotten dinosaurs.

I met a reasonably English-speaking young Lao woman in a stall on the river and recruited her as tour guide. I liked her. She was studying to the extent she could in a school of business in hopes of getting into hotel work. Waitressing in a Lao beer chute is a dead end. Our deal was that I'd pay for the cab on forays into the countryside, correct her English, and buy lunch. She would be factotum.

During a temple crawl she mentioned in passing that life had been difficult for her family after they had lost her father. How had that happened, I asked unwisely. He died fighting the

Americans, she said.

Oh.

Maybe it is better not to go back to where your wars were. Perspective is corrosive of causes unless they are very good ones. I'm not sure ours were. Three decades have passed since we were bombing the Laos. It is hard to remember why they were a threat to the United States. The Lao communists won, at least in the sense that they kept the country, and nothing bad happened to the US. The communists won decisively in Viet Nam, and nothing bad happened to the United States. They won in Cambodia, and nothing bad happened to the United States.

I, my guide, and two taxi drivers were looking at another temple, which Laos has lots of, when I asked about the French. They were gone, said one of the drivers with approval. After them came the Americans, he said, who were also gone, and then the Russians, who too were gone. They clearly thought that gone was the proper condition for all of these groups.

I don't think that Americans quite grasp that countries don't like having foreigners bomb them. We tend to justify our wars in terms of abstractions: We are attacking to defeat communism, impose democracy, overcome evil or, now, to end terrorism. The countries being bombed, devastated, and occupied usually think they are fighting invaders who have no business being there. The distinction is lost on many Yanks. I know aging veterans who to this day do not understand why the Vietnamese weren't grateful that we had come to help them fight communists.

Southeast Asia is full of the moldering offal of deceased foreign policy. In Siem Reap in Cambodia a couple of weeks ago I was delighted to find a thriving tourist economy based on the ruins of Angkor. The schools were full. Hotels went up. Yet you still see one-legged men. For years, Cambodia's chief crop was land mines.

I lost acquaintances to the Khmer Rouge after the fall of Phnom Penh and tend to be disagreeable when I think about it. Perhaps I should reflect stoically on the necessity of breaking eggs to make omelets. The wisdom of this is more apparent to those who are not eggs.

In Cambodia the United States, exercising its God-given right to meddle catastrophically anywhere it can reach, had destabilized a puzzled country of thatch huts and water buffalo and facilitated the arrival of Pol Pot. The Americans then went back to California to surf.

The communists, exercising the mindless brutality common among them, had then killed huge if uncertain numbers of people for no reason and wrecked the country. This showed that the Russians and Americans could cooperate when they wished. Call it non-peaceful co-extermination. Or call it synergy or convergence or conservation of parity. The Khmers died.

On the train from Bangkok to the Thai-Lao border I had shared a compartment with a Lao, perhaps in his sixties, from a comparatively rich family. He had spent thirty years in business in Paris. We became casual friends and he invited me to dinner at his house, where some fifty of his relatives were having a Buddhist commemoration of something or other. Members of the family had returned for the event from several countries.

They were hospitable and spoke I have no idea how many languages among them. The children were well mannered, the food excellent and accompanied by that traditional Lao drink, Pepsi. I supposed that they were the enemy, or had been, but wasn't sure why. I sometimes think the State Department needs to get out more and the CIA, less. The notion of devout Buddhist atheistic communist businessmen scoured around my mental craw but I could never get a handle on it.

While eating breakfast at the Lane Xian, I was surprised to hear Spanish. The two fellows at the next table were Cubans, doubtless in Vientiane because of party solidarity or something equally as tiresome. I chatted with them briefly about nothing in particular. They were friendly, having the notion that the American government hated Cuba but that the American public did not. To a considerable extent this is true. The analysis is complicated by the inability of many of my compatriots to distinguish between Cuba and Castro.

I don't understand our embargo of Cuba. When the Russian empire was trying to turn the island into a military base aimed at the United States, the embargo made sense. Now it doesn't. As nearly as I can tell, it continues because of the petrified vindictiveness of cold warriors without a cold war. It's funny: We don't like Castro because he oppresses his people, so we maintain a now-pointless embargo that also oppresses them. More cooperation.

If you get to Laos, the reclining Buddha a half hour from Vientiane is worth the trip. The little countries of the region were not always backwaters, or not so backwaterish anyway. In brief respites from killing each other, which they did as relentlessly as everyone else, they made some remarkable things. If you are in the business of building hotels, you might put one hereabouts. The country could use the money. I can recommend a young lady to help you manage it.

48 A SOLDIER SPEAKS

I am a Soldier. I am Dirt: Dulce et Decorum
Non Est

I am a soldier. I am dirt. With Joshua I put the cities of Canaan to the sword while women screamed and tried to protect their babies. I spent long days in Nanjing butchering and butchering civilians because I enjoyed it. For I am a soldier. I am dirt. I fire-bombed Dresden till the wind-fanned flames left nowhere to hide and the people burned screaming and their fat puddled in the streets. I am a soldier. I am dirt.

On the crumbling walls of Angkor Wat, the Cold Lairs, trees now crawling over the walls, you may see me carved, marching, marching to kill forgotten peoples, it matters not whom. In the sweltering heat of Chichen Itza and the terrible winter of Stalingrad and the flaming paper cities of Japan and on the Death March of the Philippines I killed and killed, for I am a soldier. I am dirt. I kill.

In this I glory. I spend my declining years drinking in bars with old soldiers I knew when Breda fell to us and we raped and killed and looted, when we torpedoed the troop ships and left the soldiers in their thousands to drown slowly as their strength gave out. The fierce exultation of watching Atlanta burn, Pearl Harbor, Nagasaki, these I remember lovingly. For I am dirt.

Crush their skulls and eat their faces, we say with remembered bravado. We remember the adventures fondly. They almost had us at Plei Cuy when Puff arrived with miniguns, and that put paid to them, hoo-ah.

These are degenerate days. Once I breached the walls of Ilium or Constantinople during the Fourth Crusade and killed and looted and raped girls of seven in front of their parents—how they howled! Now perforce I say I do it for democracy, about which I don't give a damn, or to end evil, though our allies are the worst tyrants we can find. Before, I could torture my captives between two slow fires, or by running a red-hot poker up their nether ends, and this in the public square for the amusement of a bored populace.

Now I water-board them, bringing them to the edge of drowning, screaming, begging, puking, yes, that does nicely, now a little more water as their minds break, and maybe I will masturbate over it later. For I am a soldier. I am dirt. I am the worst of a sorry species.

I am a soldier. I pride myself on my allegiance to duty, God, honor, country. My god is Moloch of the red fangs, who wills me to besiege a city into cannibalism, to catapult the severed heads of loved ones over the walls, with blankets infected with smallpox. My god, however named—Yahweh, Moloch, Satanas, Odin, imposes my duty, to kill, to rape.

If my country says to butcher, then butchery were no crime, but a source of honor. To kill openly for pure enjoyment, as Ted Bundy or Jeffrey Dahmer did, is thought contemptible, though we do it, but to kill because Bush II, Tojo, Bin Laden, or Netanyahu commands it—this is virtue at its highest. Though we enjoy it: Listen to us in the O Club. Killing for your own reasons is criminal. Killing someone you have never seen for the benefit of a politician you have never met is a source of medals.

I was a soldier once. I received certain medals. They were trivial medals. The meritorious variety are awarded for jumping into a trench of scared conscripted adolescents and bludgeoning them to death with a rifle butt. I lacked the character. But medals can be problems. If I put them in the toilet, they might clog it, but I certainly would not want children exposed to them. The military presents problems that Clausewitz did not anticipate.

Once, in a war of no particular importance, I lay in a hospital of little importance in a country in Asia that doesn't matter. It was just a country. Soldiers kill, who and where and why being of no importance to them. I was blinded. Soldiers are dirt, and sometimes they get what they deserve. I did. Across from me, though I couldn't see them, were the survivors of a tank crew. An RPG 2, which you probably don't know what is, had hit their M60, which you probably don't know what is, and had cooked off the cherry juice, which you probably don't know what is. They had been killing somebody else's soldiers, which is what soldiers do, for they are dirt.

I couldn't see them. I was a soldier. I was dirt. But I was blind dirt. I couldn't see them under the plastic sheeting under which they oozed serum. But they spoke of the fire within, and the loader and gunner screaming as their skin sloughed off, and they desperately tried to find the hatches and couldn't, and died screaming, screaming, fingers groping for hatches they couldn't find in the smoke and agony and terror, which is why I hate you sonsofbitches in Washing who made them into soldiers and sent them and us to make money for McDonnell Douglas.

For this we hold reunions. We get together in Wyoming and Tuscaloosa and Portland and remember when we were young and the war held off the boredom of life and the star shells flickered in the night sky over Happy Valley and life meant nothing but was at least intense. I hated the H&I fire over the dark forests of a puzzled Cambodia and I hate you cocksuckers living soft at home for sending us and I hate what I did and I hate what my friends did who were there, who are really my only friends. And I hope you one day pay, what we paid, what our victims paid and you pay it as we did. And this will bring me the only joy in my life.

I am a soldier. I am dirt.

49 TANKING

The M1 Abrams, A Maserati of Tanks

First published in Harper's

T o an observer on one of Fort Hood's flattened prominences, the Abrams M1 tank would seem a dark mote below a high plume of dust, a glint of periscopes, a small furor lost in the vastness and pastels of central Texas. Not even the grandest of tanks can intimidate a landscape. By day and night the armor rumbles across this land, seen only by tankers. Armor is a private trade.

From low in the turret in the gunner's seat, the tank (depending on what it is doing at the moment) is a terrific clatter of tracks, a howl of big turbine, a shriek of hydraulics, or a welter of strange oscillating noises of no obvious origin. Everything vibrates. Talking is absolutely impossible except on the intercom, where it is relatively impossible. There were, in the tank with me, the tank commander, a driver, and a loader. You still feel alone

The effect was almost nautical. Stuffy air, smelling of paint and oil, and heavy machinery filled every available space. There were turret controls, the primary sight, an auxiliary sight, switches, hydraulic lines, cables, the machine gun, and most notably the breech of the main gun inches to my left. Intermittently, we lurched sharply sideways. A tank steers by the simple-minded process of slowing down one of its two tracks, with the subtle result one would expect. There is a certain directness about a tank, a lack of understatement. One knows intuitively that Proust would not have wanted one. In the strange isolation born of dimness and cacophony, I braced my forehead against the brow pad and peered through the round eye of the gunner's main sight. A glowing pink reticle floated slowly, deliberately across the land; pale green Texas drifted by in the eerie clarity of good optics. The stabilization system held the turret rock-steady despite the bucking of the tank. I laid the empty gun on a distant steer-Fort Hood open range-not from any hostility toward cattle but because some limbic instinct wants to aim at living things. Beneath a huge sky we careened on, with me, two gyroscopes, a laser range finder, a remarkably precise turret drive, a fire-control computer, and a 105mm high-velocity gun fixedly watching a cow.

The public attributes a great many qualities to tanks that they do not have. It is easy to think of a tank as a sort of terrestrial torpedo boat, dashing rapidly and invincibly about and blowing things up. Unfortunately, some who harbor this notion are armor officers, who tend to be frustrated cavalry officers and believe a tank to be an intractable but noble form of horse-which is one reason why in war, tanks are so often seen in flames.

In fact, tanks are big, hard, solid, fragile, unreliable, temperamental, and vulnerable. When possible, they are carried to battle on enormous trucks called tank transporters in the hope that they will function when they arrive. They break easily, bog down at the slightest provocation, and cannot go very far without something going wrong. The fall into holes and can't get out. They are a superlative pain in the neck.

Tanks ought to be obsolete, but they are not. Civilians said tanks were obsolete when I was in armor school with the Marines in the late 1960s, and later as I followed them through three Middle Eastern wars as a correspondent for various publications. Yet they were always there, always dangerous, and always decisive. I watch them today and see no change.

The voice of Sergeant San Miguel, the tank commander in the turret with me, roared from the headphones of my CVC helmet (the initials stand for something like Combat Vehicle Crewman). The army could never bring itself to call a headset a headset. "You gotta TC an M1 different from an A3." TC, Tank Commander, is both a noun and a verb, and an M60A3 is an older tank than the M1. "In A3s you stay high out of the hatch, but an in M1s you deep low. You gotta be careful about your face." He demonstrated, lowering his seat until only the top of his head cleared the steel coaming of the hatch. "You gotta think about your teeth," he said. "You can smash them."

Tanks are dangerous to their crews, and much effort goes into avoiding injuries. They are also brutally uncomfortable. After a few hours in the hatches, you ache, unless you are nineteen and too dumb to know when you are uncomfortable. Fort Hood is uneven, pitted, ravined country. Tanks, except for the M1, which has a limousine's suspension, do not race across rough country. They pick and baby their way, like an automobile on a badly rutted road. The driver slows as he reaches a declivity, and the tank--whoops!--pitches downward, checks sharply at the bottom, accelerates, rocks back to the horizontal. Each step throws you against the hatch coaming unless you brace against it. At high speed, you have to resist with muscular tension, bend your knees, sit back hard, press your arms against the side. The world rocks u-p-p-p-p, tips sharply over, down, thump, roar of engine, bump of upslope, surge, hour after hour.

The M1 is a feline tank, quick, agile, with a smooth, honeyed ride-for a tank. This means that the crews hot-rod M1s over rough ground-being, after all, American kids-so you still get thrown around. Somewhere the army is said to have s photograph of an M1 firing in mid-air. The stabilization is good enough.

We pulled into the firing range. The range-control people were on a low hill behind us, working from an armored personnel carrier fitted with radios. A dozen dirty M1s clattered about, squeak-squeaking, rattling, turbines howling like mournful lost vacuum cleaners. Tanks are exciting for about an hour, after which they are obtuse tractors that need fixing, The are also incredibly ugly and throw up a lot of dust. For the next several hours we did endless minor maintenance. The M1 seems to need a lot of it. Like yachts, tanks never work perfectly all at once.

The sun was hot. A constant wind from the hills desiccated without cooling. I leaned against the turret and waited. From somewhere down the line came the sharp crack of firing tanks, the putt-putt of their machine guns. I wasn't sure what we were waiting for. In the army, waiting is intransitive, without an object.

I watched the crews, aware of the yawning gap of twenty years. These days they are smart, competent, and cheerful, which is astonishing to one who remembers the dregs of the late 1970s. And they can use their tanks. Yet there is a terrible innocence about them. It is a curious paradox that reporters go to more wars than soldiers do. I wondered whether the junior officers, who are conscientious, or their men really understand the business they are in. They have never looked inside a gutted tank. They were children during the Vietnam War.

From *The Sharp End*, an excellent book about soldiers in World War II:

"A tank that is mortally hit belches forth long searing tongues of orange flame from every hatch. As ammunition explodes in the interior, the hull is racked by violent convulsions and sparks erupt from the spout of the barrel like the fireballs of a Roman candle. Silver rivulets of molten aluminum pour from the engine like tears...When the inferno subsides, gallons of lubricating oil in the power train and hundreds of pounds of rubber in the tracks and bogey wheels continue to burn, spewing dense clouds of black smoke over the funeral pyre."

Not the stuff of recruiting posters. These men do not know of it, not really. Armies don't read. Even the officers have never seen the horror of a burning tank. Fire is the hideous, unspeakable nightmare of armor. So many things burn in a tank: ammunition, fuel, hydraulic fluid vaporized by 1,500 pounds of pressure. The crews don't always get out. Hatches jam, the wounded can't move, sheer panic and agony prevent escape.

The M1 uses fire-retardant hydraulic fluid and a Halon gas fire-extinguisher, which are said to greatly reduce the likelihood of fire. One hopes they work.

The gun is the soul of a tank. The M1 is computerized, electronic, and designed for accuracy at long ranges and for firing on the move. The wisdom of this design can be argued on complex grounds, yet the Israelis, presumed to know something of tanks, have remarkably similar equipment on their own Merkava. So do the Germans.

Firing is easy, although there is an ampleness of buttons. Before battle the gunner should enter into the keyboard on the turret wall to his right the bore wear, the barometric pressure, and the temperature of the air and of the ammunition, all of which influence the strike of the round at long range. There is a gadget to offset the droop of the gun as it softens slightly in the sun. Sensors automatically account for cross-wind and for the cant of the turret in case the tank is parked on a bump. Some of this works, some doesn't. At normal ranges, it doesn't matter.

Next, depending on what he is firing at and whether it is day or night, the gunner sets various switches mounted in boxes of industrial appearance and labeled in abrupt, technical Gotterdammerungian language: NORMAL MODE DRIFT, AMMUNITION SELECT/SABOT/HEP/HEAT. FIRE CONTROL MODE. EMERGENCY/NORMAL/MANUAL. POLARITY BLACK HOT/WHITE HOT. The words reek of Wagnerian drama and insulation. I found myself with wild visions of Beowulf standing in dented armor, high in the cold hills of Denmark, holding a calculator from Hewlett-Packard and figuring azimuths.

There is a peculiar appeal, perhaps original to the late twentieth century, in being low in the cramped bowels of a tank, secure behind the armor and surrounded by all manner of fierce, cryptic controls. Major weapons always seem to me to be as much civilizational Rorschach blots as reasonable solutions to problems. Beneath a superficial rationality, all of them-tanks, fighter planes, submarines-are too obviously the toys I wanted when I was eleven. They call powerfully to the male's love of controllable complexity, and they are too much fun for coincidence. They too readily offer to a romantic the grey adrenal satisfactions of doom. And soldiers, god knows, are romantics. Few of us have room to psychoanalyze others. Still, I suspect that if tanks were in decorator colors, pink and baby blue with satin trim and leopard skin, and the switches said BIG BOOMY GUN and LITTLE PUTT-PUTT GUN, war might stop.

Anyway, you set AMMUNITION SELECT to SABOT. This prepares the computer to fire a thing like a heavy metal arrow at terrific velocity. In the sight, the ominous circular pink reticle hangs in space. A pair of handgrips, universally called Cadillacs by the troops, raise the circle or move it sideways. Squeezing the grips turns on the turret stabilization so that the bucking of the tank does not affect the gun.

You put the reticle on the target, press the laser button to feed the range to the computer, and squeeze the trigger. There is a jolt, as if a giant boot had kicked the tank. Outside the noise is terrific, but inside it isn't loud. The shell case ejects onto the floor with a clang. Modern tanks can hit each other a mile away.

Earlier in the dust and heat of Fort Hood, I had watched as Sergeant San Miguel tried to start the tank. The turbine cranked around with a rising howl and sighed to a stop. An abort. He tried again. No go. She wasn't going to start.

He called another tank over and jump-started ours successfully. Yep, batteries. Many of the ailments of tanks are depressingly similar to those of the family car. We pulled the armored cover from the back deck and discovered that two batteries had been rebuilt badly. There was nothing to do but wait for new ones.

I chatted briefly with a couple of soldiers about Killeen, the town just outside Fort Hood. Tankers see an awful lot of Killeen, and an awful lot of Germany. Killeen is the usual nasty little strip of burger joints, beer halls, motorcycle stores, and loan sharkeries, all engaged in the patriotic business of separating a GI from his paycheck. Signs blare NEED MONEY? SEE HONEST JOHN THE CASH SPIGOT. Denny's, Roy Rogers, McDonald's, Arby's-all the way stations on the road to coronary occlusion are there.

I was told that Killeen has improved in recent years. For example, the prostitutes have been chased away to Austin. I said I was glad to hear this, being sure that several thousand single men would respond with gratitude. "Ain't but one hooker left," a tanker told me. "She's so ugly I wouldn't take her to a dog fight if I thought she'd win."

The principles of tank gunnery find perfect expression in the age-old military prescription, "Do unto others, but do it first." The armor may help, but no one depends on it. The tank that doesn't fire first is likely to have a finned arrow of depleted uranium, moving at a mile a second, come through the turret in a burst of metallurgically complex finality. When a tank fights in what the military euphemistically calls a target-rich environment, the result is a terrifying controlled ballet as the loader slams 40-pound rounds into the breech, while the gunner desperately floats the pink circle onto an enemy tank that is trying to do the same thing to him: boom, load, *load, godda-*

mit....

The Soviets have experimented with an autoloader which unfortunately displayed democratic tendencies, promiscuously loading crewmen into the gun along with ammunition. ("Once more unto the breech, dear friends....") This is said to have been corrected.

Once, while in the jumbled rock country of the Golan Heights covering the aftermath of a war, I drove along a winding road cut into a hill. The curves were so sharp that it was impossible to see more than a short distance around the hill. Suddenly, a Soviet-made tank loomed into view; there was a neat hole at the base of its turret. Farther around the turn was another dead tank and, farther still, yet another. As nearly as I could tell, Israeli and Syrian tank columns had met unexpectedly, and the Israeli lead tank had fired first and loaded fast. The Syrians apparently had not realized that they were in a fight.

Earlier, I had passed a small plain, green against the high crags and rocky hills. A Syrian tank army seemed to stream across it, almost pretty, pennants flying from aerials. They had been dead for a week. Where tanks had paused to take on ammunition, great piles of cardboard canisters and splintered crates lay in sodden piles. Nobody thinks of war in terms of trash. There is a lot of it.

In peace, the tanker's life is the curious combination of boredom and resignation to lunacy that has always characterized militaries. The army is ridiculous in ways beyond civilian comprehension, and tanks are ridiculous even by army standards. Attending a military exercise in Korea, I witnessed the guarding of a bridge by a tank. The exercise was hopelessly unrealistic, as most are, being intended to show our highly questionable resolve to come to the aid of Korea if need be.

It was mid-afternoon. Mountains sloped sharply to paddies frozen to steel and a frigid wind raced up the valley. We guarded the bridge by parking beside it, pointing the gun in the presumed direction of the imaginary enemy, and pawing through C-rations for the edible parts.

The day dragged on. For a while we stood in the hatches and watched in awe as Korean kids played in freezing water. Next we made wretched C-ration coffee and lay on the ground with our heads against the tracks and talked. As a pillow, a tank is flawed. Then we watched some soldiers building a barbed-wire enclosure to fence in nonexistent prisoners.

From the driver's compartment came a lugubrious wail from Hoover, the driver: "Heater's broke."

With night falling in a Korean winter, that was a knell. The tank commander responded with the natural leadership of a good NCO. "Hoover, fix that goddam thing or you're on watch for a week!"

Hoover tried. The heater began to emit thick black smoke but no heat. The sun sank behind the mountains, and the temperature began to fall in earnest. Smoke poured from the hatches of our 58-ton smudge pot. We leaned overboard, caught in a coldly burning tank, coughing like consumptives, Korean kids staring in stark wonderment....

From war movies it is easy to imagine that fighting in a tank is something like Luke Skywalker's exhilarating rush into the entrails of some death star. This sentiment killed many men in World War II and still kills, there being a profound tendency for tankers to regard themselves as diesel cavalrymen at Balaklava. Given the capacities of antitank weaponry, tankers who regard themselves as cavalry usually meet the same fate as those who charged with the Light Brigade.

In fact, the first element of ground combat, armored or not, is not elan but exhaustion-grim, aching weariness that actually hurts, that saps the will to resist, turns fingers to rubber, makes a standing man blank out for a second and catch himself falling. Eyes go gritty, armpits get raw from stale sweat, and the mind has trouble with simple things.

Then, in armor, there is the paranoia, the weird sensory deprivation that swathes a tanker in his own dim world of nerves. He can hear nothing above the racket of the tank, except through the intercom. An infantryman hears small arms fire, shouts, crackling of bushes, his own breathing. A tanker hears none of this, only the voices of the other crewmen hissing and roaring metallically from the headset and the voices of other tanks over the radio. But even these have an odd disembodied quality. They don't come from anywhere in particular, for example. All voices seem to hang six inches behind your skull.

When the tank is buttoned up, with the hatches down for protection, it is almost blind. The driver, low to the ground (almost lying down in the hull of the M1) can see nothing at all in dense vegetation. The gunner has only the narrow field of his sight to connect him to outward existence, the loader sees nothing. The tank commander is slightly better off, but not much. Behind every bush there may be an antitank rocket that will explode through the side armor and make mush of all within.

And so tanks, the ones that survive anyway, are diffident, timid things. Except perhaps on flat desert, they advance fearfully, trailing the infantry that has to screen the hedges, kill the rocket men, root out mines. Tanks stay under cover whenever possible, dislike open ground, dash from shelter to shelter like frightened fawns. This is why the army chose the turbine engine for the M1, trading fuel economy for acceleration. A bold charge of massed armor, racing across open terrain with streamers flying, leads to many flaming tanks.

A preferred way to use tanks is to put them in holes with just the turret showing. Another is to stay on what the army calls the reverse slope of hills (meaning the other side), climb into sight to fire quickly, and reverse back down. It is almost embarrassingly ungallant.

The tank remains critical to war, yet one somehow feels that it shouldn't. The mood of a tank, if you will, is not suited to the times. The thing belongs in an age of blast furnaces and raw national force, in an epoch of dreadnought navies when guns that a man could crawl into flung projectiles weighing a ton. The tank is a characteristically Soviet weapon-crude, brutal, but effective. You imagine tanks crawling like dark beetles from roaring factories deep behind the Urals.

Tanks are heavy machinery at its heaviest and simplest in a time when respectable weapons abound in microcircuitry, frequency-agile radar, focal-plane arrays, and near-sentient electronics. Modern tanks have many of these gewgaws and sometimes use them well, but they are essentially an encrustation of glitter. Remove the accretion of advanced whatnots, and the tank is still a hard object with a large gun. No matter how silly tanks may seem, no matter how archaic and unreliable, when one heaves out of the smoke and comes Do not think that because tanks are something of a blunt instrument, no thought goes into them. A tank is a cosh, but a highly engineered cosh. Open a book on tank design at random and you are likely to find a swarm of second-order partial differential equations. Lethal details are fussed over. For example, engineers give careful attention to the best ratio of length to diameter of long-rod penetrators-the "arrows" fired by the main gun. X-ray flash radiographs stop the penetration in mid-act for examination. The mechanics of plastic deformation are considered with great mathematical sophistication. The engineers are quite concerned about maximizing behind-armor effects, or BAE, a technical term that encompasses burning and mutilation of the crew. Pressure transducers measure the "overpressure" as the tank is hit to see whether the lungs of the enemy will be ruptured, a desirable effect if you can get it. The probability of flash burns and their likely severity is studied. The following paragraph is from a report on an anti-armor warhead tested at Aberdeen Proving Ground, Maryland, but could have come from the labs of any civilized nation:

"The pressure transducer was the Kistler type 6121 piezo-electric gauge. This gauge, having a frequency response of 6 kilohertz, was used to measure air-shock pressures generated in the compartment. The incapacitating effects of temperature were assessed using the burn criteria presented in figure 7."

I once lay across from a pair of scorched tankers at the Naval Support Activity hospital in Danang. I couldn't see them because my face was bandaged, but we talked. They had been hit with a rocket, they said. It didn't penetrate, so the crew, having no idea where it came from, began to fire at random, this being the embodiment of American strategy in that war. Unfortunately, a hydraulic line had burst, and the fluid had ignited. Two tankers got out. The others stayed behind, screaming considerably. This is sometimes called secondary or delayed behind-armor effects.

The fear a tank inspires in infantrymen is hard to grasp. A tank is far faster than a man-the M1 is good for 45 miles an hour on good ground--and doesn't get tired. The infantryman knows that it will run over him to save ammunition. Unless he is beside it and has exactly the right weapon, there is nothing he can do about it. He knows this. And if you haven't heard a big gun fire close up, you cannot imagine what a shattering thing it is. Seasoned troops who know a tank's limitations will stand up to one in reasonable terrain. Others will run in blind, squalling panic.

Once, late at night, I was out on the rolling dunes of Camp Pendleton with a platoon of infantry. The night was foggy, the moon a glow through dripping mist. We were in good spirits, listening to the soft swish of waves. Then we heard it: squeak-squeak-squeak.

Tanks. They weren't supposed to be anywhere near infantry at night, but somebody has slipped. I could feel unease go through the platoon. The squeaking grew in volume over a deep rumble of diesels, growling and dying, growling and dying as the crews rocked them over the dunes. We couldn't localize it; in the fog the sound seemed to come from everywhere.

We all thought the same thing: My God, they're going to run over us. They wouldn't even notice until they found the meat in the tracks. The roaring grew and grew, and with it came the seeds of panic, a panic that didn't know where to run. The fog shuddered with belching exhaust and--whumph--they rose over the dunes and stood there, idling, growling, waiting....

Three a.m., Fort Hood. Down the hill from me the tanks were firing into the blackness. Armies don't stop at night. There was no moon. The wind still soughed through the brush. From other ranges around us came distant detonations, streaks of fire across the sky, the brilliant white light of magnesium mortar flares dangling under their parachutes. From the invisible tanks low on the slope erupted violent yellow blasts and the cherry streak of main-gun tracers slashing across the unseen land. Behind us a spotting tank called on the radio, "Target...target...target..." The troops can shoot these days.

I waited for a lull and asked whether I could look at the thermal sights that allow firing in the dark. People and tanks are hotter than other things. The thermals pick up the heat and turn it into video, allowing fighting at night. They are also complex, delicate, and, it seems, prone to break down. A lot of them were burning out.

We made sure that tanks weren't going anywhere for a moment and walked down the hill with a flashlight. The night was pleasant, the company good-whatever one's political delusions, GIs are likable. For men who enjoy being outside and are not driven by the devils of the ego, tanks are not a bad field of endeavor. We found the step and hauled ourselves up the slab side-armor and lowered ourselves through the hatches.

The inside was dim with battle lights. A pile of hot shell casings lay on the floor.

The sergeant turned on the refrigeration and we waited for the noisy little unit to cool down the thermal sensors. After ten minutes I crawled into the gunner's seat and peered through the lens. Nothing. The field was a meaningless jumble of flicker and snow. We slued the sensor head, and suddenly I was looking at clear, white silhouettes of troops. The effect was strange: The surrounding land didn't exist because it wasn't hot enough, so targets appeared to hang in fuzzy nothingness. But they were shootable.

I walked back up the hill and lay on the bleachers. The radio blared and chattered. A tank had slipped sideways into a hole and thrown a track. The men repaired it. The flickerings behind the neighboring hills continued. The red streaks flared from the dark tanks, hour after hour.

50 MARINE
BOOT CAMP

Tales from the Lejeune Woods

Boot camp. Yawning gateway to military life, an adventure outrageously funny and frightening, source of a lifetime of lies, all growing worse with each bull session. No one forgets boot. Get two GIs together over a bottle of gin, talking about old times, and sooner or later the talk will turn to tales of boot, a few of them true.

Not many, though. It is all right for most stories to be based on fact, but the better recollections of boot have only a nodding acquaintance with truth. Facts inhibit flexibility. They stultify.

But boot is more than tall tales. It is part of American life. We talk of being a peaceful nation, but usually we have a couple of million men and women under arms and often a war going. A high percentage of Americans spend time in the military. They shape it, and it shapes them.

A particular aspect of the national character appears in the organized anarchy of military life. Literature finds the military a feast--*Catch 22, M*A*S*H, A Farewell to Arms, Dispatches*, and all the rest.

Boot is a gateway. Here's to basic, as I remember it, as everyone remembers it, as I saw it in going back this year. A boy's first great taste of life.

Next to finding a shark in the bathtub, the worst thing that could happen to a kid of 20 in 1968 was getting to Parris Island at a grainy-eyed two in the morning, flat exhausted, and meeting a drill instructor. Everyone has heard the tales. DIs will pull your fingernails off one by one, make you run until your knees corrode, bury you to the neck in sand and leave you for the mosquitoes.

When the bus pulls into the swampy lowlands of South Carolina and Parris Island signs appear, it all becomes plausible. And there's no...way...out.

I arrived on a chartered Greyhound crowded with Richmond boys who suddenly suspected that they weren't a Few Good Men. It was a raw deal all around--cottony taste in the mouth, somebody else sure to get the girl back home, bus reeking of stale sweat and beginning fear, no thought yet about dying in Asia, just a sort of uh-oh feeling.

The driver had picked up a sergeant at the gate to give him a ride. "You wanna get off before the stampede?" the driver asked. Stampede? It was ominous.

On that loneliest morning I'll ever see, my introduction to the Marines--the Green Team, the Crotch, Uncle Sam's Misguided Children--was a little man 32 feet wide and about as high as my chin. He had killed Smokey the Bear and stolen his hat. He had a voice like Krakatoa in full eruption, and his name was Staff Sergeant Bull Walrus. At least I think it was.

He exploded into the headlights like one of hell's more vicious demons, trembling with fury.

"*GiddawfadatgawdambusNOW!*" he bellowed, blowing several windows out of the bus--I swear it, three windows fell out--by which we understood his desire that we disembark. We did so in sheer terror, trampling one another and no longer worried about our girls. To hell with our girls. Bull Walrus was clearly about to tear out throats out with his bare teeth, that was the important thing.

There we were, The Few, The Proud, standing in deep shock with our feet in these silly golden footsteps painted on the pavement. Move one inch, Walrus screams, and he will do unspeakable things, after which our girls will no longer want us. I figured they kept Walrus in a dungeon by day and just let him out to torture recruits by night.

We were groggy with fatigue, minds buzzing with adrenaline, and Walrus is inspecting our suitcases to take away glass objects. So we won't commit suicide with them, see.

I imagine myself tearing out my carotids with an Arid bottle. Suddenly he is in front of me. I lied. He's not 32 feet wide. He is 40 feet wide. He's got arms like anacondas and his head is held on by a bolt.

He also is confiscating porn books, to protect our morals and read later. He reaches for a book in my suitcase and glares at me with eyes of tin and death. I realize, with calm that still surprises me, that he is going to murder me. The book is *Medieval Architecture.*

A recruit, a drill instructor told me much later, after I had been reincarnated as a journalist, "is the funniest goddam animal alive. He's gotta be. You get these kids, some of them are street kids from the city, some of them farm kids, and these suburban kids who just don't know nothing--every kind of kid.

"And dumb? Jeez they're dumb. And they've got about two months to adjust to a complicated life they've got no experience with. They've got to learn how to think Marine Corps. Military thinking isn't like civilian thinking.

"Half of 'em don't even know how rifle sights work. Like this friend of mine is teaching a class about the M-60 machine gun, and he's telling them its rate of fire, it's gas-operated, and this skinny recruit says, 'But where's the gas tank?'"

"Jeez, they're dumb."

Sergeant Sly is a man with a sense of humor. He's black, strac, and cocky--the DI cockiness that says there's nothing on God's green earth better than the Green Team, and I'm the coolest thing in the Army, and, Prive, you gotta sweat to be as good as me. All DIs are like that, all the good ones anyway. Sly is a good one.

Sly runs recruits along the hot, dusty weapons ranges of Camp Lejeune--hot and dusty in summer, anyway. He tries to keep his recruits from getting hurt.

"All right," he tells a platoon, standing in sweat-soaked utilities. Nothing looks quite as dispirited as recruits in a hot sun. "While you're in the field, you gotta take certain precautions against the wildlife. I don't have to tell you about some of it. Don't feed the snakes, or try to pick'em up 'cause they're pretty.

"I'm talking about the other wildlife. Most of it's harmless, but one kind is bad news--what people down here call the Wampus cat. It's related to the bobcat and it's not too big, 'bout like a cocker spaniel, but you don't want to make one think he's cornered."

Another afternoon at Lejeune. The recruits listen, barely.

A few scenes are so close to boot camp that they deserve inclusion here, embodying as they do terrors near to those of boot. A massive grinder at Camp Pendleton, California. A private, fresh out of training and spending a week on maintenance duty before his school begins, has been sent to pick up toilet paper for the barracks. Battalion issue has no box in which to carry it. He ponders, has an idea, sticks a dozen rolls on a mop handle, puts it over his shoulder like a rifle.

A bird colonel rounds the corner. The Marine is new enough to the real military that officers terrify him. Panic strikes. He hesitates and, driven by reflex or some buried death wish, gives a snappy rifle salute. The colonel's jaw drops. His hat slowly rises on a column of steam.

You learn. It just takes a while.

Boot camp is a very quick education in the ways of the world--of many worlds. For a weird collection of people, the average training platoon beats midnight in a New York City bus station.

In my platoon we had a Mexican kid named Rodriguez who couldn't speak English, a black kid who said he was Bill Cosby's nephew, three college students--one of them a physical chemistry major, one a tiny blond guy who couldn't have been more than 11 years old, and a bunch of judicial draftees. ("I'm gonna give you a choice, son," says the judge. "Four in the slammer or two in the Marines." It's supposed to be illegal. So are a lot of things.)

Many of these judicial draftees were burglars from Tennessee. Free enterprise seems to be broadly interpreted in those parts and usually begins after midnight.

One of them was named Mulvaney. He had been caught in a second-floor bedroom collecting someone else's silverware. He preferred the Marines to the slammer, not necessarily a wise choice in those days--I later heard he got killed outside of Danang.

Anyway, Mulvaney was built like one of those Martian robots on the late show, arms like logs and the legs of an offensive lineman, and he had gray eyes and a long, slow smile that meant he was about to break your legs in 20 places. He didn't get mad easily, but it was spectacular when he did.

For a college kid accustomed to settling disputes by reason, Mulvaney was a revelation. He didn't care about right and wrong. Either he liked you, or he tried to kill you.

One night Mulvaney was standing fire watch in the latrine--the Marine Corps thinks they are flammable--and he somehow got into a fight with Rodriguez. A Mexican kid from Brownsville is not the best choice to throw hands with. We could hear it all down the squad bay--terrific thumps with a splattering sound like a sack full of hog kidneys hitting a tile wall, and not a word. Neither wanted to waste energy talking. It was one of those extended fights engaged in by men who simply like fighting.

Next morning it was hair, teeth, and eyeballs all over the deck, and enough gore that you'd have thought they'd been slaughtering hogs. Both combatants looked like they had lost a discussion with a cement truck. Mulvaney's left eye looked like an egg fried in blood and Rodriguez's nose wasn't quite where I remembered it.

"What you pukes been doing?" snarled the drill instructor. Pukes was the nicest thing they ever called us. He really wasn't mad. Fighting was a sin, but not as bad as falling out on a run.

"Walked into the door, sir," says Mulvaney, deadly serious.

"Wha' sir?" says Rodriguez, looking puzzled. His English deteriorated when he was asked inconvenient questions.

For hours, Mulvaney and Rodriguez pounded round the grinder in full packs, holding hands and yelling, "I love Mulvaney more than poking my girlfriend." When they finished, I bet they did. It was justice of a sort.

McCoy was the saddest thing I ever saw. McCoy was very tall with a long, sad face. He was disturbingly thin--your impulse on meeting him was to feed him--and beet-brown from heaven-knows-how-many weeks in strength-building platoons.

McCoy didn't have any muscles to enlarge. If he had any coordination, you didn't notice it. His voice was soft and feminine and he was funny-looking, a bad thing at boot. He reminded me of a clerk from a Dickens novel.

On the grinder he stuck up above everyone else like a weed and was always out of step. He tripped over his feet and fell into other people. McCoy struggled to do pushups until tears ran down his cheeks, but couldn't do them. His back folded until his belly touched the ground, and when he got into the "down" position he couldn't push himself back up.

The DIs wanted to get rid of McCoy. He didn't belong in the Corps, they said. They offered him medical discharges and general discharges, and set him back time and time again, but McCoy wouldn't quit.

Later we learned that McCoy's older brother had gone through Parris Island and had been All-time Superprivate or something, a really hot trooper. McCoy wanted to finish to make his brother proud. He had never amounted to much and wanted to show that he could do it too. Trouble was, he had the guts for five Marines but the body for about a third of one.

The DIs bullied him to drive him out. They were practical men, and they knew he would die in Asia, probably getting several other men killed at the same time. They badgered him mercilessly and made him stand on tables and roar for the platoon. He'd stand there on a bayonet instructor's table, surrounded by the platoon, and the DIs would torment him.

"Roar, McCoy."

McCoy couldn't roar. A muted groan came from his scrawny chest.

"Louder, McCoy! Let's hear a Marine Corps roar!"

"*Uhhhhh...oooo...uhhh...*"

"Louder!"

"Make a muscle, McCoy."

McCoy, looking sadder than ever, would tense his muscle for all to see and nothing would happen. But he wouldn't quit because he was going to be a Marine and make his brother proud.

I forget how they finally got rid of him.

If there is any possible way to do something wrong, a recruit will find it.

There was the ambidextrous kid at the grenade range at Lejeune. The idea was to stand between two walls of sandbags and throw the grenade over a high parapet. He pulled the pin and rared back to throw. Then he stopped. You could see the puzzlement in his face. No, that hand didn't feel right. He casually tossed the thing in the air, caught it in the other hand, and threw it. By the time it exploded, the instructor was in the next county and accelerating.

I remember lying in lovely cold muck behind a log at Lejeune, firing at enemy oil barrels a few hundred yards away. It was one of those weird situations that occur regularly in the military.

Cold rain drizzling down my helmet and running neatly down my spine, my helmet slipping down over my eyes, and I'm in a firefight with a bunch of extremely dangerous barrels. The rifle is a worn-out M-1 probably left over from the Napoleonic Wars, in use only because the government has several hundred billion rounds of ammunition for it.

The trigger mechanism is broken. Every time I fire it, the damned thing falls out and hangs down like a wounded clock. I slap it back. Bang, slap, bang, slap. Every fourth round, the clip pops out of the top of the rifle--*spoing*--and lands on my helmet.

Bang, slap, *spoing*, clunk, adjust the helmet. Bang, slap. I begin to see that it could be a long war.

A recruit was standing on a roof at Parris Island in the burning sun at parade rest. His DI had put him there to work on the roof and somehow had forgotten him. A passing sergeant noticed, stared curiously for a second, and bellowed, "Git down from there, prive."

The private didn't move.

"Goddamit, git down here," bawled the instructor, unused to being ignored.

Nothing. The private looked deeply unhappy, but didn't so much as twitch.

Another DI came along and yelled, but nothing moved the recruit. He gazed desperately ahead, either deaf or crazed by the sun. A group formed on the sidewalk, including a warrant officer, a lieutenant, and, finally, a passing light colonel.

The colonel snapped his crispest order. The private stared ahead. The crowd conferred, decided they had a mental case on their hands and prepared to send for a struggle buggy and some big corpsmen. Then the private's DI returned.

"Jaworski, *Ten-hut!* Git your butt down from there."

Down came Jaworski. From parade rest, you see, the only acceptable order is "attention. The manual of arms says so.
"You see," a drill instructor explained to me, "a recruit's in a place he doesn't understand at all, and nothing ever works for him. Back home, he knows the rules. Maybe he's a big dude on the block, got it made. Not here. Everybody's yelling at him and he can't ever do anything right.

"So he figures he'll do exactly what he's told. It's his way of protecting himself. If something goes wrong, he thinks at least it's not his fault. This is what a drill instructor's got to learn-- nothing's too crazy for a recruit to do if he thinks it's what you told him. And you really got to think about it. Otherwise you can get him hurt.

"One time in winter a friend of mine, Sergeant Grunderling, had evening duty at some building and he wanted to go take a leak. So he tells this recruit who's with him, 'I'm going out for a minute. Don't let anyone in who doesn't know the password. You got that?'

"The recruit says, 'Yes, sir,' so Grunderling relieves himself and realizes he can't remember the password. So he hollers, 'Minter, open the door."

"What's the password?"

"I forget. Open the door."

"I can't do that, sir. You told me not to let anybody in who doesn't give the password, sir."

"Goddamit Minter, now I'm telling you to open the door."

"'No sir, I can't do that."

"Minter, it's cold out here."

"No, sir, I can't do that."

"By now Grunderling's mostly frozen and so mad he can't see straight, but he sees threats ain't going to help him.

"Please, Minter, let me in. I ain't gonna yell at you. I won't do anything to you."

"Aww, you're trying to trick me."

"No, Minter, honest, I ain't trying to trick you. Open the door.'

"You're gonna yell at me, aren't you sir?"

"No, Minter, I promise."

"Finally, old Minter opens the door and Grunderling nearly kills him. But he should have expected it. A recruit does exactly what you tell him."

"You probably won't see a Wampus cat," Sergeant Sly continues, "but if you do, remember he's fast. A cat isn't built for endurance like a dog is, but he's lightning in a dash. Don't think you're gonna tease a Wampus and run away when it starts spittin' and howlin."

"They're not that fast--I mean, a Wampus cat can't keep up with a cheetah or anything, but they've been clocked at 50. It takes a damn good shot to hit anything at that speed."

A September day in a clearing at Camp Lejeune. Our company of trainees sits in weathered bleachers, scratching and, after three months of training, feeling as salty as three bosun's mates.

A massive black sergeant with a velvet Georgia accent is teaching us the care and feeding of a white phosphorus grenade, otherwise known as Willy Peter (and several other things unfit for a family magazine).

Willy Peter is an unpleasant weapon that throws white phosphorous around, a nasty substance that sticks to you and burns.

He holds the lethal cylinder in his hand, tells us what horrible things it can do to Luke the Gook--who was then the hated enemy--and announces that he will trot into the field and demonstrate.

That is fine with us, as long as we can sit in the sun and relax. We watch with interest as he lopes into the grass.

For days we'd been watching weapons specialists trot into Lejeune's clearings, and something spectacular always happened. Something blew up or went bang or made colored smoke.

So the sergeant gets out there next to this little steel hut he's supposed to hide in while Willy Peter does his stuff. He chucks this incredibly vicious grenade downfield and ducks into the steel hut.

Two seconds later he streaks out at roughly Mach Four, like Tony Green on a punt return. He has the unmistakable gait of a man who is flat terrified. About that time Willy Peter goes *whoomp!* and the air around the sergeant is filled with long smoky trails of flaming phosphorous. He streaks on as if he took showers in the stuff, ignoring it, a mountain on the move in blind fright.

Somehow all that smoking agony misses him and he reaches us panting hugely.

"Goddam wasps."

Training has changed. Ten years ago, reveille at Parris Island meant a GI-can lid sailing down the squad bay at oh-dark-30. The lights would come on suddenly and 10 seconds later a hundred recruits would be standing at attention in their skivvies, half-conscious and miserable.

Now the GI-can lid is gone. So is much of the stress of training.

"What happened, some kid's mother heard about it and wrote her congressman. He came down and said, Oh dear, ain't this awful, what if they hit somebody with that lid. So they made us stop that.

"And one time a recruit died of heat stroke carrying his first issue to the barracks, so everybody's mother started writing her congressman. Now we gotta carry recruits around in cattle cars.

"Hell, you can't put thousands of people through military training without somebody getting hurt. It just ain't possible. If they don't train hard, they get killed in combat. They ought to shoot the doctor that let that kid in here in the first place. Congress doesn't give a damn about training.

"And you know what? The recruits want training to be rough. That's why they joined--to do something hard."

Parris Island can make a Marine out of almost anything with a detectable heartbeat. What a kid wants most at Parris Island is out, and the quickest way out is to behave. Most kids have a well-developed sense of self-preservation and see the wisdom of obedience. A few are hopeless.

I remember a tall black kid named Gurdy from the slums of Chicago who was terrified of the water. He had a tiny cue ball of a head and held it to one side, like a rattlesnake. There was a mean, cautious defiance to him, the look of a trapped animal. Gurdy had lived so much on the outside of society that he didn't realize you ever had do anything.

We were lined up at the pool for the swim test, if you could call it that. I think you had to swim about as far as most of us could broad jump. Gurdy stood there wild-eyed and strange, leaning his head one way and rolling his eyes the other. He didn't say anything.

The rest of us were going through boot camp, but Gurdy didn't know what he was going through. I guess he thought we were going to make him walk the plank. He was out of some remote urban tenement world, and beyond even the military's ability to handle.

We could see him getting crazier and crazier as the line got shorter. Tension was building up in him like a head of steam. Finally he broke and ran like a jack rabbit--just shot out the door and kept going.

God knows where he thought he could run to on Parris Island, where it's hard for a fugitive in a bathing suit to hide. I don't think he much knew himself, probably figured it was like ducking a cop in the city. It was the last we saw of him.

I had thought it was baloney from some book like *Battle Cry*, but it happens: You don't call your smokepole a gun. It is a rifle. Private Mulligan walking down the squad bay at Parris Island, chanting, "This is my rifle, this is my gun, this is for killing, this is for fun...," firmly holding on to both.

The worst hazard for a recruit is not shrapnel or even dismemberment by Sergeant Bull Walrus. It is tattoo parlors. These garish dens abound near big bases and prey on recent recruits longing for any evidence of manhood. New soldiers spend an hour getting that impressive eagle, and then they spend 20 years pricing plastic surgeons to get their boyhood back.

Some recruits go stark nuts over tattoos--Wasloski, for example, a red-headed Polish kid from Chicago I met in the drab barracks of Pendleton.

Wasloski was crazy. He had an angular, pugnacious face with half the world's strategic reserve of freckles, and claimed he had graduated from the University of Pennsylvania, which for obscure reasons he called UPI, and had less judgment than a volunteer for kamikaze school.

God help him, Wasloski discovered tattoo parlors. It had to happen. He showed up at the barracks one night with a half-naked Vietnamese girl tattooed on his forearm. It was conspicuous to say the least. I mean, it had colors like a Day-Glo detergent box and probably had batteries.

Before it had healed the poor maniac had another on the other arm, and then on an upper arm. I don't know where it ended, if it did. He's probably got naked bar girls running up his spine.

Nothing is quite so military as a tattoo, and he wanted to be military. He just didn't know that guys with tattoos spend the rest of their lives trying to get rid of them. If Wasloski ever has a girlfriend, which is barely possible, he'll have to have his arms amputated. And maybe his back.

Junior enlisted men have a limitless capacity for avoiding work. Among the better recruits, this talent verges on religious inspiration. Trainees learn it quickly.

My first experience with this useful ability was watching a platoon that was walking in line across a sandy field to police up cigarette butts. Instead of picking up the offending butts, each man carefully pushed sand over them with his boots. They hadn't planned it or seen anyone else do it. The idea simply came to them as the obvious response to the situation.

They left a spotless field. Thirty minutes later, wind blew the sand away and the place looked like a public dump. I suppose those butts had been accumulating for 30 years, buried repeatedly by generations of recruits.

Then there was McClinton, assigned to water the grass at a chow hall on a blazing California day. There wasn't a puff of wind. The heat would have baked a camel's brains, and asphalt was turning to a sticky ooze. McClinton was supposed to walk back and forth across the lawn, spraying each patch until it was thoroughly wet. A Russian would have done it, but the American trooper thinks for himself.

McClinton found the opening for a storm sewer in the ground in the shade beneath a tree. For three hours he stood in the shade and watered that grate. The grass never got wet, so he always seemed to be watering a dry patch. A hundred yards below, the gutter flooded.

"Now the Wampus cat isn't any damn killer bogeyman, no matter what the locals say. All that stuff on TV about how it killed seven Boy Scouts in a swamp is so much crap. At least in my opinion. But it can get real savage, like any cat, and we do lose three or four recruits every year to it. It's mostly their own damn fault because they don't take the right precautions.

"When you put your tent up, just make sure you're at least four feet from the tree line. Four feet, got it? And the Wampus cat tends to hunt on a north-south line, so I want those tents facing east and west. That's all it takes, and the colonel won't be chewing my ass because the Wampus cat killed one of my recruits."

The beach at Lejeune, a chill gray day with fog wafting over greasy Atlantic rollers. A platoon of infantry trainees stands shivering beside the looming bulk of an amtrac--the old LVT P-5, the beach assault of the Marines in those days.

It's shaped like a steel loaf of bread with tracks. It runs up on the beach and drops its ramp, whereupon the grunts run out and get machine-gunned.

At least, that's what the crewmen tell the grunts. The grunts are trainees. They'll believe anything.

The corporal in command yells and the trainees scramble aboard--37 of them. A trac is like a steel coffin, dark and cold inside, with only two small windows on the sides.

Sometimes they become coffins for real. Once, a hatch was left open and a big roller came aboard, dragging the trac down in 150 feet of cold water. Nobody has heard from the occupants and, as this was some years ago, they are presumed dead.

The crew tell the grunts about it as the ramp closes.

The engine revs up to a deafening roar, hollow and sepulchral, for the dash into the breakers. The beast crashes into the surf and sinks to within a foot of its top, which is what it is supposed to do. Green water comes over the windows and shoots in streams through the minor leaks a trac always has.

The recruits don't know this. They are very, very uneasy in this death trap, imagining the terrified scramble should it sink. There would be no hope of avoiding a watery grave.

A hundred yards from shore, the crewman stands under the machine-gun periscope and looks out like a U-boat commander.

He eyes the rollers, which break over the top, and says laconically, "It's too rough up there, Charlie. Let's take her down to 50 feet and hope the bulkheads hold."

Three recruits faint. Trainees will believe anything.

"I had this guy Handley, couldn't do anything right," one DI told me. "I mean, he was the kind of guy who tries hard, but everything he touches turns to crap. Big doofus guy outa Miami. You can't persecute that kind of guy, because he genuinely is trying his best.

"One day Handley is sitting in this 10-holer latrine we had, along with about six other guys, all with their trousers around their ankles. Well, the colonel comes in to take a whizz, and Handley stands to attention and yells, '*Ten-hut!*'"

Oh-dark-30, a frigid morning at Lejeune. Our last day of training. We line up single file to go into the dark administration shack and collect our boot pay. We are harder and heavier than we were three months ago, a little cocky, confident, aware of new muscles. Inside the shack we have to stand to attention and do some silly boot rigmarole: "Sir! Private Smith reportingforpaycall, serial number twothirtyonetwentysixfiftyone Sir!" all in one breath.

We also have to stop just outside the door and count the crisp new bills. One of the squad leaders--Bergland, a beefy kid from Alabama--has been ordered to be sure we do.

He is feeling full of himself on the dark sidewalk and well he might. For the first time in his life, he is in charge of others.

A figure comes from the shack, like 20 before him, but counts nothing.

"Marine, count them bills!"

The figure doesn't stop, so Bergland grabs him around the waist and pulls him back, unaware that he has grabbed the meanest gunny sergeant in Camp Geiger.

"Gityourbuttback...here...oh...my...gawd...."

"Sir, what's a Wampus cat look like?" a recruit asks Sergeant Sly.

"I wish I could tell you. You see, a Wampus is unusual in one way: It only runs backwards. It's one of the mysteries of science. A lot of people have seen the back end of a Wampus, but nobody's seen the front. That's why you gotta run your tents from east to west, so the Wampus cat doesn't back into it. And let me tell you, if you ever see the butt end of a Wampus cat coming in, you better kiss your ass goodbye, 'cause it's all over."

Noon in the Lejeune woods, chilly with autumn and the slowing drizzle, gooky red mud making sucking noises under our boots. Rain-laden pine branches brush across faces like cold hands. "S" Company is coming off the flame-thrower range for chow. Why the scene sticks in my memory I don't know, but it is my most vivid impression of training: a company of sodden recruits, shivering.

There were inexplicable moments when it all came together and we were proud to be in the service, the real world, not pumping gas or pulling frogs apart in some tedious laboratory. A fair number of us would be dead in ten months, but we didn't believe it yet.

Steam rose from the field kitchen, the only warm thing in the entire world, and we held out mess kits for the cooks to fill with savory glop. At 19 you're too dumb to know when you're uncomfortable. We were used to 3 1/2 hours sleep, at ease with rifles and seven-eighty-two gear, beginning to feel like Marines.

One blond kid with huge, round, blue eyes has lost his mess kit. He takes chow in his canteen cup--stew, spinach, bread, canned peaches dumped on top, string beans. It all goes to the same place, he says. When you've been up and running since 4:30, you don't care what it looks like.

Sergeants bark at us, but act like we're human, which may or may not show good judgment on their part. I line up with the rest of these olive-drab warriors at chest-high log tables. We eat standing up in the soupy clay, gray clouds rolling and twisting overhead. Someone passes a rumor that we have declared war on Red China. Some believe it. Some always do.

There is no such thing as a recruit with enough to eat. Chow wasn't bad--not like at the chow hall where, when the cook scooped up the powdered eggs with an ice cream scoop, green water filled the hole.

Along the log tables are jars of peanut butter and jelly for making Geiger-burgers--two-pound sandwiches that keep you going through the training ranges of Lejeune's Camp Geiger. Huge wasps and yellow jackets crawl around in the jelly jars.

The man next to me eyes a hornet the size of a heavy bomber in his jar. The beast is obviously dangerous. On the other hand, the Marine wants a sandwich.

It doesn't pay to stand between a recruit and food. With a quick twist of his knife, he forces the hornet deep below the surface of the jelly and makes his sandwich with the top layers.

Others before him had done the same thing. I count seven buried wasps, some still twitching. You do what you gotta do.

51 THE GREAT FIZZLED PLAYBOY UNDERSEA BLACK TIE AND ORGASMIC MALE-FANTASY DIDN'T HAPPEN PHOTO SHOOT

We Wuz Almost Contenders, But Heartbreak Got There First

First published in Playboy

I t was three a.m. in late December and I and Stu Miller, a federal lobbyist and former motorcycle racer, were zooming around the DC beltway in his male-menopause red Miata and discussing what to do for the Millennium. The possibilities were dismal.

"God, some black-tie thing on the Hill? I'd rather slit my wrists," Stu said.

"Let's blow it off and go diving."

We're scuba loons. Blowing it off and doing something else is my response to most of Washington.

"Yeah," he said, attempting humor, "We can dive in black tie. Hey? Hey!"

The idea burst on us like a squeezed grape.

"What if we really dive in black tie? Take a bottle of champagne. Take photos?"

The light was dawning hard. Stu nearly hit a tree.

"We'll take the millennium *Playboy* down with us, sell them the shots. Yeah."

"The magazine will get soggy."

"Not if we laminate it. I'm gonna call *Playboy*."

Right, I thought. Sure. The idea was admittedly cute, and we'd both written for *Playboy*, which might add to our credibility, especially since the editors didn't know us. On the other hand, magazines work months in advance. We'd have to leave town in four days for the Keys. At bottom we didn't have a corn dog's chance in a hog trough.

Sure enough, *Playboy* responded that it was thinking about the idea, which is magazine-talk for we aren't thinking about it very hard but don't want to crush your spirit. By then we were committed. We were going to do it anyway. We packed several cubic yards of scuba gear into a station wagon and pointed it down I-95 toward Miami.

All the way down we fantasized. What if we did the shoot and just sent the pics to *Playboy*?

God worked in strange ways, we said. And with strange people, which gave us a shot. What if? what *if*??

You gotta understand. When we were growing up, or at least in college getting older, *Playboy* was our philosophical guidebook. We all thought we ought to be at the University of Virginia, look like a young William Buckley, and drive a Lamborghini. *Playboy* gave us the polish, if not the Lamborghini. It was where we learned who Mancini was, what existentialism meant, and how to behave around people who wore shoes. We dreamed of Vargas girls and wanted to be like Hugh Hefner, to whom we referred to familiarly as Hef.

Playboy actually sophisticated us. And we really did read the articles. Too.

So the thought of actually being in the magazine–having a photo of us in black tie with champagne and lovely babes in the altogether or at least mostly together–wow! Sure, a wetsuit had the erotic appeal of a cold shower. Maybe a reef wasn't a blues club in Chicago.

But we were talking image. And as a glittering male ego-fantasy, it was up there with Marlboro Man, or a restored '57 Chevy with 454 cubes and a mild blower and 73 coats of hand-rubbed Kandy-Kolor cherry metal-flake lacquer.

Even though it wasn't going to happen.

We made 800 miles the first day, 300 the second, and pulled into Key Largo in early afternoon. Hotels were insanely pricey because of the Millennium. We went back up the road to Florida City and got a room in the Econo-Lodge near the Last Chance Saloon, a biker bar in which we felt at home.

For the next two days we dived in the mornings to check our gear and figure out how to do a shoot under water. I'd used a camera in the ocean enough to know that I couldn't. We needed a cheap photographer. We found one.

In the afternoons we got props. OfficeMax laminated the cover of the Millennial Playboy for us. Fortunately it was brightly colored for good contrast against a midnight ocean. The centerfold was trickier. We did it in two parts and taped them together.

Then we got plastic "Happy New Year 2000" party hats and cheap red cummerbunds and bow ties (something told me the resale value would be marginal), a bottle of incredibly lousy champagne called Dom Bahde Stufe or something, with a gaudy label, and a box of frozen peas to attract fish for local color. (Hef probably didn't do this at his parties. Well, we were going to.)

Since *Playboy* wasn't going to happen, we laminated the cover of *Soldier of Fortune* magazine, for which I once worked in another and stranger life. The editor, Bob Brown, was a buddy of mine, and I knew he'd run it. We wanted a published record.

OK, Plantation Key, nine-thirty on New Year's Eve. We showed up at Conch Republic, a dive operation running a reef trip for people who wanted to be underwater at midnight.

The photographer showed. Seas were flat, the night warm. We loaded gear, boarded, and went to Davis Ledge, a nice easy reef at thirty-five feet. The other divers suited up and went in. Stu and I looked like idiots in cummerbund and party hats. We probably were idiots, so it didn't bother us. He went in. I followed.

At which point everything went wrong.

His hat tore in two in mild chop. The centerfold slipped from our hands. He dropped the Dom Bahde Stufe, having forgotten that he'd need one hand free to clear his ears. We finned around the bottom like neoprene bats and found it. The photographer had vanished.

We followed the reef and reacquired him. He looked unhappy.

The camera had flooded.

It was definitely the end of our great all-time wet dream of glory, of our quest for ultimate meaning, the closest we would ever come to the Playboy Mansion. True, the magazine wasn't interested–but what a photo for the office wall.

What the hell. The water was clear and lovely, the reef burning in reds and orange where our lights touched it, goofy fish slowly swimming and wondering what we thought we were doing. We stayed down for forty-five minutes, surfaced, had (good) champagne and shrimp on the boat, and started back.

Ashore, I went to the car and found a message on my cell phone. My daughter, I figured.

She was at the Phish concert in the Everglades.

It never occurred to me that it might be *Playboy* calling.

And it wasn't. It was my daughter.

But it *could* have been *Playboy*.

The Last Chance saloon was rocking. Bikers and local watermen were partying with their ladies, and a country jukebox was wailing laments about sorry paychecks and bad divorces. Stu and I were on our fourth Rum Runner, a devastating drink for whose acquaintance we would pay dearly in the morning. It didn't matter. Nothing mattered.

"Y'all want two more?" asked the barmaid.

"Yesh. Rum Runnersh. Hold the Runner."

We stared at each other in sorrow, trying not to put our heads on the bar and sob. It isn't a good thing to do in biker bars.

52 LA FUENTE

Slow Afternoon in Guadalajara: The Virtues of
a Misspent Life

So I was sitting with Tom the Robot and Jonesy in La
Fuente, an old and cavernous beer bar hard by the cathedral in Guadalajara, and swapping lies. Except they
weren't lies, because some people can't lie to equal the truth.
Otherwise I guess they would. Thing is, lying is a limited form.
Life isn't.

La Fuente is dark and inelegant. It covers about a roaring acre
of locals hooting and hollering and you pay for beers as you get
them.

The Robot was talking about social interaction. Like Jonesy,
he has what writers call a checkered past, but chaotic is more
like it—ground Marine in Nam, paramedic in New York, curious jobs in remote parts of Alaska. He once played a bottlenosed dolphin in a movie, hovering two feet below the Gulf
of Mexico in scuba gear and waggling a plastic dolphin's head
above the water.

The Robot is crazy. He is also a dangerous brawler and has
anger-control problems. Actually, he doesn't see a problem.
He's perfectly happy smacking the hell out of people who need
it.

Anyway, social interaction. He comes out of a bar in Guad late
one night, three sheets to the wind, and probably the blankets
and pillow cases too, and these young bad-asses come up with

a knife and request his wallet. When that happens, the smart thing is just to give it to them. So the Robot reaches for his wallet and nails the sumbitch with a drop-shouldered sucker-punch, hard, and the jerk goes down leaving teeth on the concrete, and the others decamp.

"Bloody chicklets," said the Robot, referring to the teeth. "I was stupid. I coulda got killed." He has anger-control problems. And his wallet.

He wasn't bragging, just telling beer stories.

Jonesy is a retired bush pilot out of Alaska with a soft Southern accent like Karo syrup dripping on busted china and he'd talk about flying way up north with ice on the wings and in a fog in places that made nowhere look like somewhere. Maybe he was in a high-wing Cessna, but I forget.

"What happens if you can't find a place to land?" asked the Robot, who knew the answer.

"Shucks, you can land anywhere," said Jonesy. "Nothing to it. What you want to do is find a airfield before you do it."

I guess you could drink beer with a tax accountant. But I wouldn't want to try it.

The waiter came by on a resupply run with more Corona and I mentioned coming out of Angola on a story for *Soldier of Fortune* in a DC-3, flying ten feet over the trees to keep SAM-7s from getting a lock. This was this when Cuban soldiers, whom I rather like, were supporting the evil commie government in Luanda. I didn't care. The world is complex. I didn't need to solve all its problems, or take sides.

Anyway, among a certain kind of riffraff and rabble, such as us, the DC-3 is a legend. It first flew about 1936, and still does, age seventy-five and re-engined, and it was the platform for an early attempt at Puff the Magic Dragon, a gunship popular in Asia. More popular with one side than the other, I guess. With Gatlings firing tracers it looked like it had ray guns.

But that's neither here nor there. La Fuente was getting noisier as people came in for an after-work brew. There was nothing hostile about it, just good times and bad acoustics.

Mexico changes fast. You see women in lots of bars. You've heard a lot about machismo, but it's on life-support, at least in the cities. Which is a good thing. In the US you can see some diesel-dyke feminist with spiked hair like an alarmed porcupine and hollering about what she thinks is machismo because she caught some guy leering at her tits. Mexican machismo isn't funny. It often involved broken jaws. Still does in the wilder parts.

You might think guys who know more about guns, engines, and questionable bars than about polishing doilies, or whatever you do with doilies, would be untouched by civilizing influences, and regard women as furniture or captive hookers. No, actually. I know lots of pilots, former door-gunners, cowboy divers, and generally very tough guys. They think women are nuts, but don't speak badly of them, even in private. Except gringas. Jonesy will gaze at an ambient lovely and opine wistfully that she could suck-start a leaf-blower. But he would never say it to her. He's just dreaming. He treats his wife with kindness and respect. But then, she's Mexican.

The Robot looks like a skull with skin stretched over it. Hollowed out, he'd make a good lamp shade. He has don't-fuck-with-me eyes that make you want to be his friend, or somewhere else. I've never figured it out. Some guys you look at and you know mayhem is readily available. It isn't a scowl, threatening manner, over-hanging orbitals, or angry voice. But you know. You just know. "Cops eyes," they have been called.

He talked about motorcycles he'd had, which was lots, and falling off them occasionally to no good effect on bad turns, and long lonely rides down to Florida on a Harley panhead to dive and hang out with people your mother wouldn't like at all.

The better forms of human detritus tend to travel in similar social tunnels. The Robot and I both knew the Last Chance Saloon, a biker bar at the top of the Florida Keys. My lunatic friend Stu and I had spent time there when we drove down to pass the turn of the millennium underwater, which we did at Davis Ledge, trying to drink, at forty feet, a bottle of rust-cutter champagne called Domme Bahd Stufe, or something similar. It didn't work too well.

A couple of hours and considerable Corona later, I'd heard about getting dropped off in distant lakes in Alaska to fish by a float plane that wouldn't come back for two weeks so you better be alive then. About the shark that swept in on an attack run in cloudy water and veered off when it realized that divers weren't in its food chain. About the bomb squad in DC that sent robots to investigate what seemed to be a bomb, but turned out to be bull sperm in liquid nitrogen. About cold rain over a disintegrating M60 tank on the mud ranges of Fort Hood. About....

I don't guess we saved the world or cured cancer. But I thought it was a pretty good way to spend a slow afternoon, way south of the border.

53 WUNXPUTL GOES TO HARVARD

The Tloxyproctyl Justice Gap

By 2018 the market for social indignation had bottomed out. America's War on Injustice had entered the doldrums. There seemed to be no inequities left to conquer. The major aquifers of discrimination had been pumped dry. Hate-crime protection had been extended to blacks, Hispanics, mulattos, women, bisexuals, homosexuals, Lesbians, Native Americans, transsexuals, asexuals, transvestites, the transgendered, sadomasochists, pedophiles, and the bestiality lobby (NAMFLA, the North American Man-Fido Love Association). Affirmative action had been so successfully extended that all governmental departments were uniformly diverse with no whites at all. The Washington Redskins had been renamed the Federal Folders, and three congressmen had lost office for using the word "Oriental" to refer to Orientals.

Across the country bored adolescents in universities sought something about which to be indignant. Hunting was poor.

Then, thank God, an activist in Swarthmore's Lesbian Chicana, Gay, and Bicephalous Studies department pointed out that not enough Tloxyproctyls were enrolled in Ivy nurseries. This was genius, though not immediately recognized as such. A collective "Huh?" rang out in progressive circles. No one knew what Tloxyproctyls were. Traffic at Wikipedia rose thirty percent for several days.

It was discovered that the Tloxyproctyls were an obscure tribe of some two dozen mostly naked Indians living in the Amazon rain forest and the Stone Age. They ate only tree leaves and large white grubs found in rotting logs. Their language, unrelated to any other, consisted of twelve words, none of which meant anything. Their intellectual development was approximately that of a cassava root.

Clearly they were victims of discrimination by...by...well, that could be decided later. Now they needed political action. Exactly why was not clear, but did not seem important.

On campus, the best instincts of the Improving Classes roared into action. Goodness raged. Further research showed a shocking lack of 'Proctyls, as they came to be called by the knowing, almost everywhere. It was just...Wrong. At Wellesley, puzzled co-eds marched for Lesbian and Biramous Tloxyproctyl Rights. Universities established 'Proctyl quotas. A mad scramble ensued to recruit the unwitting Indians. The campaign was somewhat hampered by the fact that there weren't any.

More were needed to keep the wheels of justice turning. At Princeton the Department of Black, Transaxle, and Amphibian Studies found a solution: Imputed Tloxyproctyls or, as some called the idea, Inferential Tloxyproctyly. Students of other oppressed categories, such as Lesbian, Gay, Vegetarian, Bicyclic, and Transphylum students would be assigned as 'Proctyls by imputation. The argument was that if one could be transsexual or transgendered, why not trans-ethnicked?

The noted feminist professor Dr. Cecina Pocilga-Dworkin, whose academic credentials consisted of looking like an orangutan, said, "Race, gender, and ethnicity are socially constructed by white-supremacist capitalists to oppress the black and brown races, which don't exist because they are social constructs. Since 'Proctyls would suffer discrimination if

there were any, we can appoint proxy Proctyls, and seek re-
dress for the discrimination they would suffer if they existed."
Several upper-middle-class date-rape activists were chosen
as stand-ins. They stopped bathing and began eating ersatz
white grubs made of sashimi to raise public consciousness of
Tloxyproctyl issues.

With support from NPR and *Mother Jones*, a gala fund-raising
masquerade ball was held in Washington. Proceeds were to
go to the various organizations that had sprung up to end
oppression of 'Proctyls, none of whom were actually in the
United States. It didn't matter. Justice does not know national
boundaries.

The ball was a great success, attracting many prominent
figures. Hillary Clinton attended as an aging blonde ruin,
and won the prize for most-convincing costume. She said,
"Injustice is injustice, whether there is any or not." Nancy
Pelosi came as a slightly decayed cadaver, apologizing that she
hadn't had time to find a costume. "Not even grubs can escape the curse of whiteness," she stated, and pledged Congressional funding to find Grubs of Color. Barack Obama arrived
disguised as usual as a President. No one was fooled. Barney
Frank , gay as an Easter Bonnet, came as, well, Barney Frank,
and gave the keynote address, saying, "I stand hard and fast behind the Tloxyproctyls of America."

While the inferred 'Proctyls did raise 'Proctyl awareness in
the country, mostly by convincing the public that a lot
of people were crazy, a vague suspicion continued in aca-
demia that funding would be more reliable if based on real
Proctyls. Consequently the Anthropology Department at Harvard suggested sending a hunting party to the Amazon Basin
with nets. The university's conservative professor expressed
reservations at this. Yet the consensus was that the national
interest in equitable treatment of Tlosyproctyls outweighed
considerations of their civil rights. Anyway, sanity was a social construct.

Support for 'Proctyl issues came from unexpected quarters. The Pentagon set up a Department of Tloxyproctyl Acquisition so as to stay ahead of the Chinese. The Secretary of Defense said the Tloxyproctyl Gap represented an existential threat to the United States, as did everything else, and requested a seventy-six billion dollar fighter plane. Thought was given to encouraging the Proctyls to breed, perhaps by offering them strings of brightly-colored glass beads. Maybe their grubs could be doctored with fertility enhancers.

After three weeks in the rain forest, the anthropologists succeeded in gathering up Wunxputl, an actual Tloxyproctyl, who stood four feet nine and weighed eighty-three pounds when he was buck naked, his usual state. When offered a loin cloth, he spent half an hour trying to put it on before giving up due to the unaccustomed complexity, and said, "Gurp."

On his reaching Harvard it was discovered that "Gurp" was all Wunxputl ever said. Neo-Nazis, racists, and Republicans snickered that Wunxputl was retarded, but Dr. Herzog-Mariposón, head of Indigenous and Native Peoples Studies, pointed out that intelligence was a social construct. He explained that Wunxputll's silence was just the natural reticence of Native Peoples, who lived at one with Nature. Wunxputl's continued attempts to climb the curtains of the faculty lounge, said Mariposón, merely represented his desire to share his folkways with a civilization that had lost contact with the natural world. We should be humble, he said, recognize the wisdom of Native Peoples, and Learn from Them.

The retrograde responded with their usual lack of progressive insight. The conservative professor at Harvard said privately that Wunxputl seemed no more benighted than most of the incoming freshmen, though he conceded that these usually did not climb drapes except after major football games.

Having been given a simplified loin cloth, Wunxputl was brought to classes in anthropology, seated at the professor's desk, and given a banana. He said "Gurp." The students took extensive notes. A graduate student began a doctoral thesis on the various meanings of the word, which many thought embodied the wisdom of the Tloxyproctyls. The conservative professor agreed that it probably did.

The matter came to a close. The remaining 'Proctyls had fled deeper into the rain forest and begun hiding in caves to avoid Justice. The Imputed 'Proctyls held a few marches, graduated, and went into I-banking. The conservative professor at Harvard said that the Anthropology Department's head should be repositioned by a Proctylologist, but was ignored.

54 HANT VII

Bulk-lot Wisdom from Up the Holler

Saturday morning was sunny and bugs screaming and buzzing, at least in my part of West Virginia, and it was nice and cool. Bugs is pretty much like folk. The boy bugs holler or buzz or I don't know what all so the girl bugs will love them and they can get laid, and then the boy bugs run off and leave the girl bugs with the eggs. You'd think the girl bugs would learn, but they never do. If you have a choice, it's better to be a boy bug.

Anyways, I was planning to go see Uncle Hant that makes skull break moonshine back in the woods so he could tell me how to make a living. Hant knows everything. A few years back, he sent the Poverty Office in Wheeling a letter that said he was a one-legged Injun princess named Sighing Cloud with black lung, and they started sending him money in trucks. Then they wrote him a letter saying did he have any children he didn't know who was the daddy to, so they could send him more money. He told them he had thirteen and he didn't have no idea where they came from but they all had Down's Syndrome, whatever that is, and now he's the richest man in McDowell County. So don't nobody who says gummint is a bad thing know what he's talking about.

But Hant don't get up too early in the morning, so first I went up the holler to see my old school teacher, Mr. Entropy McWilliams that's got a internet television and lets me look at it sometimes. He was watching what he said was a Sympathy Orchestra and a noise was coming out of it like a blow-out plug on a high-pressure drill rig. It was real awful and I asked Mr. McWilliams what it was and he said somebody was blowing a hobo. I thought that was pretty ripe for a show anybody could watch, even little children, but it turned out it wasn't so much a hobo as a oboe, which is like a three-foot duck call. I didn't see much future in it. Neither would our McDowell County ducks, that don't have much schooling. It might work with city ducks, though.

Anyway, he said it did sound kind of like a cat squalling because of Affirmative Action, which I didn't know what was. He said it was a newfangled law in Washington, that's the Yankee capital, that says if you want somebody to do a job, you have to hire someone that can't do it. I said that made sense, about like taking poison. He said I thought that because I wasn't in Washington and it was God's own truth, and it was for Social Justice. The more you couldn't do a job, the more you had to get it.

That was too many for me. I thought, what if I had cancer in the head and the brain doctor showed up with a claw hammer and a ice pick and didn't know where to start, so they put a sign on my foot that said Open Other End or something. I'd shoot the sonofabitch before he got in striking distance. Maybe there's such a thing as too much social justice. At least if it's my head.

Mr. McWilliams said the Sympathy, that was in New York, used to hire music people by setting them down and listening to them play the fiddle or duck call or banjo and taking the best ones. But then women got into a uproar and started yowling that the Sympathy only got men. They said women could play fiddles and all just fine and it was affirmative action for men and they was madder than wet hornets. So the Congress made a law that the Sympathy had to string up a bed sheet and them as wanted the job had to play behind it and the judges didn't know who they were and couldn't let in their sisters and uncles. It made sense, but they did it anyway, and pretty soon the Sympathy was full of ladies blowing and honking and sawing away, and everybody was happy because they did it right.

Well, everybody except American Africans, that said none of them was in the Sympathy. They wanted Social Justice. Best I can tell, Social Justice means getting anything you want or you'll scream and yell and bite and wet yourself like a two-year-old that needs a whupping and a new diaper. So now they're going to choose by colors, like they was painting a '57 Chevy. I guess that'll work.

Mr. McWilliams said I just didn't understand Advanced Thought. Well, I didn't. I guess it's because I'm not real smart. I used to be, though. The first time I was in the fourth grade my teacher, it was Miss Purity Perkins, said I was real special and she hoped I'd go far, but I guess she would have settled for the next county over. I told Mr. McWilliams if Affirmative Action meant getting a job Titilebecause you couldn't do it, I wanted to be a Space Rocket Driver. At least if I could be one from Lou-Bob's Billiards and Rib Pit. I was having a lot of fun with my girlfriend Jiffy Lube and I figured I couldn't drive a Space Rocket at the Rib pit just as good as I couldn't drive it from Australia or Wheeling or wherever they have Space Rockets.

I said so much Social Justice was giving me a motingator head-ache and I wanted to go off to Lou-Bob's that serves bust-head shine under the table if you don't look like a damn Revenoor.

Then the television started talking about Reparations for Slavery, that I thought they got rid of after World War Two. He said it didn't matter and it was to pay you for bad stuff that never happened to you, just like Affirmative Action was to give you jobs you couldn't do, but that was a whole nutheer bucket of crawdads and we could talk about it later. I don't know. It all sounded like a crooked poker game to let grifters and frauds get paid without going into the mines and getting killed like Christians.

It was still early so I went off to tell Hant about Affirmative Action. He was at his still. Like I said, he makes panther sweat that takes the enamel off your teeth to sell to yuppies from Washington that want a Cultural Experience. He puts it in genuine authentic mountain stone jars he gets from Taiwan. Some folks say he gets a cut from liver doctors in Bluefield, but I don't know.

Hant's a tall skinny rascal with arthritis so when he bends over it looks like folding a Buck knife and he's got a jaw like a front-end loader. Later he said he told the Poverty Office he wanted to be a Orthostatic Ontological Proctologist. I asked him what that was. He said he wasn't sure but he sure as hell didn't know how to be one so they had to pay him for it. He said they would never dare say no to a one-legged Injun princess with black lung.

After, I went down the hill to look for Jiffy Lube that I hadn't seen for weeks. What happened was, Jif is real pretty, and she was in Lou Bob's, and Lester 'Callister got smart with her like he didn't know what parts of her was handles and what parts wasn't. She laid him out cold with a pool stick and went to hide in the mountains. But after a while the sheriff said he figured the Statue of Limitations was about a month for smacking Lester, and anyway the doctor said he probably be out of a coma in a week, so weren't no harm done but his teeth might be all cattywumpus. Jif was smiling all happy like. That's a good sign if you know Jif, and I felt like a man with five aces and a date with somebody else's wife, so we went off to my doublewide. I figure there's nothing better on a mountain night than a good girlfriend, a six-pack, and a Bug Zapper.

55 ELVIS

*Elvis His Own Self: Consult Your Grocery-Rack
Literature for Details*

You gotta understand the grip Elvis has on the automobile-loving basically Iro-Celtic libido of the southern United States. Maybe you think Presley was just the first white rock-n-roll singer. Naw. He's a state of mind. Anybody who has spent time in the smoky evening fields of the Mississippi Delta, where people talk slow like sorghum dripping onto cheap china and mosquitoes gang up in packs and carry off cattle, knows, just knows, that Elvis is *meaning*. It's in the culture. In fact, it has been scientifically proved that eating Moon Pies and drinking RC Cola makes you love Elvis. It's true. MIT did it.

And that's why Elvis will live forever. Especially in grocery stores.

Every time I go to Safeway to buy more of whatever bachelors eat, the grocery-rack tabloids always have a sighting of Elvis as the third lead. First comes, "Women with Three Breasts and The Dwarves Who Love Them." Then there's "Lose Thirty Pounds in a Month While Gorging Yourself with Chicken Fat." Finally comes, "Elvis Seen Alive In Las Vegas Or Paris Or the Back Seat of a Greyhound Leaving Nashville." Or floating over Graceland in a cloud of light. Or in a flying saucer.

The other night I was on the beltway with a friend who has a Miata in male-menopause red with awesome speakers. The top was down, the volume was up, and Jailhouse Rock was celebrating homosexual love among the incarcerated. What more could man born of woman want?

The announcer crooned, "That was Elllll -*viss* the King who may not actually be dead because *yesssss,* he's been seen again according to the AP wire in Mississippi near Tupelo."

It seemed, the announcer said, that the Mississippi troopers had found some high-school kid and his girlfriend parked naked on a back road at two a.m. with a pile of beer cans on the floorboards. The kid explained that a few hours ago they had left the movies and were driving to the churchyard to think about Jesus together. Suddenly this, like, you know, weird bright *light* from above enveloped their car and they could feel a strange force sucking the car upward.

They found themselves inside a big glowing room like a doctor's office and met with Elvis and then passed out and found they'd been put back on earth on a back road, far from the church. And all those beer cans tossed in. Who would have thought it, space aliens drank Budweiser. They'd probably been experimented on, the kid said, 'cause they found this used condom....

See? Elvis lives.

In the mid-Fifties, when I was a Huck Finn simulacrum of eleven in Limestone County, Alabama, and spent my days eatin' goober peas (known as "peanuts" to the unworthy, chiefly Yankees) out of the fields and letting fly at mosquito hawks with my BB gun, Elvis ruled. I wasn't sure what he ruled, because I hadn't figured girls out yet, but he wafted through everything. I mean, in the seventh grade kids jitterbugged to Hound Dog at lunch and girls, who actually wore bobby socks, carried around magazines with his picture.

People even looked like Elvis. Boys had long Scots-Irish visages with angular facial planes. They looked as if they had been carved with Exacta knives. Most of them had the same hair as Elvis, and practiced letting a cigarette droop from their mouths with a sneering expression (which Elvis didn't, but never mind.) You could tell they had been raised on buttered grits with lots of black pepper sprinkled on top.

Elvis wiggled like he knew about sex, which was thought revolutionary and dangerous because teenagers would never have thought of sex their own. But pretty soon he was eclipsed by higher forms of expression. It had to happen.

In the Sixties in a club in Austin I saw a band called Klok Mortuary and the Gadarene Swine, consisting of three chords, two bare bellybuttons, and enough hair for a mattress factory. It would have been avant garde if anyone could have spelled it. During the show Klok, an adolescent furball who looked like half a spider, smashed his guitar on the amplifiers, bit the head off a live chicken, and threw the remains to a nest of pet army ants. (I later heard that in Detroit the ants got loose into the crowd, ending the meteoric career of the Swine.) Anyway, the critics were smitten by the performance. It was so...*dynamic.* Klok, who by now had trouble remembering what country he was in, said the chicken expressed his deepest musical thoughts. Which I was prepared to believe.

Anyway, Elvis briefly seemed by comparison as tame as Pat Boone or unflavored Jell-O. But lo, the Sixties passed like a cautious poker player and people noticed that there was something eternal about Elvis. He was good-looking and spoke of heartbreak, love, good dogs, sweet-lovin' women, and poontang. These were things we could all identify with. He came back.

Last week I went to Safeway to get things to heat in the microwave. The first lead on the *National Enquirer* was, "Midgets, Evicted from Posh Hotel, Honeymoon in Cardboard Box." Next came, "Secret Pentagon Report: Army Growing Dinosaurs to Eat Enemy Soldiers." Finally, "Priscilla Says Elvis Took Nazi Immortality Drug, Drives Pizza Truck in Tupelo."

What did I tell you?

56 A COSMIC POOL SHOT

The universe as Billiards: A Galactic Five-Rail Bankshot

We will start this magisterial explanation of everything with the time-honored approach of the philosopher, beginning with the things we know beyond doubt and then reasoning from them to suitably astonishing truths. As we know, Descartes began by saying, "Cogito ergo sum," I think therefore I am." (Ambrose Bierce, a more profound thinker, said, "Cogito cogito, ergo cogito sum. Cogito." But this way lies madness.) So with what certain knowledge can we begin our quest?

Our only certain knowledge is that we don't have any. Acceptance of this condition will diminish the world's output of philosophy, or so we may hope, but this column faces reality with a brave front. We may now list our certainties:

We don't know where we came from, where we are, why, what if anything we should do while we are here, wherever here is, and where if anywhere we go when we die.

On this bedrock we shall construct our philosophy of everything. However, before we begin thinking about these profound matters, we need to take into account one more certainty:

Thinking is impossible.

I will explain. But what it comes to is that while we know nothing about which to think, it doesn't matter because we couldn't think about it if we did know something.

Why? Consider the brain. It is an electrochemical mechanism, blindly obeying the laws of physics and chemistry (chemistry being the physics of the interactions of atoms). For example, consider a nerve impulse propagating along a neural fiber, depolarizing, sodium in, potassium out. Pure chemistry and physics. When the impulse comes to a synapse, a neurotransmitter diffuses across the gap, pure chemistry and physics. It can't do anything else. Even chemicals with long, imposing names cannot make choices. The neurotransmitter then binds to receptor sites, because it has to. Textbooks of neurophysiology state it thus: "A brain has less free will than a wind-up clock." Or at least if it were so stated, it would be. This is close enough for philosophy.

Putting it precisely, the state of a physical system is determined entirely by its previous state. This establishes beyond doubt that we have no free will, and that what we think are thoughts were determined at the time of the Big Bang, if any.

Now, no philosophical essay can be held in repute unless it contains words ending in "ism." The reigning creed today is materialism, the philosophy of the wantonly inattentive. Many who believe in materialism are of high intelligence, and so can only be sufficiently inattentive by great effort.

Anyway, a materialist believes that nothing exists but space, time, matter, and energy, however hyphenated. That is, physics. As the physicist Joe Friday said.

"The physics, ma'am, just the physics, and nothing but the physics."

This means that the Big Bang, if any, was set up, or I suppose I should say, set itself up, like one of those billiard-table trick shots. You know the kind: The balls seem randomly placed on the table but bounce around a lot before miraculously running into the pockets like birds returning to their nests. In the Bang, if any, all those subatomic whatsamajigggers erupted forth at exactly the right angles and velocities so that, billions of years later, they formed Elvis, San Francisco, and Hillary. (The latter *had* to be by chance, since no one in his right mind would form Hillary on purpose. QED.)

Next, consider plane geometry as taught in high school. (You may wonder why we have to consider it. Well, we just do.) Plane geometry deals with planes, lines, points, angles, and nothing else. It is useful and interesting, but it cannot explain a cheeseburger, Formula One race, or political hysteria. Why? Because cheeseburgers exist in three dimensions, which plane geometry doesn't have. Formula One races involve matter, energy, and motion, which plane geometry also doesn't have. Hysteria is an emotional state associated with liberal co-eds in pricey northern colleges who, thank God, do not exist in mathematics.

What it comes to is that a logical system is defined by its premises, and all downstream results are mere elaboration. (Of course, as established in the beginning of this luminous essay, we have no premises except the lack of premises, but philosophy readily overlooks such hindrances.) Plane geometry is not wrong. It is just incomplete.

To state it in mathematical terms, you cannot flatten a cheeseburger enough to fit into a plane.

Physics, the foundation of the current official story of everything, also depends on its premises. Physics is just mathematical materialism. From its equations one may derive all manner of fascinating and useful things, such as planetary motion, npn transistors, smartphones, nerve gas, and hydrogen bombs. (Some of these may be more useful than others.)

But, just as you cannot get strawberry milkshakes from plane geometry, because they are not implicit in it, there are things you cannot derive from the equations of physics: Consciousness, free will, beauty, morality, or curiosity–the whiches there just ain't in physics. This would not worry a rational thinker. He (or, assuredly, she) would simply state the obvious: Physics is not wrong, but incomplete. It does what it does, and doesn't do what it can't. Not too mysterious, that.

However, the true-believing physics-is-all Neo-Darwinian matter-monger cannot admit that anything–anything at all–exists outside of physics. Since some things obviously do, the only-physics enthusiasts have to resort to contorted logic. I think of kite string in a ceiling fan. Or simple denial.

For example, sometimes they say that consciousness is merely an "epiphenomenon." Oh. And what does that mean? Nothing. (Actually it means, "I don't know, but if I use a polysyllabic Greek word, maybe nobody will notice.") Epiphenomenon of what?

Sometimes they will say, "Well, consciousness is just a byproduct of complexity." But if consciousness is a byproduct, what is the primary product? A computer is somewhat complex, so is it somewhat conscious? Is a mouse less conscious than a human or just, in some cases, less intelligent?

A materialist ignoring consciousness is exactly equivalent to a geometer ignoring cheeseburgers.

We will now examine the question, where did we come from? The answer is ready to hand: We don't have a clue. We make up stories. The physics-only folk say, see, there was the Big Bang and all these electrons and protons and things flew out and just by chance formed Taiwan Semiconductor Manufacturing Company in the most motingator a-stonishing pool-table trick shot ever set up. Just by accident. Damn! Who would have thought it?

Of course any sane person, to include materialists when they are thinking of something else, would say that TSMC was designed by hordes of Chinese engineers. But designing anything requires mind and intelligence (or a computer designed to simulate these things), But Mind cannot be derived from the equations of physics. Therefore we are all mindless. In general human behavior supports this.

Other stories exist. Yahweh created the world, or maybe Shiva, or Allah, and I think some remote tribes believe that it just appeared on the back of a giant turtle. I have no information on the matter, though frankly I incline to the turtle story, but will let the reader know the instant I find out.

The weakness of creation myths from Bang to Turtle is the question of the five-year-old, "But Mommy, where did God come from?" or "Who made God?" Fifteen years later in dorm-room bull sessions he will phrase it differently, "Well, what came before the Big Bang?" Same question.

A sort of second-echelon creation myth now in vogue is Darwinian evolution, also a subset of physics and therefore completely determined. Mutations are chemical events following the laws of chemistry. Thus trilobites had no choice but to form, and so they did. Metabolism is physical from the level of ATP to animals eating each other.

There is of course no such thing as a sex drive, teenagers notwithstanding, since no sort of drive can be derived from physics. (This will no doubt devastate Pornhub.) From this the inevitable conclusion, proven by physics, that we cannot reproduce. Therefore we either have always existed or do not exist at all.

To give oneself an aura of overwelling wisdom, one may say things like ontology, epistemology, entelechy, and teleology, but these do not detract from mankind's underlying and perfect ignorance.

It's all a trick shot, I tell you.

57 CAVE DIVING

Feeble-minded in Quintana Roo: What the Hell
Am I Doing Here?

C ave divers are the world's most witless people. This
is not mere Freddian assertion but a neurological fact.
They have fewer brain cells than normal people. MIT
did a massive study, and concluded that a cave diver has the
reasoning capacity of a lemur. A smaller study by CalTech
equated them intellectually with woodchucks, though a peer-
review team noted that no one had ever seen a woodchuck
diving in a cave. All agreed that people who strap on scuba
gear and swim far back in dismal grottos full of water repre-
sent a dangerous counter-evolutionary trend.

I decided that Quintana Roo, in southern Mexico near the
Yucatan, was the place to do it. The region is pockmarked
with *cenotes*, which are caves called something else to gull the
unwary. I had seen pictures taken in *cenotes*. Invariably they
made these sordid pits look like the cathedral at Chartres submerged. Rays of sunlight from openings to the world speared
through gorgeous clear water and divers hung in green tran-
scendence. Lovely.

My flight landed at Cancun and I found a bus to Playa del Car-
men and then a van to my hotel on the beach between Playa
and Tulum. It had all the credentials of a (you will admire my
linguistic originality) tropical paradise: Water, sand, and an
insufferably arrogant Mexican owner who believed himself to
be a Buddhist. Off to the dive shop, clutching mask, contact

lenses, and dive computer.

I booked a dive in Chac Mool, a *cenote*. I also met, I'll call him, Pablo, who was the cave guide. I'm not going to name the shop because I suspect most of the others in the region are as bad and I see no reason to pick on one. Anyway, Pablo was short, brown, maybe twenty-six, amiable, and a cowboy. Mexicans are. It's part of why I like them. Anyway we agreed that he would pick me up at the arrogantly-owned pseudo-Buddhist hotel in the morning. He did. We bounded through the jungle in a four-wheel drive toward Chac Mool.

Now, a certified American cave diver (and, believe me, they're all certifiable) will tell you don't just plunge into an intricate cave as if it were a warm bath after a night of dancing in a dirt bar. No. Cave diving involves certain compelling realities, such as the difficulty of surfacing through forty feet of rock if something goes wrong. It is therefore thought expedient to have some faint idea of what you are doing. You plan. You discuss contingencies. You agree on hand signals. You have three dive lights per diver. Caves by their nature are not well lit.

None of these thoughts disturbed the tranquil surface of Pablo's consciousness. We hopped out, suited up, and staggered off toward a tree-fringed hole in the ground as if we knew what we were doing. When you put on a wet suit in the tropics you have about thirty seconds before going into sunstroke. We staggered into dank obscurity and fell—*aaaah!*—into cool water, below the surface of which was the entrance to Chac Mool.

Whereupon Pablo handed me one of those lame little tourist dive lights that dive shops use. That was it: Four tired C-cells and three ounces of plastic. So much for planning, recognition of inherent risk, the Anglo-Saxon penchant for control. You know, like the Apollo landings.

So we were floating half over our masks in dark clear water and I tested the sad little light and it didn't work. Nada. Pablo looked puzzled and took the light. He slapped it hard. It began to emit a sort of fungal glow. The batteries were probably the original beta versions of Duracell. He indicated that we should submerge.

Now, anyone who engages in risky sports—skydiving, caving, rock climbing and so on—will tell you that there is a difference between courage and stupidity. When things just don't feel right, or the equipment isn't up to par, it is not cowardice simply to say, "This isn't a good idea. I'm not going to do it." Intelligent sportsmen always recognize when it is time to choose judgement over bravery. This was one of those times.

Inside, Chac Mool was a grey, rock-walled, ugly, preternaturally uninteresting tube, maybe five feet wide and four high. Nothing whatever recommended it, at least nothing I could see with the wan glow of my alleged light. It reminded me of caves I had been in during my above-water caving days. Cruddy tumbled rock. More cruddy tumbled rock. No slanting beams of sunlight, no stalactites like fluted Corinthian columns and suchlike nonsense. Crud. I felt like a geologic tapeworm in its natural habitat.

I've been had, I thought. I'm going to find that photographer and kill him.

Some people are courageous. I am not. My response to unnerving situations is to turn my head off and not worry too much, except about relevant readings on the computer. I followed Pablo's fins darkly flapping in front of me, thinking roughly, "This is incredibly boring and I'm probably going to drown. How *very* reasonable. Eeyore would understand."

I once wrote a diving song to the tune of "Oh Lord Won't You Buy Me a Mercedes Benz." The words ran through my mind like squirrels in an exercise wheel.

Oh Lord, woncha help me
Nursa dese bends
My friends got computers

I jes jumps in....

On and on we went, back back back into the small intestine of Mexico. "This is really stupid," I thought with delayed reason. *Sssssss*-wubbawubbawubba. I kept my fingers lightly on the first stage of Pablo's regulator: If both our lights failed at once, I was going to go out with him, or he wasn't going to go out. I had no idea where we were. I wondered whether he did.

My light slowly dimmed. We came to a fork in the tunnel. A sign with a skull and crossbones warned us that one branch was dangerous. Oh. We were hundreds of yards, nay, perhaps miles, maybe parsecs, away from life and air in the bowels of nowhere in particular—and cave divers wanted us to know that *somewhere else* was dangerous. Roger. Got it. I wondered what lay down the bad branch. On thought, I stopped wondering.

Finally, purely by accident I am persuaded, we got back. My computer told me thirty-eight minutes with a max depth of forty-two feet. I had 1200 psi of air left. I told Pablo that it had been a dive of surpassing excellence. Idiocy abetted by mendacity. But that's how the thing is done.

58 1953

An Exhaustive Sociological Analysys

E ight years after the end of WWII, 1953 sprang upon America like a tabby cat on a mouse. Children abounded in profusion (if you can do that). Thousands of virile men had returned from long years of such erotically depressing things as floating around the Pacific on a destroyer. They meant to make up for lost time. Boy did they. Thus America brought forth moiling swarms of children exactly nine months and fifteen minutes after dad returned home. The unsurprising surprised no one, except demographers.

Dukesy and I were sheaves among this bumper crop of human wheat. Dukesy (technically Michel Duquez) was a dark dashing kid of Frog extraction who assisted me in crime--for example, the great fraudulent Plastic Man for Polio crusade. He was quick-witted, good with his fists when he needed to be, and a wicked second-baseman. Later he joined the Foreign Legion and died gallantly, repelling a camel charge against Fort Digby by 12,000 hashish-crazed Bedouins waving poisoned scimitars.

Well, I expect he did.

Ours was a sunny world, hopeful and prosperous. We lived in new suburbs of pleasant brick boxes in Arlington, Virginia, each with one tree in the yard, laid out with as much imagination as the stringing on a tennis racket. We Americans had won the war. Evil had taken it in the shorts, at the end of an

American boot. Now we were going to buy washing machines.

Everything made sense. We knew who we were, what we wanted, and how things should be. Our patch of Arlington had no diversity, (and therefore) no crime, no drugs, no illiteracy. In its exoticism, divorce was stranger than human sacrifice. Life was endlessly wholesome. Kids, itinerant herds of them, amused themselves with yoyos, glorious Gilbert chemistry sets with, yes, fifty bottles (Let's see, sodium thiosulphate, cobalt chloride, sodium silicate....) and of course baseball.

But I digress. I'm trying to tell you about Plastic Man and how he disguised himself as a Thanksgiving turkey to catch a malign force that was eating all the food in whatever city he lived in. (Maybe you didn't think you needed to know this. Well, you do. Read it.)

Now, Plastic Man–I know, this isn't obsessively organized– was an elastic hero in comic books, which we read along with anything else we could find. We could read: Feminism hadn't taken the intelligence out of the classrooms, producing a vacuum that sucked in the national dregs like a bored-and-stroked Hoovermatic that needed a better filter. The Waspish belief in work and study sat well upon the nation. You could have asked my friends Michel Duquez, John Kaminski, and Lynne Sverdlov.

On long summer afternoons when we couldn't find a pick-up ball game, and we wearied of climbing the willow in Bradley Furman's front yard and throwing spit-bombs at each other, we'd go to the drug store in Westover on Washington Boulevard and burrow into the comic racks. There were three of them, the kind that spin, close together so you could squeeze into the middle and hide. They enclosed a dim papery space like a fort, which appeals to all proper boys, and you could peer out between the comics and watch the customers. When we turned the racks from within to get new comics, they moved as by a ghostly presence.

Anyway, Plastic Man. (This is *important*. There may be a pop quiz.) He was a fixture with us, like Wonder Woman who had an invisible glass airplane and a magic lasso. He wore a red-and-yellow spandex suit (if memory serves) and blue sunglasses, so that he looked like a French bicycle racer. He stretched. If he wanted to see what was on top of a building, he just elongated his neck like a forty-foot soda-straw. He could make himself into any size and shape he wanted. He did this to fight crime. Dukesy and I hadn't reached puberty so this seemed the most profitable use for a protean talent.

Plastic Man hardly stood out in a crowd in 1953. Those were the days when Superman was always jumping out of windows amid much whooshing with the announcer intoning something about a Strange Visitor from another planet who fought for Truth, Justice, and the American Way, then thought to be coextensive.

I guess Ol' Plastic got all stretchy because his father, who was probably a scientific genius, accidentally spilled radioactive gunch on him. It's how things happened in 1953. Scientists often spilled stuff on a shrew or scorpion or something, and it would grow and grow into a terrible movie. He had a vaguely Chinese sidekick called Woozy who was shaped like a wonton with legs.

Anyway, the bad guys would plot nefarious deeds and never notice a red-and-yellow umbrella in the umbrella stand. In one episode the Thanksgiving turkey was suspiciously red and yellow, but they didn't notice *that* either. Maybe they thought it was just moldy or something, till it turned into Plastic Man and wrapped around them like grinning rope till the cops came.

Polio, though. Dukesy and I came up with the idea of Plastic Man for Polio. At the time the disease did a land-office business and the March of Dimes was always collecting money to do something bad to it. We gathered our substantial supply of comic books and began going door to door in the neighborhood, telling all the mothers that we were selling them to eliminate iron lungs.

"Yes, Ma'am, we're selling used comic books. It's to help polio. Got some really good ones, see?" we'd say to the wife of a demobbed B-29 captain.

Of course no one believed us, but they didn't want to seem to be in favor of respiratory paralysis, so they smiled and gave us nickels and dimes. Soon we had several dollars, mostly in small coins that made it look like more. It suited us. Like Heraclitus, we believed in change. We'd count it and play with it in the manner of Scrooge McDuck. And then go spend it. I'd like to say that the enterprise taught us something lasting about commerce or the virtue of initiative, but mostly it let us go to Westover and buy more Plastic Man.

I'm not sure where this column is going. I had a feeling that Godzilla was about to come into it, trampling paragraphs while searching for something to eat—most likely Tokyo. He did that a lot at the Glebe Theater, while we hooted and threw popcorn boxes. I guess it's too late for the old lizard, and I don't have space to tell you about the Great Squash Wars on Soapstone Hill. Some other time.

59 GODZILLA, THE BLOB, AND RODAN THE REPTILE BAT

True Art, American Flavor

Hooboy, am I tired of arty movie critics. You know, the ones who talk about Fellini and Rigatoni on National Public Radio, in low gaspy voices that sound like asthmatics on Quaaludes, so you'll know they're intellectuals and dreadfully earnest. Me, I'm going to study real movies, for Americans: movies with grit and diesel fumes to them, and maybe some home fries, and application to everyday life. I mean the masterpieces that shaped this country: *Godzilla, Mothra, The Blob, Killer Shrews*, and *Rodan the Reptile Bat*. (Actually, I thought Rodan was a sculptor. Maybe he was a reptile bat too.)

Now, if you go to Europe, they *will* get arty on you. Like as not, they'll screen some grainy black-and-white atrocity about two tiresome people in love, and some reason why it won't work, and their sighs, and significant expressions, and soul-searching, and agonies, and eventual suicide. It will probably be based on an unnecessary novel by a French existential *philosophe*. You'll end up wishing you had never been born, and probably get drunk afterwards. The message will be that life is insecure, and unreliable, and sad sometimes, and doesn't make a grain of sense.

I bet you needed a French director to tell you that, didn't you? Only the Frogs would need a thousand years of intellectual posturing to learn what any C&W band knows at birth. Besides, if you want insecurity, Godzilla teaches that at any moment you can be stomped on by an enormous dinosaur. Maybe I'm just a country boy, but that seems like enough insecurity for everyday use.

If you want a movie up to the eyeballs in textured meaning (that's critic talk), watch *Killer Shrews*. It's real American Art—art you could sell at a NAPA outlet, forty-weight, with detergents and a discount if you buy it by the case. Great movie. See, there were a bunch of scientists on this island, maybe in the Fifties. They were experimenting with Radioactive Gunch or something. It's what scientists all do. They spilled it on some shrews.

Now, a shrew is about two inches long, and eats 27,000 times its weight in bugs every fifteen minutes. You can see that a big one would be a problem. Well, the Gunch made these shrews grow. Big shrews.

Trouble was, the movie had about a twenty-cent budget. The best they could do for giant shrews was to get collies and put shrew masks on them. (So help me: Watch it yourself.) You'd have an expendable character pursued through the woods by a herd of deadly shrews, all wagging their tails. There was no audio editing. Sometimes you could hear the shrews saying, "Woof woof."

Then there was *Jaws*. I didn't see it until last year, so maybe my experience with computer animation has prejudiced me. Everybody had told me about how terrifying the shark was and how they all had nightmares for weeks. (That's a good reason to pay seven dollars for a movie ticket.) To me, ol' Jaws looked like a rubber raft with teeth and a pole-axed stare, as if someone had put chloral hydrate in his last drink. And he ran into things, clunk. I was afraid the poor stiff might get blunted.

Artwise, though, I figure America hit a pinnacle in about 1957, when *The Blob* debuted, or debutted, or anyway came out. A meteor or space ship or something was zooming around the universe and crashed in Alabama, it looked like. Space aliens must have quality-control problems. They drop like flies, mostly near trailer parks in the South. Anyhow this one was full of slime. It jumped onto your hand and then dissolved you, and got bigger: Slime writ large.

For most of the movie a nomadic schwudge (I think that's how you spell schwudge) of sociopathic jello oozed around ominously (note the alliteration: it's literary), dissolving people. You'd see some guy in a vulnerable position, maybe under a car working on it. The camera would cut to gelatinous evil, *urgle blurg, glop.* Then to the guy under the car. Then to urgle blurg. The tension became unbearable, closely paralleling the cinematography. In a thousand theaters girls clutched their boyfriends extra tight. Those guys still eat jello in gratitude.

By the second reel the Blob was well on its way to metabolizing small-town America. One night it was eating Joe's Diner. Someone discovered that it didn't like being sprayed with fire extinguishers. (How smart was that? Who does like it?) It seemed that cold was the soft underbelly of intergalactic slime. Fortunately Joe's was in the only town in the country in which everyone had three fire extinguishers. They all came out and extinguished at it, and it chilled to death.

Then the movie ended. Good thing, too. It gets warm in the South, come morning.

There was a movie called *I Was A Teen-Age Werewolf*, but I never got to see it. In fact, there was a whole slew of movies about teen-agers who turned into various disagreeable things, a distinctly minor metamorphosis. In fact, teenagers being what they are, most parents wouldn't have noticed the advent of a werewolf. (I was inspired later in high school to write an autobiographical screen-play called *I Was A Teen-Age Breast Pump*, but I had to abandon the idea due to a shortage of material.)

However, the apotheosis of nuanced paradigmatic *fin de siecle* in the genre of *le filme atrocieuse* (I made that up. Am I a critic, or what?) was *Godzilla*. He was a bedraggled tyrannosaur, displaying signs of autism, who repeatedly came from the sea, breathing fire, and ate Tokyo. You could set your watch by it: Every Saturday afternoon at the Glebe theater, chomp, chomp, chomp. *Godzilla* was an allegory of unreached potential. He could have gone to a shipyard and worked respectably as a welding torch, but, no, he had to eat the city. Here we have a literary subtext on the repudiation of conventionality and society's inevitable punishment of the rebel. (He got chased into the sea where earnest-looking scientists dissolved him with oxygen bombs.)

Millions of kids, throwing popcorn boxes in Saturday matinees across America, learned from *Godzilla* lessons about the inexorability of fate, and about insecurity (at least in Tokyo)– not to mention how to sail a popcorn box for maximum range.

If that ain't Art, I don't know what is.

60 A LUGUBRIOUS SUCCESS

Oh help! Oh help! Oh help!: Getting What We Seem To Want

H ere is a news item that I once might have made up as parody. It is hard, though, to imagine anything too absurd not to exist in a university.

"Female Arizona State University students can receive extra credit for defying social norms and refusing to shave for 10 weeks during the semester."

Accompanying the news of this enlightened policy was a photograph of the beneficiaries triumphantly exhibiting their armpits. The children were of course trying to shock, which is normal among adolescents. What once would actually have shocked is that the alleged adults in the alleged university encourage their alleged scholars in extended juvenility. (Stray thought: Why are so many feminists ugly enough to make a freight train take a dirt road?)

Said one of the participating students (I use the word so loosely that it might well cast off and set out into life on its own):

"The experience helped me better understand how pervasive gendered socialization is in our culture. Furthermore, by doing this kind of activist project I was no longer an armchair activist theorizing in the classroom. So much is learned by actually taking part in the theory or idea we learn in the classroom, and we could benefit from this type of pedagogy being taken up by similar classes."

This solemn gibberish begs for parody, but on contemplation I am more sad than amused. These pitiable girls go through the forms of schooling, but learn nothing beyond a pseudo-intellectual drivel of pubertal rebellion. The story is not an anecdote but a condition, repeated at hundreds of pretend-universities across the land.

And this in institutions that once existed to pass along civilization.

The bleakness of American culture leads one to despair. Subtract technology and nothing is left. Music? Classical composition is dead. The symphony orchestras hold on by their teeth. Opera is unheard and almost unheard of. Book sales drop, and those that sell are mostly trash. Poetry is dead, Shakespeare a comic shorthand for ridiculous irrelevant pedantry.

Talented painters abound, but the nation has no interest in them. Sculpture means curious blobs and shapes said to be art and chosen by suburban arts committees. Theater? How many people have seen a play recently other than a high-school production?

In all the things that once marked civilization, the United States has become a desert, a waste of self-satisfied, pampered, arrogantly ignorant sidewalk peasants. This is curious, since anything the cultivated might want awaits on the web. One may think of Amazon as an automated fifth-century monastery, saving things of worth for an awakening centuries hence.

The female of the race being more susceptible to hysterias than the male, it is not surprising to see theatric idiocy of lofted armpits in departments of Women's, Transsexual etc. Studies. Males seldom show such symptoms of psychiatric stress as bulimia and anorexia. Yet a similar infantilism seems to affect the boys. Girls exhibit a desperate feminism while boys retreat into video games. In their mid-twenties both seem farther from adulthood than my generation was at sixteen. Why?

When I was a stripling in rural Virginia a dispiriting number of years ago, we rebelled with expected hormonal punctuality, knew more than our parents about everything, and behaved with the proper amount of reckless stupidity. Yet we did not cling to our pubescence. The reason, I think, was that we were trying to be adults before we were ready, rather than avoiding adulthood after it was proper. These are very different things.

It is traditional for the old to view their youth in roseate hues it never had and speak of walking barefoot twelve miles daily to high school through eighteen inches of shark-infested snow. We didn't. Nobody in King George Country was hungry or close to it. I certainly was not.

Yet I remember getting up before first light in January (in, yes, sometimes a foot of snow) to run my paper route, which I did partly because it made me feel semi-grown up, and partly because I had my eye on a thirteen-foot Grumman canoe. It was no big deal. Kids did these things. We were, as they say, transitioning out of kid-hood.

To be sixteen, working the graveyard shift alone at Kriegstedt's Esso on Route 301, fueling the big eighteen-wheelers that came howling in for diesel at three a.m., talking to the drivers as almost an equal—it was close to manhood. I liked it. We liked it. It was preparation for the big world. Marching for transgendered rights or getting our navels pierced would have seemed lunatic.

It still does. Different world..

61 APLOMB

*Aplomb, Debonerness, and Class: A Harley
Aistocracy*

Let me tell you about aplomb. I don't mean watery New-Age aplomb, suitable for a fern bar. I mean the real article, forty-weight, that you could lube a diesel with.

This was in the early eighties. I was still a staff writer on *Soldier of Fortune* magazine. This was years before Craig, the staff artist, killed himself riding drunk on his motorcycle somewhere outside Boulder. (He died, everyone said, as he would have wanted. Horribly.)

In those days Craig and I hung out for a while in the Berkeley Bar in a bad section of Denver. Craig was a big, baby-faced street fighter out of Chicago with a Special Forces past and a mean streak. He was the staff artist and layout guy at the mag. He mostly drew skulls. He also like the Brandenburg concertos, and used to listen to them at his easel with headphones built into a World War II leather flying helmet.

The Berk was the home pit for the Sons of Silence, a bad biker club. If you haven't been in dives like this, don't start now. They swarm with huge bearded bozos with tattooed eyeballs and missing teeth and slow ominous grins and the IQ of a camshaft. You get the impression that they are evolving, but just not as fast as the rest of us. They'll hurt you. Either they like you or you're jelly. They don't worry about consequences. They can't remember them.

The Berk had Formica wood tables and smelled like a weight room. Rows of bottles waited patiently, but not for long, behind the counter and corpulent biker babes lolled about like stranded elephant seals. No one else did. When you have a biker clientele, you don't have any other kind of clientele. Craig and I were guests. I had sold Bob Brown, the editor of *Soldier of Fortune*, on a story about the warm patriotic urges of the Sons, who didn't have any. The Sons were charmed. They might get on the cover. They knew they would never get closer to significance.

It was cold enough to freeze the personals off an iron dog and dirty snow gleamed yellow under the streetlights. We showed up in Craig's pickup truck, wearing our credentials: cammies, antisocial T-shirts ("Happiness Is A Confirmed Kill") and jump boots. A Tribal Meeting followed, heap big pow wow, talk'em. Craig and I sat in a booth with Torque, the honcho, and a brain-fried guy called Lurch, and Mountain Jerry, who was a pretty Tarzan replica with long golden hair like Rapunzel and gold-flecked eyes that spoke of psychopathy and bone fractures. He sort of looked through you.

"We don't like the press," Torque said. So what? Nobody did. I didn't. Torque had a face like a gorilla's armpit. "You can do your story. SOF's a righteous mag. *Righteous.*" I guess it was a recommendation. Like having Carlo Gambino say that you were a Really Good Person.

"We do what we can," Craig said.

Lurch just stared at his beer with his mouth hanging open. He didn't actually drool, probably because he couldn't remember how. I figured he had smoked too much brass polish or sniffed some bad glue.

During this prayer meeting, Lurch had An Idea. You could tell it was bubbling up inside him. His jaw closed slightly and a crazed focus came into his eyes. He was going to say something, as soon as he figured out what. His head came up. Yes, an idea. He almost had it.

And then it left him. He collapsed with a soughing sound, like a punctured tire. Gone. A Real Idea, probably the unified field theory. And it got away. He stared sorrowfully at his beer. Eeyore of the Bikers.

We went back to the tribal thing.

Manners, though. This is about grace, elegance, and aplomb. Yeah.

Later we were boozing at the bar, doing what women call male bonding. It means talking to each other. I was chatting with Mountain Jerry. Craig was talking to some guy farther down the bar and drinking peppermint schnapps. Which was amazing on two counts. First, that the Berk had such an effeminate candy-ass yuppie-swine liqueur. Second, that Craig would drink it in a biker bar. It was grounds for execution.

Thing was, Craig was scary. He'd cripple you. You sensed he was ready to rock-and-roll, and you really didn't want to rumble with him. Some guys you leave alone. The Sons could smell it.

About then one of the biker babes got into it with the barmaid. I don't know what the raison de guerre was. The challenger was a gas-station Brunhilda like a sack of potatoes, except potatoes have better skin. Shrieking ensued. Barmaids in motorcycle hangouts do not back down. You could tell this one wasn't a Latin professor at Bryn Mawr. She screamed obscenities in a florid cloacal gush. The potato sack gave as good as she got.

The bikers ignored them and kept drinking. Jerry and I were discussing social encounters in rural bars in West Virginia, where we both came from. The chief instrument of intercourse in those regions was the pool cue. It was simple and direct and provided the hospitals with a brisk business.

Over Mountain Jerry's shoulder I saw the challenger's arm

flash forward. She was throwing a bottle at the barmaid. Either her aim was bad or the barmaid ducked. Bottles shattered behind the bar and the mirror pretty much exploded. Slivers rained down on me, but missed my drink.

Mountain Jerry never flickered. He grinned his slow mean golden grin and said, "Git it on." And kept on talking. He was amused.

The bar top glittered with glass fragments. The barmaid was about to leap over the bar to do battle with Spud Sack. Screaming continued. Nobody paid the slightest attention. Down the bar I saw Craig absently, without looking, pull a sizable sliver of glass from his schnapps without interrupting his sentence. He dipped a finger to see whether more shards awaited. No. All was well. He lifted the glass and drank.

That's aplomb.

62 CODPIECE

A Codpiece for Hillary. Gucci, Maybe with Pocket fo Car Keys

The other day I saw a photo of Hillary Clinton going into the Senate. I have a kind heart, so I won't say that she looked like a teenager's room, but I did conclude that she must have had a better maintenance contract when she was First Basilisk. You could tell that she needed new siding and maybe her lawn mowed and some paint on her trim.

I saw a science fiction movie once, the kind with a twelve-dollar budget and actors they probably found in a bus station. Anyway these scientists were doing experiments with radio-active gunch. It's what scientists do. They'd pour it into test tubes and it would bubble like grits if you don't watch them and turn colors.

I guess it didn't work because they threw it in a landfill and went off to shoot pool. Well, that landfill started to jiggle, and humph, and sort of pile up on itself, and finally set off to eat Boise. It left a trail and looked like it needed combing.

I don't know why I thought of that.

We were talking about Hillary. When she and Bill lived in that nice double-wide on Pennsylvania Avenue, she was sleek, probably because she had terrific make-up people who did in-jection molding, and she'd say, "Cookies," and "Children," and all the ladies would vote for her so she could be the Senator from New York. It helped that New Yorkers are dumber than rutabagas.

But people who knew her said she was icy cold and crocodilian.

So I reckon we've got one of those profound social questions that you can do a doctoral thesis on:

"Hillary Clinton: Cookie Monster, Walk-In Fridge, Or Dumpster?"

Thing is, you can't look at Hillary in isolation. (Actually, I don't feel a pressing need to look at her at all. But we're being sociological.) If you want to make sense of the Clintons, the best way is to understand them as the revenge of the Confederacy. Nothing else makes them plausible.

My guess is that a secret society, in Montgomery or maybe Chattanooga, figured that the South would never Rise Again, but if they could bring the North low enough, it would be the same thing. I reckon the conspirators meet in a duck blind out in a swamp and drink Franklin County shine ('cause it's the best) and eat okra. Then they plot.

Now, think about this. Suppose you wanted to destroy the Union, and humiliate it, and make everybody cross the street when they saw it coming. You'd probably start by making some hamhock grifter President. You can actually embarrass a country into submission, except maybe the United States. So I guess they called Little Rock, and got What's-His-Porkchop to run. They knew Yankees didn't have better judgement.

Hillary was part of the plan from the beginning. The Committee for Southern Revenge knew that Bill had a character that made tapioca look like reinforced concrete. A vertebrate influence was needed to steady him. Besides, Bill would have to leave the White House in eight years, taking everything in it with him. They saw Hillary as the iron spine of formless mendacity. She was their hope for continuing the havoc.

It worked pretty well. Ol' Willy Bill came into Washington

honking on a saxophone like a cheap rock band and proceeded to grope women and rut and lie more than he breathed. The Yankee Capital had always had the charm of a theater seat's bottom. Now it had become ridiculous. Can you imagine what the French thought? They didn't have Elvis or an army that you'd notice, but they did have taste.

The Union had been brought low. It was revenge sweeter than a pair of Moon Pies stuck together with sorghum syrup.

For eight years, Willie Bill was a serviceable embarrassment. In fact he was spectacular. He sold secrets to the Chinese and did chunky interns. He'd look you in the eye like a sincere cow with an uncle complex and say, "Ah feel yore pine," and maybe your leg too. Wise men locked up their daughters and the dog and the whole business was funnier than a toad frog in a milk shake. I guess people in Little Rock laughed and laughed, 'cause they knew it was going to happen.

The next trick for the boys in the duck blind was to get Hillary to be President. I'm serious. They knew she would wreck the Union as Marse Bob and Stonewall never could. She would be like getting a second shot at Gettysburg, but as an inside job.

Sure enough, Willy Bill's eight years ran out, and he left, selling pardons like New Year's at Wal-Mart. This, what with looting the White House, proved to be a problem. The duck blind worried that even the American public might not be crazy enough to elect Hillary after that. She did her best to help. She said that, why, she was just shocked about those pardons, and how she was just a li'l ol' housewife, and baked, and thought about children, and didn't worry her silly little head about politics or what her husband was doing.

Everyone figures that when the White House comes open, she's going to run like bad nylons and, if she wins, then Bill could be first lady and they could steal everything in the White House they didn't carry off the first time. Political insiders in Washington think she'd mostly likely pull it off.

She'd get all of the black vote, most of the women, and the men would all move to Canada.

The Committee for Southern Revenge didn't want to take chances. They wanted her to get male as well as female votes. This required a balance between virility and domesticity. Domesticity was easy. She could just say "Cookies" a lot. But... virility?

So they got a custom-leather store to make Hillary a codpiece, and Fed-Exed it. Suede, with alligator straps, and a little pocket for car keys. It should get here in a week or so. I hear it's stunning, and ought to intimidate hell out of the Chinese.

63 A VETERAN WRITES

Reflections on a Sorry War

Originally published in Harper's

I weary of the stories about veterans that are now in vogue with the newspapers, the stories that dissect the veteran's psyche as if prying apart a laboratory frog--patronizing stories written by style-section reporters who know all there is to know about chocolate mousse, ladies' fashions, and the wonderful desserts that can be made with simple jello. I weary of seeing veterans analyzed and diagnosed and explained by people who share nothing with veterans, by people who, one feels intuitively, would regard it as a harrowing experience to be alone in a backyard.

Week after week the mousse authorities tell us what is wrong with the veteran. The veteran is badly in need of adjustment, they say--lacks balance, needs fine tuning to whatever it is in society that one should be attuned to. What we have here, all agree, with omniscience and veiled condescension, is a victim: The press loves a victim. The veteran has bad dreams, say the jello writers, is alienated, may be hostile, doesn't socialize well--isn't, to be frank, quite right in the head.

But perhaps it is the veteran's head to be right or wrong in, and maybe it makes a difference what memories are in the head. For the jello writers the war was a moral fable on Channel Four, a struggle hinging on Nixon and Joan Baez and the inequities of this or that. I can't be sure. The veterans seem to have missed the war by being away in Vietnam at the time and do not understand the combat as it raged in the internecine cocktail parties of Georgetown.

Still, to me Vietnam was not what it was to the jello writers, not a ventilation of pious simplisms, not the latest literary interpretation of the domino theory. It left me memories the fashion writers can't imagine. It was the slums of Truong Minh Ky, where dogs' heads floated in pools of green water and three-inch roaches droned in sweltering back-alley rooms and I was happy. Washington knows nothing of hot, whore-rich, beery Truong Minh Ky. I remember riding the bomb boats up the Mekong to Phnom Penh, with the devilish brown river closing in like a vise and rockets shrieking from the dim jungle to burst against the sandbagged wheelhouse, and crouching below the waterline between the diesel tanks. The mousse authorities do not remember this. I remember the villa on Monivong in Phnom Penh, with Sedlacek, the balding Australian hippie, and Naoki, the crazy freelance combat photographer, and Zoco, the Frenchman, when the night jumped and flickered with the boom of artillery and we listened to Mancini on shortwave and watched Nara dance. Washington's elite do not know Nara. They know much of politicians and of furniture.

If I try to explain what Vietnam meant to me--I haven't for years, and never will again--they grow uneasy at my intensity. "My God," their eyes say, "he sounds as though he liked it over there. Something in the experience clearly snapped an anchoring ligament in his mind and left him with odd cravings, a perverse view of life--nothing dangerous, of course, but...The war did that to them," they say. "War is hell."

Well, yes, they may have something there. When you have seen a peasant mother screaming over several pounds of bright red mush that, thanks to God and a Chicom 107, is no longer precisely her child, you see that Sherman may have been on to something. When you have eaten fish with Khmer troops in charred Cambodian battlefields, where the heat beats down like a soft rubber truncheon and a wretched stink comes from shallow graves, no particular leap of imagination is necessary to notice that war is no paradise. I cannot say that the jello writers are wrong in their understanding of war. But somehow I don't like hearing pieties about the war from these sleek, wise people who never saw it.

There were, of course, veterans and veterans. Some hated the war, some didn't. Some went around the bend down in IV Corps, where leeches dropped softly down collars like green sausages and death erupted unexpected from the ungodly foliage. To men in the elite groups--the Seals, Special Forces, Recondos, and Lurps who spent years in the Khmer bush, low to the ground where the ants bit hard--the war was a game with stakes high enough to engage their attention. They liked to play.

To many of us there, the war was the best time of our lives, almost the only time. We loved it because in those days we were alive, life was intense, the pungent hours passed fast over the central event of the age and the howling jets appeased the terrible boredom of existence. Psychologists, high priests of the mean, say that boredom is a symptom of maladjustment; maybe, but boredom has been around longer than psychologists have.

The jello writers would say we are mad to remember fondly anything about Nixon's war that Kennedy started. They do not remember the shuddering flight of a helicopter high over glowing green jungle that spread beneath us like a frozen sea. They never made the low runs a foot above treetops along paths that led like rivers through branches clawing at the skids, never peered down into murky clearings and bubbling swamps of sucking snake-ridden muck. They do not remember monsoon mornings in the highlands where dragons of mist twisted in the valleys, coiling lazily on themselves, puffing up and swallowing whole villages in their dank breath. The mousse men do not remember driving before dawn to Red Beach, when the headlights in the blackness caught ghostly shapes, maybe VC, thin yellow men mushroom-headed in the night, bicycling along the alien roads. As nearly as I can tell, jello writers do not remember anything.

Then it was over. The veterans came home. Suddenly the world seemed to stop dead in the water. Suddenly the slant-eyed hookers were gone, and the gunships and the wild drunken nights in places that the jello writers can't imagine. Suddenly the veterans were among soft, proper people who knew nothing of what they had done and what they had seen, and who, truth be told, didn't much like them.

Nor did some of us much like the people at home--though it was not at first a conscious distaste. Men came home with wounds and terrible memories and dead friends to be greeted by that squalling she-ass of Tom Hayden's, to find a country that, having sent them to Viet Nam, now viewed them as criminals for having been there. Slowly, to more men than will admit to it, the thought came: "These are the people I fought for?" And so we lost a country.

We looked around us with new eyes and saw that, in a sense the mousse people could never understand, we had lost even our dignity. I remember a marine corporal at Bethesda Naval Hospital who, while his wounds healed, had to run errands for the nurses, last year's co-eds. "A hell of a bust," he said with the military's sardonic economy of language. "Machine gunner to messenger boy."

It wasn't exactly that we didn't fit. Rather, we saw what there was to fit with--and recoiled. We sought jobs, but found offices where countless bureaucrats shuffled papers at long rows of desks, like battery hens awaiting the laying urge, their bellies billowing over their belts. Some of us joined them but some, in different ways, fled. A gunship pilot of my acquaintance took to the law, and to drink, and spent five years discovering that he really wanted to be in Rhodesia. Others went back into the death-in-the-bushes outfits, where the hard old rules still held. I drifted across Asia, Mexico, Wyoming, hitchhiking and sleeping in ditches until I learned that aberrant behavior, when written about, is literature, and can be sold.

The jello writers were quickly upon us. We were morose, they said, sullen. We acted strangely at parties, sat silently in corners and watched with noncommittal stares. Mentally, said the fashion experts, we hadn't made the trip home.

It didn't occur to them that we just had nothing to say about jello. Desserts mean little to men who have lain in dark rifle pits over Happy Valley in rainy season, watching mortar flares tremble in low-lying clouds that flickered like the face of God, while in the nervous evening safeties clicked off along the wire and amtracs rumbled into alert idles, coughing and waiting.

Once, after the GIs had left Saigon, I came out of a bar on Cach Mang and saw a veteran with a sign on his jacket: VIET NAM: IF YOU HAVEN'T BEEN THERE, SHUT THE FUCK UP. Maybe, just maybe, he had something.

64 BAR FLIES

Drunks, Time, Life, Death, and Such

For most gringos, Mexico is a place to retire. The Mexicans say, "The Americans come here to die." Not exactly. It isn't why they come, but it is what they do, there being eventually no choice. Everybody has to croak somewhere, so why not in the sunshine with little brown kids running back and forth and the street dogs lounging contentedly about? It beats, for some anyway, a wretched sanitarium and lots of tubes.

In the hills on the north side of town, where the nice houses are, you see aging couples like couples anywhere. It could be Lauderdale. They have each other and insurance and pensions and savings. In the bars you see the old single guys. They have close to nothing.

At nine in the morning they sit on green iron benches in the plaza and wait for the cantinas to open. Little beyond white hair unites them in appearance. Some are thin, others fat, others whatever you can think of except moneyed. "Drunks" is not quite the right word for them. They are just old guys whose lives are spent and they sit around and drink beer and wait. It's what they have. They seldom fall off stools or get into fights. They are anything but dangerous. They are just old guys with nothing, waiting.

Some would find them reprehensible. Why don't they *do*

something improving, learn to knit, or take up square dancing? This is harsh. What does a man do when he is seventy years old, his wife died eight years ago in Louisiana, and the trucking firm no longer wants him as a driver? Social Security and a small pension don't go far in America. He comes to Ajijic and moves into the residential hotel, Italo's, a block from the plaza and easy walking distance to the bars. It's cheap and decent and the rooms come with kitchenette and the maids clean them. I've stayed there.

He's seventy and tired, too old to learn a language and probably not of that bent anyway. He doesn't want to learn to square dance. He is not looking for a cultural experience, not looking for much of anything. Women no longer interest him except as nice people, and anyway the diabetes doesn't help in that department. So he talks to his friends. And he drinks. It takes the curse off. Besides, if he bothers no one else, it is the business of no one else—*n'est-ce pas*?

It is a mistake to think these men to be of no account because they are ending their days on a bar stool. They have had lives, traveled, drifted, worked, loved, had families or not, seen things and done things. Often they are intelligent and thoughtful. They are just through.

We live in a censorious age in America, an age of "Gotcha!" in which drinking looms loathsome, smoking is a crime to be punished, second-hand smoke a fearful threat to children and plants and wallpaper. Oh dear. We all must be vigilant for racism, sexism, and the rest. Psychologists call it "passive aggressiveness," though I think that "the Higher Priss" does nicely. Well, I say, each to his or her or its own. Still, I have always found people who smoke and drink and do the occasional doob to be more interesting than those who don't—certainly than the drab Comstocks of the current Carryan Nation. So I'll cut these guys some slack. You choose an exit door, or fall through one. They have. So will you.

Not all stay in one place. In Italo's when I was there I met a guy well into his seventies who was about to get on a third-class bus to Guatemala, I think it was. He didn't walk too well and moved as if he had sand in his joints. He seemed sad but was keeping his chin up. He knew a hotel in a nice town outside Guatemala City where the food was cheap and the young girls just so pretty. He meant nothing sexual. They were just pretty, like pictures. He liked watching them and the kids and Guatemala.

Now that's rough, I thought. To be at the end of his days and bouncing around bad roads on a Guatemalan bus, alone, going where he probably knew nobody—that's not the feather-bed route out the door. But he didn't want to spend the winter in Ajijic. At least he was free. I wished him well.

Some drunks have other stories. There was a fellow, in his thirties I'd guess, who always wore a white cowboy hat and lied compulsively about what daring things he had done. This is common. It's called "border promotion." You know: "I was a SEAL team leader before I was an astronaut, between being a fighter pilot and president of IBM." Sometimes it seems like half the gringo population used to be in the CIA.

Anyway, the guy with the white cowboy hat said he used to be a dead-end drunk, and had the tremor to prove it. But he was over it, he said, and in fact seemed to be. Then one night he got a ride home with somebody, pulled a pistol from somewhere, put it under his chin and blew the top of his head off. AIDS, or at least HIV. We make our choices. The consensus was that he should have done it somewhere else, where it wouldn't have put a hole in the roof of the car and generally made a mess.

Sometimes one of the old guys will take up with a poor Mexican gal of twenty-five with four kids. They move in together. You could say that it was absurd, that neither knew the other's language and he was a dirty old man and she a gold-digger. You could also try to exercise a little decency. Not everybody has choices. Usually he treats her well, puts food on the table, maybe gets her some dental work or insists that the kids go to school. It's better than nothing. She cooks and keeps house and has a few years of security, and he leaves her whatever he can. I've seen such couples who seemed happy together. You play the hand you draw.

Things are different for those of intellectual resources, who take up photography seriously, fly ultralights, read, or keep on at whatever they did for a living at a reduced level. I'm not sure how different it is. They too are waiting. So are we all. But there were drunks before there were moralists, and I hope there will be drunks after, as they are so much less tedious, and closer to the human condition.

65 DOWN AND OUT

Life on the Underside: Scenes Better Not Seen

P orn store on Times Square, NYC, before they cleaned it up. Early evening—by New York's standards. Bright yellow light, walls lined with bins of magazines arranged by subject, Peeing, Cream Pie, Big Tits, Face Sitting, Threesomes. Scurfy men grody and half-shaven flicking through the pages like rats in a garbage dump. Others, respectably dressed, embarrassed to be there, furtive, but grimly determined. They are more lonely than sexually desperate, would trade all they have for a nice girlfriend. They avoid eye contact. The place is an urban coral reef by night.

There is a wall of garish sex toys, edible panties, silicone dildos in dayglo colors, some with strings embedded so gays can avoid the ER, double-dongs, complex condoms with odd appendages. An inflatable woman; the box shows a smiling man in a convertible with her beside him: your date with a beach ball. Loneliness, not sex. "Live mouth action!" says the box. "Just squeeze the back of her head."

Toward the back, behind milling men trying not to touch each other in the egg-yolk light, the Mother of All Grotesqueries: A circular room maybe twenty feet across, a huge wooden drum with doors around it every three feet. Each opens into an unlit booth with a small window at the back, obscured by an external curtain. Each has a coin box. You put a quarter in the box and the curtain rises to reveal a turn-table with a naked woman on it. She is dimly lit by more yellow light. All around her are the little windows, each with a man inside peering out and probably choking his chicken. After a couple of minutes the curtain automatically falls and you have to drop another quarter in. The woman squats, crawls, spreads, juts in mortal boredom. It is as erotic as watching toast burn. Round and round, the windows open and close. What does she do in the day? A med student, maybe. It happens.

A bad section of DC, which is most sections, late night, summer, on a foot beat with the Metropolitan Police. Sidewalks are devoid of pedestrians. It is not a good place to be a pedestrian. Everything lies colorless under a weak street light. A white woman, blonde, maybe forty-five, clutches a bottle of whiskey on a random stoop: A street person in jeans and very stained blouse. She is slobbering drunk. The cop asks how she is. He knows how she is.

She slurs in anguish over something she can't communicate, not quite sobbing. The cop says ma'am, maybe we better take you in. He is not being a bastard. Cops don't hate cirrhotic unhappy women gurbling and puking through their last few days on earth. But what do you do? Nobody wants her, not the hospital, not the jail.

She protests unintelligibly. Well, ma'am, maybe you ought to pour the rest of that out.

At this she tumbles off the stoop and begins crawling toward the mouth of a near-by alley, holding the bottle as if defending a baby. She is visibly wetting her pants. Some things you can't fix. We walk on.

Bangkok, the Patpong brothel district, early Eighties, in the Takara Club. You sit at the bar and chaff with the barmaid. At the end of the room a plate-glass window opens onto bleachers on which sit a dozen young women in pretty dresses; each has a number pinned to her top. You tell the bar-maid, "Nin2," and she goes to get her. You talk a bit, buy Nine a whiskey or two consisting of tea, pay the bar fine, and go upstairs.

As prostitution goes, it is civilized. As prostitution goes, I said. The girls are free to leave, unlike the peasant girls who sleep chained to beds in the soldiers' brothels, and occasion-ally burn to death when there is a fire. The Takara girls service foreigners, who usually treat them well, and sometimes take them to the beach. Some are not so nice, the Japanese in par-ticular often being sadists.

Ask the girls why they work at the Takara and they say, I've got a little boy, and I make more here than I would going blind in an electronics factory. Me, I still think they should have more name that Nine.

A sweltering night, mid Seventies, in Wan Wha, the old part of Taipei, out of the depths of an old, old China. Narrow al-leys, push-carts with charcoal braziers and pink squid draped like moist jointless fingers, and—the snake butchers. A dozen kraits, cobras, god knows what hang from a dowel on a cart, alive, tied just behind the head, many of them deadly—the *y-bai she*, hundred-pace snake, thus called because that's how far you go after one bites you.

A hard-faced laborer points to a snake and asks the price. With a razor the butcher slits the animal from head downward, massages the blood into a glass, and squeezes the gall bladder, if so it really is, into the glass. The customer drinks it. *"Dwei shen-ti, hen hau."* Good for the body. The snake is still twitch-ing.

Manhattan, the Vault, now closed, an S&M joint in a catacomb-feeling basement like an industrial hell by Dickens—a tourist destination for those who want to get off the beaten track, or maybe I mean onto it. When the theaters closed on Broadway, elegant people came in to see how the other half lived, and perhaps experiment. At the bar, preposterously elegant in the surrounding grunge, a couple of high-end executive types stand chatting of stock portfolios. They are suntanned, frizzy-haired, in pricey suits, maybe from the publishing district, with their trousers down around their ankles. A young woman wearing more leather than Trigger comes by, smacks hell out of their butts with a paddle, and leaves. "Thank you, ma'am," say the men, and go back to comparing their portfolios.

Night in the Pot Yards,

Correctly, the Potomac train yards, now closed, in the Virginia suburbs of DC. Jimmy Auld and I are waiting in the bushes while a yard mule howls in the fog, putting together a train which we hope to hop. There comes a crunch of footsteps. We tense, figuring a yard bull and we'll run for it.

It is an old black guy, walking stiff and slow, carrying something—a jug of water if memory serves. He is surprised to find white boys awaiting a train. We talk in low voices.

A natural camaraderie grows between those down on their luck or a bit on the wrong side of the law or just apart from society. He gave us advice on the yards and said he lived in a shack nearby. It had to be a shack if he was fetching water in a Clorox jug. We knew him for one of life's discards, a type you encounter often on the roads. He had nothing, never would, no insurance, no family, just living because that's what people do until they don't. We wished him well, and he went off into the fog.

66 MISCREANT COLUMN

Padre Kino, Dogs, and the Broad Blue Sky: A Column I Probably Should Hide

I am sitting today on the upstairs balcony, communing with our three useless but agreeable dogs and ingesting the mortal remains of innocent grapes. I am conducting a veritable holocaust of grapes. It comes of following the news. My favored instrumentality of inebriation is Padre Kino, cheap Mexican red that you could remove barnacles with. Think of it as the poor man's Lethe, a two-carbon Mickey Finn. Trying times call for desperate measures. Things being what they are, immoderate sobriety suggests mental imbalance.

The Great Purple Father incites me to physics. I have spent the last half hour on the back of an envelope, trying to calculate the Schwarzschild radius of Detroit. In my current state it is too much for me.

This is not going to be an organized column. Deal with it.

When I was fifteen and read *New Scientist*, which was then well-written, someone wrote in and asked, "Why does a mirror reverse things horizontally, but not vertically?" A couple of weeks of discussion ensued with weird mathematical explanations. A third-grader could have figured it out. It It may be why I didn't become a scientist.

The worthy grape cannot actually eliminate the horrors of today, such as Justin Bieber, but it can make them harder to remember. And absinthe makes the tart grow fonder, a service to the young.

Oh god, I feel poetry coming on.

Vatican, Vatican, shining bright/Are your cardinals transfinite?/ I wish I may, I wish I might/Trace my descent from a trilobite.

I rather like trilobites. I am a serious traditionalist, harking back to primeval seas. Cambrian arthropods at least had dignity. And if girl trilobites didn't have very good legs, they had lots of them.

Obama. We should think about Obama. Some students of IQ have estimated his at 126 to 129. It's hard to know. The first thing a president's ventriloquists do is hide his tracks, SATs, IQ, and grades so as to make him an amorphous plastic concept suitable for sculpting. Actually, presidents do not exist. A "president" consists of four advance men, three pollsters, two speechwriters, and a partridge in a pear tree. No, I meant to say, two speechwriters, a make-up artist, a gestures coach, and assorted fixers.

You could do them in software—you know, a slider marked Firmness and Resolution at one end, and Compassion and Empathy at the other. Another saying Confidence-Inspiring Calm at one end and Human Emotionality at the other. Intelligence at one end, and Jes' Folks at the other. Dial in a corn-pone accent for campaigning in the South, and, for Boston, make him honk through his nose like a Canada goose. Poll results would come in over WiFi and the software would add Appropriate Social Values.

The only part missing is three-D holography. Then, instead of spending fortunes on air fare to places like Beijing, we could email him as an attachment.

Anyway, Obama. A 128 IQ is respectable, well up in the 90th percentile, suitable for being a pretty good doctor, or student in a fairish university, or a door stop in Silicon Valley. There you find numbers like 190, which might be better for running a nuclear-armed country with pugnacious kindergarteners in Congress.

Now we come to CERN, which is Frog for Center European for Research Nuclear. Latins always talk backward like that. Anyway, under Switzerland CERN has a supercollider, which is like a huge hatband for a man with a round head, that cost more than a billion shaky green ones and makes subatomic particles go round and round and run into each other. Why would anyone in his right mind want to do it? Never has so much money been spent to make so little go so fast. (All right, for pickers of technical nits: It makes them go minutely faster but lots heavier.)

Anyway—the world is swirling strangely, must be some sort of gravitational flux—I wanted to tell you about the Biggs Hoson, which is a sort of Heffalump particle, which if you go around the bush however many times, or the collider, you never find it, just its tracks.

Come to think of it, you could use Padre Kino as pretty fair rust-remover, I think. Or as anvil-dissolver. And it poisons flies.

Onward. For the technically minded: I have found a way to make programmers obsolete. Yes. Mumbai will fall back into rag-picking and Google shares will tank, but there is no stopping progress. Anyway:

We can regard the entire memory, RAM and disk, of a computer as one long binary number. We set it to zero, and then increment it repeatedly by 1. This will eventually generate all possible memory states, and thus all possible programs, plus a great deal of trash.

We feed each state into a disassembler program, which will turn the binary into assembly language, LOAD, ADD, STORE, MDX, SPSW, that sort of thing. Then an identical computer will endeavor to execute the resulting code, to find out what it does. Most strings will do nothing at all. Many will do something useless, such as loop forever. These can be stored in a file for sale to the federal government.

Those remaining will be the set of all useful programs possible for the computer. It will be necessary only to catalog each with a description of its function. Then, instead of importing geeks named Khan and Wong to write programs that our increasingly useless young no long can, we just use a look-up table. See? It's brilliant.

Skeptics will say that on a computer with a terabyte drive, there will be more than 10^{12} states and the process would take too long. Actually, more than 2 raised to 8 x 10^{12}. Pfah! That's what graduate assistants are for.

Padre Kino is said to lead to brain damage, causing psychosis and separation from reality. I'm hoping. It must be true. It seems to me this headline actually appeared in the *Huffington Post*:

"Vaginal Knitting Is Here to Make Everyone Afraid Of Performance Art Once Again."

If I were a woman, that would definitely make me afraid. I'm clearly delusional. The story seemed to say that some silly wench, one of those eternally-thirteen self-absorbed tediously-outraged feminists, stuffed yarn into her, uh, self, and now pulls it out, as if she were a spinning reel, to knit things. Wouldn't a knitting bag be more comfortable?

This is happening in Darwin, Australia, which confirms all my fears about human evolution. The evolution part is right, but we got the direction wrong. And we think the English-speaking world is going to compete with China?

The delusions are coming on again. I am imagining that colleges are offering scholarships for video-gamer s. See? Padre Kino is like the better grades of peyote. Onward into the fog.

67 SUNSET AND MOSQUITO HAWKS

Why You Should Never Be a Queen Ant

O f a late afternoon long ago I sat in the clearing above the swamp, headwaters of Machodoc Creek, where my parents lived in Virginia's Tidewater. I was reading. The air was thick with summer almost silent, except for the occasional bird and bug going about their affairs and the distant cough and roar of big trucks gearing their way up the hills on Route 301. Dragonflies flittered about in light that began to slant through the trees. Odd. Usually they kept to the wetlands below the hill.

Something fell on my pages and thrashed awkwardly about. A bug of some sort, but not one that I had seen, and it seemed to have trouble walking. Above, the dragonflies flashed and hovered. I dumped the stranger on the grass and kept reading. Shortly another of the curious creatures fell on my leg. It couldn't walk either.

At last I understood. The ants were queening. Hopeful chitinous maidens were taking wing to mate, and the dragonflies were eating them, nipping off the juicy abdomens and dropping the rest on me. That was why they had left the swamp.

I knew dragonflies well. As a boy in Alabama with a BB gun, I had hunted them, and moccasins, in the wet region near the

Valley Gin Company, which didn't make gin but took the seeds out of cotton. The town was Athens, then small and almost rural. The air there was alive with snake doctors, as dragonflies were locally known, though elsewhere they are called mosquito hawks or the devil's darning needles—fast, muscular insects, with huge compound eyes like radomes. They are fearsome to look in the face and, for small prey that fly, agile death. They glittered iridescent blue and green in the sunlight. I could never hit them.

In Virginia, ant parts rained down. The world, I reflected, seemed friendly only because people were too large for most things to eat. The world we live in bears little relation to the smaller world roundabout. In our pretty clearing with the smell of warm vegetation and the babble of birds was a realm of nightmare mechanical monsters, unnoticed because small. I have seen ants tear apart a wounded hornet, a mantis eating a struggling bug held in brawny green forearms. It is well for us that mantises don't weigh three hundred pounds.

I sometimes think I am the only man who doesn't understand wherever it is that we are.

As the light failed and I could no long see my page, I wandered across the bean field to where the old road, once a wagon track, ran between high banks into the woods. A flaming sunset had come over the sky, rolling off forever in what looked like ocean waves or burning dunes. The air smelled of damp earth and leaf mold. Night came early in the road cut. The first bats began to flicker through branches dark against the flames.

The droning announcers of the endless nature shows on television, full of the confidence born of limited understanding, tell us that bats and cockatoos and locusts are the necessary consequent of blind chance, speaking in the next breath of Mother Nature's intentions. For them everything is simple. Starlings are drab so that nothing hungry can see them, and cockatoos are gaudy so they can find each other to mate. Yet I note that starlings seem to mate prolifically if drably and, given what cockatoos sound like, it is hard to see how anything could fail to find one that wanted to be found.

I think those big birds are too pretty to be accidents. Those of religious nature have attributed such things to any of several thousand gods, some more attractive than others. They, like the acolytes of evolution, are perfectly sure of the rightness of their views. I am not sure of anything. Alone in a darkling wood, with things all about flying and hunting and growing in a vast ungraspable dance, I suspected that I was in the presence of something above my pay grade. Just what, I couldn't say, nor of what intentions or provenance. I didn't think it was much concerned with me. It wasn't physics.

Recently I found the noted astrophysicist Stephen Hawking quoted, perhaps correctly, as saying that humanity may be on the verge of understanding everything whatever. Physicists often say such things, speaking of string theory, singularities, and the 3K background radiation-words redolent of insulation and sixty-cycle hum. If one may differ with a cosmogonist, I suggest that we understand almost nothing. And without the slightest disrespect, I note that the brightest of a large population of hamsters is, after all, a hamster.

I suppose that people believe that they understand this mysterious universe because it is more comforting to think that one understands than to worry uneasily that one mightn't. The faithful, Darwinian and otherwise, persuade themselves that they have The Answer. The fury of their defense of their creeds suggests a nagging doubt. Others focus on the here and now and deny the question. Few say, "I don't know."

The sky glowed in gorgeous oranges and reds like a Chinese lamp lit from within and slowly burned out to blues and ashen black. Yes, I have heard of water vapor and indices of refraction, but I don't think that was what was happening, or not all that was happening. In the marsh below things would be coming out to eat.

I wish explanations explained better. There is a peculiar wasp that kills tarantulas, buries them, and lays eggs on them. I have tried to imagine how an infant wasp, crawling unschooled from where its mother left it as an egg, knows how to find a tarantula, where to sting it, and how to bury it. One would think the world would be a confusing place to such a newborn with no experience of it and only the outline of a nervous system. Yet they do it unerringly. More is going on here than I think we know.

My idiot dog Deacon showed up and set about whuffling in the black undergrowth. He was an agreeable if foolish brute, and appeared to be the product of illicit coupling between a German shepherd and a boxcar. Why he whuffled, I don't know. I didn't need to know. He did what is proper to his place in things and I, what is proper to mine. He sniffed, and I supervised sunsets. It suited us.

68 FRUIT JUICE GIRL

Schwei Gwo Syau-Jye and Life Under a Bridge

I t was 1975, just after the fall of Saigon, and I was in Taipei, studying Chinese and waiting for the next war, which didn't come. I abode downtown in the winding labyrinth of backstreets inhabited mostly by workers since I was pretty broke. My roommates were a Chinese teenager, Dingwo, who wanted to be a rock star, and Sakai, a diminutive Japanese mathematician with penis envy, and Ron, a Peace Corps guy back from India who astounded hotel guards by speaking to them in good Punjabi.

Chinese back alleys are wonderful places, or were anyway before Starbucks. They reek of spices and good cooking and kids sat outside to avoid the heat and studied at orange-crate desks. The Chinese study. We will one day think this important. We ate in tin-roofed restaurants with trays of little baby squid like grey vitamin pills and things less identifiable.

Near the apartment was a sort of concrete overpass with the space beneath it walled off to provide a low-rent place for food stalls. It was hot and steamy inside because of long rows of women frying this and steaming that. We ate sheets of fried squid, *youyu*, and then went to the fruit-juice stall.

I forget her name. We just called her *Schwei-gwo Syau-jye*, Fruit Girl. She was about twenty-five, roughly my age at the time and spent all day behind a white-tiled counter, selling fruit juice. Her mother was dead, her father eighty-something, and she had to take care of him. *Schwei-gwo* was slim and pretty, a common condition among Chinese, but tired.

I'd order a complicated juice concoction and sit there for an hour, practicing Chinese. Unless you want to read it, it is an easy language. She was usually in jeans and sweatshirt, and was trying to learn English, having a subscription to *Newsweek*. Have I said that the Chinese study? Somehow she remained cheerful despite brutal hours and not much of a life, which made me sad but that's how Asia was. Between customers she would flip through her dictionary and a copy of *Newsweek*.

In the East you meet many people like *Schwei-gwo Syau-jye*, intelligent and decent, who deserve better than they will ever have. It can get to you. She had a little white powder-puff dog that ate rice to keep her company. At night she walked home through the dark streets, a little nervous but feeling less alone with her dog. Crime was low because the government didn't tolerate it, but still....

Nights were different for Ron and me. Sometimes we went to Wan Wha, where you found the snake-butchers, and rough looking men came to the worker's brothels. (Preposterously, *Wan Wha* means "Ten Thousand Glories." It was pretty much a slum.) The butchers had cobras and the occasional *y-bai shuh*, which means one hundred paces because that's how far they think you would get if bitten. They slit the beasts from head to tail, massaged the blood into a glass, and sold it to workers. *"Dwei shen-ti, hen hau,"* good for the body. I always figured watermelon juice was a better idea. But I ramble.

The next war didn't come, and I left Taiwan. Marriage came, much water under various bridges, and my daughter Macon, Blonde Poof as we called her, made her appearance. I was working for a paper in Washington. The Taiwanese PR operation offered me and my wife a junket to Taipei, which we took, carting along Blonde Poof. I forget how old she was but she sat up successfully the first time in Taiwan.

We were staying, all expenses covered, in the Grand Hotel, Madame Chiang's gorgeous pile on a hill overlooking the city. We went downtown to my old haunts, Poof included, and found *Gwo-yu R-bau*, my old school. Was my teacher, Jang Lau-Shr still about, and would they tell her I'd like to see her? They would.

She showed up and we were both astonished that I could still carry on a conversation. It was odd after so many years. The neighborhood wasn't much, just low stores selling ordinary things, but there is a flavor to Asia that seeps into you and you never really leave. My wife, who had never been to that part of the world, said half-seriously, "Now, why are we going to go back?" Yes.

Then, on the off-chance, we went to the bridge.

There, in the same stall, hardly looking older, was *Schwei-gwo Syau-jye*. Nothing had changed. She was delighted to see us and we ordered the old concoctions. Same steamy heat, same smells. I don't know whether the dog-puff was the same or new. Her father was still alive and she was still working herself to death to care for him.

For a bit she played with Blonde Poof. The Chinese regarded a golden-haired child as almost a tourist attraction. They are a pretty people, the Chinese, but not a blond people.

No, she still wasn't married. She didn't have time to do much because she had to keep the stall open. We talked of fond memories of no importance and my wife and I left, vowing to write. I would have if I hadn't managed to lose the address. We never saw *Schwei-gwo Syau-jye* again.

Maybe she is still under the bridge, squeezing melons. Possibly things somehow got better for her. Taiwan has prospered mightily since those days. Maybe she got a job in an office. But I doubt it.

Forgive the horrible Romanization. Too many systems scrambled in my head.

69 BAR GIRLS AND WHY NOT

Part Two of How to Marry a Third World Woman and Live Happily Ever After, Somewhere Else

Bar girls are a mistake that countless guys make when they first leave the United States. they are a mistake in two ways. First, lots of gringos think that the girls are typical of the women of the country. Second, they get tangled up with a hooker and perhaps marry her. This is bad juju. Not a good idea at all.

Let's use Thailand as an example. Everyone has heard of the sex trade there. Most Americans seem to think that Thailand is a nation of prostitutes, and that seven out of every three have AIDS. This isn't true. The sex trade exists, but the overwhelming majority of women have nothing to do with it. The problem is that very few outlanders get beyond the whorehouses, so they think there is nothing else to Thailand.

The fact is that the Thais are culturally conservative, have fairly high standards of sexual morality, and regard foreigners (*farangs*) as depraved barbarians who want only sex. This typically is accurate. But the women you first will meet will be hookers. Let's go through the drill.

You land in Bangkok and check into your hotel. Of course that evening you head for one of the *farang* bar districts because, well, it's easy, and although in principle you are looking for a wife, in practice a little practice never hurts. I mean we are, after all, guys. And Bangkok at night is a sexual candy store.

There are three girly districts of note, Patpong Road, Soi Cowboy, and Nana Plaza. Patpong is perhaps the best known and the nicest. (Actually there are Patpong I and Patpong II, streets right next to and parallel with each other.) The taxi drops you off. What do you see?

A narrowish street, garishly lit, jammed with at least three-quarters of the entire population of Asia, milling and shoving and squirming through densely packed rows of stands selling clothes, trinkets, souvenirs, pirated music, antisocial tee-shirts, everything. Keep your hand on your wallet. (I wear a photo vest with inside zippered pockets.)

The street is lined with bars, many of them thumping with godawful disco music too loud to allow conversation. Go into a couple just to see what they are. There will probably be a long stand in the thumping murk raised a couple of feet above the floor. From this a dozen brass poles will rise to the ceiling. Dangling somewhere will probably be one of those beachballs covered with fragments of mirror to reflect the lights, which will be red and green and purple. Some of these places look to have been designed by Dante, but this has never been established.

On the stand, one per pole, will be Thai girls in bikinis or hot pants or whatever. They will be bumping and grinding in boredom. Depending on your age, recent deprivation, ethanol intake, experience in Asia, and testosterone levels, you may find this titillating, tiresome, or sad.

A girl will very quickly come to your table and offer you, well, herself. She will speak little if any English and be a peasant girl from up-country. She will have the appeal of the young, willing, and female. Do as you choose. She has nothing to do with our goal of finding a permanent squeeze, so we will drop her at this point.

Now go to one of the non-disco bars. The last time I did such things, a good example was the Takara, on Patpong I, upstairs by way of an elevator. It may still exist. Here, given your quest, you could get into trouble. The Takara, technically a massage parlor, is small, quiet, pleasant, with a bar and a couple of tables. The barmaid, overage at thirty-two or so, speaks English well. She is pretty and seems nice. She is in fact nice.

At the back of the room is a plate-glass window. Behind it is a series of platforms, one above the other, like very wide steps. On these sit a dozen lovely Thai girls in what look like gauzy evening gowns. Each has a tag pinned on her with a number. You can drink a beer or two at the bar, chaff with the barmaid, and then, if so inspired, ask for Seven. The barmaid will inform Seven that she is wanted, and Seven will then come sit by you at the bar.

.Here is where, if you have not encountered third-world bar girls before, especially Asians, you need to be very careful. Seven will be sweet, and sleek, and charming. She will not have any of the iron-clawed vulture in her that one encounters with many American hookers. She will smile and seem to mean it and she will be...that word again...feminine, and she will give you a neck massage and, if you buy her a second beer, a third-leg massage. She won't be crass about it, though. Thais aren't.

And you will think, "My god, she's really...nice. Not what I expected. Why, I like her."

The combination of loveliness, femininity, and sex is potent stuff. Sure, after a bit she will want you to buy her another drink, but at the Takara they aren't pushy about it, and anyhow that is how the game is played. She has to make a living. And of course before too long she will ask if you want to go upstairs. Of course you will want to.

So you will go into a little cubicle, one of many, with a massage table and a big bathtub, and she will tell you to strip and do so herself. This will not lower your opinion of her attractiveness. She will tell you to get into the bath tub. Thais are a clean people and believe in bathing before further proceedings. She will wash you, which will not decrease your enthusiasm. Then you will find yourself lying on a long rubber mat while she massages you by pouring warm soapy water on you and sliding up and down you. That is, she serves as an animated sponge. During all of this she will laugh and chat and be a sweetheart. The Thai experience is not like a quick-and-nasty against an alley wall in Washington, DC.

Being new to all of this, your thought will be to come back the next night and buy this wonderful creature out of the bar. To do this you pay the "bar fine" to the barmaid, usually 500 baht or about twenty-five bucks. Seven is now yours for the night. You can take her out to eat, then back to your hotel. Sex will be good, if a tad mechanical around the edges. Thais are not sexually inhibited.

Here is where the trouble can start. You can easily begin to bond with her, to become enamored or, as we used to say, fall in love with her. She will not discourage this. After all, bonding is her business. Her less-agreeable side, which we all have, will not appear. You will eventually hear about her five-year-old boy that she had by a boyfriend who abandoned her, and how she was half-starving selling soup on the street but went into hooking because it paid better.

And you may begin to see yourself as a Galahad rescuing this sloe-eyed princess from the vicissitudes of life. Of course part of your spirit of charity will flow from her having really nice tits. It is easy to confuse love with horniness.

But a fair number of inexperienced guys end up marrying a sweetie out of a bar, who turns out to be screwed up in the head, which is true of most bar girls, and makes his life hellish.

You find that she isn't as bright as you thought, has a fourth-grade education, or just wants to lie in bed all day and watch television. For good reasons they are often ambivalent about men, and their whole lives revolve around getting men to give them things. I have known a couple of marriages to bar girls that worked, but it is rare.

They are not evil people, or no worse than the admittedly sorry baseline for the human race. They are human beings. They have real problems and a tough life and it is reasonable to be sympathetic. But you can't solve their problems. After the body massage, give her a big tip, buy her a last drink, and disappear over the horizon.

70 AN INNATE
STUPIDITY

War, Over and Over and Over. And Over,
World Without End

W ars are seductive as women in the night. Past midnight in February of 1967 we stood, the platoon and I, on the flight line at El Toro Marine Air Station, gateway to Asia. On the tarmac big jets howled and moaned. The smell of burned jet fuel blew in the Pacific breeze. We felt the exhilaration of being part of something huge moving in the darkness, of going to the action, of leaving the mundane. The attraction of war verges on the lascivious. It gets into your blood.

And so we went. Young men always go. Always there is another war. Always there are reasons. In the past these were straightforward: lust, booty, excitement, empire, a way to escape the family yurt, sheer joyous combativeness, the king was bored. Not much has changed.

Long hours later we landed in the sweltering sauna of Danang with its gun emplacements and fwop-fwopping helo traffic and sunbaked Marines with slung rifles; 105s boomed in the distance. It was, in the vulgar but irreplaceable expression of the times, a mind-fuck. We weren't back on the block combing our hair for Sally Sue and facing a career selling fanbelts at the local NAPA outlet. We were real soldiers, who couldn't find Vietnam on a map, fighting VC who couldn't find Vietnam on a map. We didn't reflect on this. Marines fought. Somebody else decided who they fought.

Perspectives change. Later, for veterans who no longer had legs or eyes, who had lost their guts or become paras and quads, the splendor dimmed. I came home, my face bandaged, in a packed Medevac 141 with a guy slung above me sprouting tubes that led into bags. He died en route.

Those who survived soon realized that in six months no one would care what they had gone through, yet they would spend the rest of their lives in the wheel chair. A colostomy bag, they found, was not a great conversation piece in a singles bar. For them, the war never went away.

Spend a year on a casualty ward. You will see much. When the girlfriend from Chattanooga, aged seventeen, finds that Mikey, her betrothed, is blind and doesn't precisely have a face, her expression is something to see. Or not to see.

You can become disposed to ask: Is this war for anything? Or is it just a war?

Mostly they are just wars. Vietnam was just a war. We lost, and nothing bad happened. You might be surprised how many in the Disabled American Veterans quietly hate those who sent them.

Yes, I will get angry mail, from those fiercest of warriors, the 103rd Combat Virgins Division, *grrr, bow-wow, woof,* telling me that that I am a commie and a coward and wear lace under-wear. I'm impressed in advance.

Later, as a reporter, I spent a year between Saigon and Phnom Penh, leaving both cities with their evacuations. The Asia I saw in the complex warren off Truong Minh Ky was not the Asia of the GIs. It was complex, variegated, enduring. I liked the Vietnamese. I still do. I am glad that we killed only a million of them.

This you must never say. Wars are better if you don't look too closely. Never, ever, think about what is actually happening.

The Americans believed, or said they believed, that we were battling the evil of communism to save the Vietnamese, who Such a deal. wouldn't even help. To this day former GIs hate the Viets for not being enthusiastic about the war, which in fact they weren't. They wanted the war to go away so they could grow rice.

The Right thunders and the Left squeaks over the motives of the war, each bleeding cataracts of virtue. I remember the succinct analysis of a Vietnamese girlfriend I lived with: "At night, VC steal our rice. In morning, Marines kill us for give rice VC."

They were ambivalent about having a half million gringos running around their country and blowing things up, such as themselves. The GIs never understood. They didn't know that when an artillery round killed a villager's wife, all the young men picked up rifles to kill Americans. They should have thought of this.

After the GIs left Saigon I returned to Southeast Asia as a reporter for *Army Times.* For a while I lived in a rooftop apartment on Jawaharlal Nehru Street in Phnom Penh with Steve Hedder, a young stringer for *Time,* and his Khmer wife Devi. With us were the twins, pretty, playful girls of sixteen perhaps who spoke reasonable English. They were the people with soft hands that Pol Pot would shortly kill.

At night the smell of charcoal and flower trees drifted from neighboring roofs and people murmured in Khmer. Reporters–mostly stringers–lay on the roofs in a fog of gin and Nembutal and listened to the rockets whistle in from the swamps. When the KR took over, Steve and Devi got out. The twins didn't. I don't know how they died.

I will be told I have a bad attitude. You bet I do.

Years later I went back on a magazine assignment, and saw Toul Sleng. Once a high school in Phnom Penh, it was used by the KR as a place of torture. It had become a museum. On the walls were photos of those who died there. I couldn't remember the lone Caucasian's name, but I had seen him around town. A friend of mine who went back found the picture of his girlfriend. All dead.

Another time I returned to Vietnam, again on assignment. In Saigon the Continental Shelf, once a hotel restaurant with sides open to the street, was glassed in and air-conditioned, not necessarily an improvement. For two weeks I worked my way upcountry from Saigon to Vung Tau, Nha Trang, Hue, to Danang, near where I had been stationed. Marble Mountain had become a pleasant tourist stop with shops selling stone carvings.

Further north, Hanoi bustled with shops and the insane but invisibly ordered traffic of Asia. My pretty little governmentally-supplied guide asked whether I wanted to see the Ho Chi Minh museum. I said I'd rather have my teeth pulled. Oh, she said, apparently relieved, then let's just look at the city. We did. Nice place. I tried to remember what the war had been about.

As I say, it gets into you blood. For a couple of decades I worked as a military reporter. I liked the travel, the troops, the airplanes and ships. Eventually it wore thin. Over and over, in some place like remote Olancho province in Honduras, or Cuando Cubango in Angola, or this dusty clearing or that dusty clearing, the press would chopper out to be shown The Great Victory.

In the jungle would be three or four bedraggled bodies of teenagers fighting a shabby war for some dismal Marxist cause they couldn't spell, and a trove of captured weapons--couple of AKs, the stray M-16, maybe a FN/FAL or Galil. We were told it was progress. Some great cause was being served. Maybe it was. I got tired of seeing it.

Plus ca change, plus ca doesn't.

71 BESTIALITY FOR THE MASSES

Fido Reconsidered: Toward a More Inclusive Sexuality

Having read the course listings for several departments of Women's Studies at places that were once universities, such as Dartmouth, I am considering becoming a deep-sea squid. Many considerations recommend this course. Squids are more dignified than people. They make less noise. Universities run by squids do not have Departments of Lesbian, Gay, Cross-gendered, Transaxle, Transvestite, and Deeply Puzzled Squid Studies. Lady squids are less infuriated than feminists, and frequently better-looking.

Departmental offerings of fascinating import abound:

WMST488R Senior Seminar: Queering the Global South (D)

Or:

WMST698D Special Topics in Women's Studies: The History of Drag. C. Schuler

I can't imagine anything more appropriate to a college education than the history of drag. Perhaps there is a chapter on Elizabethan Englishmen, who wore brightly colored pantyhose and swords. Where I come from in West Virginia, any man who wore panty hose would need a sword, so maybe it made sense. I am not sure how one queers the global south, but I believe I will move north and, just in case, get a Kevlar codpiece.

There was a time, long, long ago, in another universe, when universities were not chiefly comic. We have evolved. Today you can pay fifty thousand withering dollars a year to let your daughter be an extra in Saturday Night Live at, say, Yale, solemnly studying erotic peculiarities. The appeal is multi-faceted. A major in Women's Studies (or would it be a majorette?) would simultaneously satisfy the teenager's natural prurience, allow her a pleasant sense of advanced moral superiority, and permit her to avoid any danger of an education.

A tone of aggressive smugness pervades these hives, and a whine of misandry like the sound of a dentist's drill in an adjoining room. Many have noticed that immaturity in today's society lasts years longer than it did when the young had to work and raise families. This, plus the control of universities by the students, has allowed the coagulation of adolescent consciousness into whole departments. In these academic sandboxes the idea of critical thought seems to have died, equipping students with the self-awareness than one would expect of a peanut-butter sandwich. A department of militant sexism warring against sexism would be an embarrassment to more-logical beings, such as, I suspect, any other beings.

There is in such courses much nattering about Women of Color. The inmates of these refuges from adulthood apparently regard themselves as being at one with oppressed women of the Third World, which in all likelihood they have never seen one of. If they had any idea of what an actual Nicaraguan woman thinks of pampered brattesses lolling about a pseudo-educational theme park paid for by their fathers, they would hide under their beds.

However, I subscribe to the Californian principle that if a thing is not worth doing at all, it is worth doing to wild excess. After exposing myself to an afternoon of such course descriptions, I decided that I would get into the spirit of the thing, that perhaps I was being retrograde in not having a sufficient respect for cross-gendered, bicephalous, transalpine, trisexual people of pigment. I decided that maybe the dyspeptic children of Dartmouth and worse had a point. Maybe we should study aberrant, non-traditional sexualities. I'm not sure why, but these days the question appears not to be important.

It seemed reasonable that bestiality should be our next front in the ongoing battle for sexual liberation. While our Victorian and Puritan inhibitions have driven this form of love into the shadows of fear and repression, history shows that it has had a vibrant existence in more-tolerant societies of the past. Among the ancients there were Europa and the white bull, and Leda and the swan. More recently we have had the Lone Ranger and Silver, and Bill and Hillary. Many clandestine amors have been reported of shepherds in the lonely moors of the Scottish Highlands. (It is reported that Scotsmen wear kilts because sheep can hear zippers, but this may be slander.) Taxonomic miscegenation is thus seen to have a lengthy lineage. It merits exploration.

In furtherance of this idea I tossed together a few collegiate courses that seemed to me a good beginning at legitimizing trans-species relations. Proposed offerings:

BSSAP 101
Introduction to Bestiality. This marginalized sexuality will be considered in the light of historical intolerance, oppression, and the liberation struggle. Basic concepts to be explored: The sheep as social construct. Countering institutional humano-centrism. The eroticism of the orangutan in the cultural context of the rain forest. The Bolivian anteater, insertor or insertee? A Latina perspective on the donkey and the Tijuanan folk tradition. Laboratory twice weekly, covering practical techniques to include stepladders and the camel, and positioning the iguana.

BSSAP 301

Managing Cross-Phylum Relationships, with interdisciplinary emphasis on the Cephalopod. The role of tentacles. Animals of Color, centering on the cockatoo.

BSSAP 302

The Concept of Species: Socially Constructed or Injection Molded? The course will consider this complex subject from perspectives of sociology, gender struggle, and plasma physics. Accommodating differing reproductive sexualities: Budding vs. the egg strategy. Instructor: Señora Rosalita Consolador y Mermolada

BSSAP 348

Bestiality and the Law. Barking and the principle of informed consent. Recent Supreme Court decisions. Date rape: When "Moo" means "No." Negotiating with parents: the danger of trampling.

In my paroxysms of liberational afflatus it occurred to me that a truly inclusive sexuality would have to embody necrophilia, which suffers today from grave discrimination. It seems unmodern to bar people from the consolations of love merely because they are dead. Cannibalism being nothing but culinary necrophilia it seemed reasonable to combine the two. As the reader can see, I'm nothing if not reasonable.

NECCAN 202 Snuff: The Problem of Finding a Lasting Relationship. Techniques for digging up a date on short notice.

NECCAN 402 Fattening prisoners. Soy substitutes in time of peace. Sausages, gravies, and organ meats. The problem of deserts. Kosher. When baby dies. Road kill. Cannable vs. bottleable.

Enough. Much as I want to contribute to social advance, I believe I will stick with becoming a squid. It will be less embarrassing.

72 THE GREAT POSSUM-SQUASHING AND BEER STORM OF 1962

A Tale of Death and Horror in the Old South

Y ou gotta understand that we were stone crazy back in 1962, in King George County, Virginia. The county was mostly woods. We were mostly country kids. Unisex hadn't hit in those days, nor sensitivity, and certainly not judgement.

High school boys burned rubber along the winding forest roads in smoking jalopies that usually ran on a few cylinders less than they had. We drank beer, pulled on cheroots hanging low and sulky the way James Dean did it, and talked of cars and poontang. Some few of us, not to be named here, occasionally fired out the window with a twelve-gauge at cats. Usually I missed.

Anyway, we figured there was nothing in life but engines, guns, brew, and girls. And fishing poles. Even today, I'm persuaded that if there is something else in life, there shouldn't be.

As they say in Alabama, we didn't have the sense God give a crab apple. You know something? I'm glad we didn't. I've never done anything sensible that was fully satisfying.

Anyway in tenth grade I drove a '53 Chevy the color of dried mud. (I'm coming to a point. I think. Involving possums.) It cornered like a giraffe with its feet roped together and topped out at eighty down a sheer cliff, but it ran. That was enough.

Our standards were low. If a car didn't have rod knock, we thought something was wrong with it. The country boys were my friends, because they had a pleasant suicidal elan that bored me less than other things.

There was a kid we called Itchy, because if he was out hunting and saw a bug crawling up a plant, he'd give it both barrels. He wasn't a repressed killer or anything. It was just how he responded to bugs. I understand he later became a sane adult. We all knew he'd come to a bad end.

This isn't very coherent, but we're getting there. Patience.

So one Saturday night itch and Jimbo and Bobby, I'll call him, were out motivating along Route 218 with me in the '53. It could have been 2 a.m. The road was narrow, and wound through the forest like a python with epilepsy.

Jimbo was a muscular farm hoy with an IQ approximating his shoe size. Bobby, like me, was a mathematician's kid from the Naval Research Lab in the county. He was blond and skinny and looked like a tubular Viking.

Trees sailed by in the headlights and we had a case of Budweiser. Drinking and driving at age sixteen wasn't a good idea. On the other hand, if any of us had encountered a good idea, we would have reported it to the police:

The air was chilly with October. We felt free and wild, young males in the night. Conversation was articulate and sophisticated.

"Gittin' any strange?"

By this was meant the favors of a yearning maiden.

"Here and there."

Lying is easier when not encumbered by details.

"Would be strange if *you* got it. Gimme another beer."

In the midst of this philosophy, a possum scurried onto the road. In the headlights it looked like a vast rat that needed braces. I hit the brakes, having nothing against possums. Not fast enough.

Blub-blup.

Jimbo thought this was splendid, exciting, as if we had inexplicably come upon a pile of unwatched racing camshafts and log-manifold carburetors.

"Back up! Back up, Ricky! Let's look," he hollered.

He had curious tastes in things to look at. In those days I was called Ricky.

We backed up until the steaming carcass lay in the headlights and got out, leaving the car running, and walked over to it. Yellow teeth snarled up from mangled fur. If anything ever needed braces, that possum did. For a moment we stood there, listening to the engine whuffing behind us. Then, without consultation, we all peed on the beast.

I don't know why. We didn't think it was funny. It just seemed... right. Maybe the beer inspired us. Maybe we were marking our territory. (A flat possum?) I don't recommend it. I'm just telling you what happened.

Anyway, things proceeded to get strange, and they were starting from a pretty good baseline. Jimbo decided he wanted to ride in the trunk. The point was hard to argue. I mean, who else could tell what he wanted? There in the star-sprinkled night, trees everywhere, possum cooling, I opened the trunk and Jimbo sat, beer in hand, on the spare tire. He looked like Buddha with muscles. That too seemed right. It probably wasn't, though.

Then Bob decided he wanted to ride on the roof. That wasn't smart. Neither was Bob, which preserved symmetry. (I think he went to Princeton, which proves it.) We'd had an awful lot of beer.

I thought about the roof. Everybody had to be somewhere. It was a law of physics. Bob went topside. We actually drove off like that. How any of us survived to adulthood is a cosmic mystery that only God can answer, and even He would have to think long and hard and maybe drink some strong coffee.

Anyway, Itch curled up on the seat next to me. He was muttering about alligators, why I don't know. Some things it is better not to think about. .In any event, I'm pretty sure we didn't have any alligators. We throbbed along.

Occasionally I checked to see whether Bob was still on the roof. I could tell he was because his fingers hung over the edge of the windshield. Jimbo whooped and hollered in the trunk.

A tremendous downpour began. The windshield just streamed water. I turned on the wipers. Itchy began muttering more enthusiastically, but less articulately. I glanced at him. And noticed that it wasn't raining on his side of the car. That was odd, I thought. My experience had been that storms weren't so local. They usually got both sides of a car. It was like a rule. Further, the road was dry. As storms went, this one was on the peculiar side.

As it turned out, Bob was holding his beer by the wrong end on the roof, and it was running down the windshield. I yelled at him to stop.

I don't know what to tell you. It's how things were. And, when you get down to it, I wish they still were.

73 HUNTER THOMPSON

All Gone Now

T he Sixties look drab now—unkempt Manson girls, the lost and unhappy, kids bleak and bleary-brained after waking up with too many strangers in too many sour crash pads. There was that. It was not a time for the weakminded. But for those whose youth passed in the freak years, there was something gaudy and silly and even profound, something delightfully warped, that nobody else would ever have. Thompson caught it.

I didn't know him. Others have written better than I can of his work. But I knew the world that gave rise to him.

Starting around 1964, a restlessness came over the land, an itch. Kids trickled and later flooded onto the highways as if called by something. I can't explain it. Few had done it before. Few do it now. They—we–set forth and created the only country in which Thompson could have made sense.

It wasn't the war, at first. Nor was it only the usual impatience of youth with authority. Nor was it even that we were young and the world was wide. There was a revulsion against suburban emptiness, against the eight-to-five Ozzie and Harriet gig, a rejection of the Establishment, which meant boring jobs and singing commercials.

We discovered drugs, then regarded as worse than virgin sacrifices to Moloch, and looked through a window we could never name. If the times were out of joint, we were seldom out of joints. Chemistry defined the life. You found a freak in some rotting slum and said, "Hey, man, got some shit?" You toked up. You got the munchies, the skitters, the fears. Parents really didn't understand. Dope, we said, will get you through times of no money better than money will get you through times of no dope. It did.

Thompson, a savage writer, a grand middle finger raised against the sky, essayed drugs and found them good. And said so, and we loved him. When he wrote of getting wacked out of his mind on seven illicit pharmaceuticals, and wandering in puzzled paranoia through the lobby of existence, we shrieked with laughter. We knew the same drugs. We too had tried desperately to look straight in public when the world had turned into a slow-motion movie. When it was over, everybody went into a law firm.

Our socio-political understanding was limited. After all, we were pretty much kids. I remember having a discussion in Riverside, California, of how Republicans reproduced. We didn't think it could be by sex. I figured it was by budding.

For a while though, it all worked. Apostles of the long-haul thumb, we hitchhiked in altered mental states. I don't recommend it without guidance. We stood by the western highways as the big rigs roared by, rocking in the wash and the keening of the tires, desert stretching off to clot-red hills in the distance. At night we might buy bottles of Triple Jack at some isolated gas station and dip into an arroyo, roll a fat one and swill Jack and talk and hallucinate under the stars. An insight of the times was that if you got fifty feet off the beaten track and sat down, you didn't exist. It still works if you need it.

None of it was reasonable. I've never found anything worthwhile that was.

Then there was politics, the war. Thompson was rocket smart and knew you couldn't work within the system since that meant granting it legitimacy. Peace with Honor, the Light at the End of the Tunnel, all the ashen columnists arguing about timed withdrawal and incremental pressure. He knew it was about profits for McDonnell Douglas and egotistical warts growing like malignant goiters on the neck of the country. He was Johnny Pot Seed, a Windowpane Ghandi, dangerous as Twain.

The times brought their epiphanies. I remember being gezonked on mescaline in a pad in Stafford, Virginia, and realizing that existence was the point of execution in a giant Fortran program. So it's all done in software, I thought. I was floating in the universe. In the infinite darkness of space the code stretched above and below in IBM blue letters hundreds of feet high that converged to nothingness: N = N * 5, Go To 43, ITEST = 4**IEXP. For an hour I was awash in understanding. The stereo was playing Bolero, which was written by a Do-loop, so it all fitted.

Thompson savaged it all, lampooned it, creating a world of consciousness-sculpting substances and bad-ass motorcycles and absolute cynicism about the government. Today, after thirty years of journalism, I can't find the flaw in his reasoning. The other writer of the age was Tom Wolfe, but he wasn't in Thompson's league. Wolfe was a talented outsider looking perceptively at someone else's trip. Thompson lived the life, liked big-bore handguns and big-bore bikes and had a liver analysis that read like a Merck catalog. His paranoia may be style, but you can't write what you aren't almost.

I remember standing alone in early afternoon beside some two-lane desert road in New Mexico, or somewhere else, that undulated off through rolling hills and had absolutely no traffic. I don't know that I was on anything. Of course, I don't know that I wasn't. A murky sun hung in an aluminum sky like a fried egg waiting to fall and mesquite bushes pocked the dry sand with blue mortar bursts. The silence was infinite. I lay in the middle of the road for a while just because I could. Then I followed a line of ants into the desert to see where they were going.

A grey Buick Riviera, a wheeled barge lost in the desert, slid to a stop. The trunk creaked open like a jaw. A squatty little mushroomy woman behind the wheel motioned me to get it. As we drove the cruise alarm buzzed, and she told me it was a Communist radar. They were watching her from the hills.

It was a Thompson moment.

Then it was over. Everybody went into I-banking or something equally odious. We gave up drugs as boring.

You can see why he ate his gun. Everything he hated has returned. Nixon is back in the White House, Rumsnamara risen from the dead, bombs falling on other peoples' suburbs. The Pentagon is lying again and democracy stalks yet another helpless country. This time the young are already dead and there will be no joyous anarchy. The press, housebroken, pees where it is told. But he gave it a hell of a try.

74 THE, OR SOME, SOURCES OF PHILOSOPHY

Charlie Dog, Golondrinas, and the Impossibility of Ants

This morning when I emerged groggily into something resembling consciousness, I didn't know that I was going to establish the impossibility of ants. Here was a deep philosophical matter, creeping up on me surreptitiously. The dogs as usual came thundering in to see whether we still existed and, having ascertained that we did, offered to have their ears scratched. Such are dogs. Our felines, Cat and Other Cat, sleep on the bed with us—north of the border, there is probably a federal law against this—and also want our attention. Why? They get nothing by sleeping with us. We feed them anyway.

Dogs intrigue me by their distinctiveness of personality and range of emotions: Anger, affection, fear, curiosity, jealousy, concern, and guilt. Scientifically speaking, I am not sure whether this is proper. They were street dogs however, and perhaps not cognizant of the more advanced theories. They do understand guilt, whether they are supposed to or not. When we come home and Charlie has a hang-dog expression, and grovels in submission, and doesn't run over to greet us, we know he has been digging in the garbage, which is forbidden. He knows it too.

Our dog Africa, who is very long and low and pretty and seems to be a cross between a Border Collie and a fire hose, is an hysteric. When I walk downstairs she barks joyously and rushes madly about, as though I were Zeus Descendant, even though she saw me go upstairs half an hour earlier and knows that I always come back down. You can't be out of your mind unless you have one to be out of, is what *I* say.

Which brings us to *golondrinas*, swallows. (You may not see why it does. Well, it does.) We have a nest of them in a corner of the downstairs terraza. They produced five eggs this year, and sat on them as is right and fitting for *golondrinas*. When the nestlings appeared, the parents tirelessly brought them, every few minutes, a portion of whatever swallows eat. When the little buggers reached the age at which flying began to seem a good idea, the parents began hovering inches from the nest, as if saying, "See? This is how you do it." They had not done this before.

...

When we enter the garage, our ornitho-chillun peer over the edge of the nest, deeply suspicious because they know Someone Is There. They sink back, only their eyes showing. Better safe than sorry, I suppose.

One of the new birdlets flew tolerably well for a beginner, but landed on the ground where there are cats. (Actually we had locked the cats inside for precisely this reason, but mother swallows don't always know this.) The parents landed next to it and began pecking the little fellow unpleasantly, until it took off and went back to the nest. I have read that they do such things purely on instinct and do not know why they do them. How would one know this? Personally, I think they suspect cats.

.I know that birds are biological automata running on chemically programmed code, and have no feelings or idea of what they are doing. I know this. I just do not believe it. Further, I do not understand the almost universal affection people feel for the very young. The very young of about everything: young puppies, kittens, burros, *golondrinas*. In terms of evolutionary biology, which we are told governs everything, affection for young swallows is hard to figure. They are fearfully ugly, being all mouth and no brain, which I concede suggests an evolutionary connection with network anchors. But we are quite fond of them. (Not the network anchors.)

I invite the reader to consider those extraordinarily small ants, the sort that can fit through the eye of a needle, unlike Biblical camels. With their help, I will now offer a formal proof of the nonexistence of ants. First, we will note the above ant on top of the eye of a needle. We will further note that there is almost no ant there. We will now ponder the size of its brain, to include distributed parts of it. If an ant is so small that it almost isn't there, and most of an ant consists of legs, chitin, digestive things, and so on, then its brain, to include all of its nervous tissues, is greatly more isn't-there.

We will now consider what an ant can do. First, it can walk. If you think this is no great shucks, talk to a robotics engineer with a cable-connected supercomputer. Ask him how easy it is to make six legs with multiple joints each work together while climbing over things. If you think about the amount of sensory feedback necessary to know where these legs are at a given moment, and what the pressures and angles are, you will get dizzy. The ant does it effortlessly, with about as many brain cells as a congressman has IQ points. This would suggest perhaps three brain cells.

There is worse, much worse. That same ant, with only three

congressional brain cells, can interpret the data from both of its compound eyes and its ocelli—tiny non-compound eyes. Now, the guys who wrote PhotoShop could merge all those inputs from a jillion ommatidia and come up with something reasonable as an image, but doing it in real-time, in the equivalent of about six lines of code, with three brain cells for processing power—they would run screaming to the nearest bar and begin living under a park bench.

The same ant knows, somehow, to dig a nest properly, to run like hell when it is scared, and to care for the queen and the eggs and larvae. It manages its internal organs and antennae. It knows how to groom itself, putting it ahead of many teenagers, and how to find food, which requires operating the senses used to do this. I could go on. But since each of these things is impossible, so is the ant. Therefore, ants do not exist. QED.

(I suspect that the impossibility of several things in one non-existent ant is the product the individual impossibilities. I will leave this matter of multidimensional impossibilities to the reader as an exercise.)

If I may lapse momentarily into unwonted seriousness, I claim these picnic micromonstrosities pose a baffling question of cybernetics. They must be doing something far beyond the grasp of our tiny boiling imaginations. Replicating an ant in hardware of the same size is out of the question. Molecular computing? Well, the little beast does it some way. Humans with our quart-and-a-third of mushy brains can do much more than ants can, but not proportionately more. The nerve tissue of how many ants would be needed to fill on human cranium? To which I usually get the witless response, "But Fred, ants have an entirely different kind of brain." That's not the answer. It's the question.

75 QUACKIING TOWARD KANDAHAR

Power and Fuzzy Ducks in Washington

This first appeared in Harper's

Recently I attended a costume party of what appeared to be several hundred Republicans from the Reagan Administration, which took place in a pricey forested suburb of Washington. The guests were a mixture of Somewhat Important People and a few Very Important People, by which is meant that had they vanished without trace, nobody would have noticed. This is a curious aspect of importance, that it varies inversely with the damage that would follow upon one's loss: when the plumbers strike, chaos results, but if the National Security Council ceased to come to work, nothing would happen.

Anyway, I found myself standing in a glossy kitchen covering several acres. Next to me stood an enormous pink rabbit, who perhaps devised economic policy for the nation, clutching a Heineken and chatting with the Lone Ranger, who doubtless hailed from the State Department--which would explain a lot. In the foreground, silhouetted against a writhing sea of varicolored ears, antennae, tentacles, feathers, and further Heineken bottles, was what appeared to be a male prostitute from the plummier days of the Weimar Republic. (Recent administrations have been able to achieve the overall effect without costumes.)

I wrapped myself around my Heineken bottle for security like an anchovy around its caper. A a short cherubic lady came ooching toward me the crowd. My recollection is that she was dressed as an inflatable rubber boat, but that can't be right. Was it true, she asked eagerly, that I was a military writer? Some thought so, I replied, and some didn't. Oh, wonderful h how perfect, and did I know the Afghan guerrillas were her hobby? Perhaps this wasn't her word but it was what she meant. At any rate the revelation did not bode well for the guerrillas. And had I heard of her scheme to help them? The idea was to send them freeze-dried backpackers rations in military aircraft extorted from the Air Force under an obscure provision of the law proving for charitable flights in time national catastrophe. Why this would have any particular effect on the war was not clear to me.

Having to say something, I said that in my estimation the proper study of Russians was Russia, and that the Soviets could work much good by paddling back across the Oxus and raising goats. Or not raising them.

The boat, if such she was, decided that I was a fellow spirit and bared her soul to me. In this unveiling I had no choice: she went at it with the reticence of an exotic dancer who wanted dollars stuffed into her garter. Such terrible things are happening in Afghanistan, she said, as indeed they are. The plight of the Pathans aroused her maternal instincts, she said. Soon she was cooing as if to a hurt puppy: "Oh, those poor, poor people, how I feel for them, poor dears ... oh, my little fuzzy ducks."

Her little ... what? I thought about it carefully. Yes, that was what she had said. Ducks. Fuzzy ducks. Now, I have known a good many of these guerrillas, and rather like them. They are among the few people mean enough to stand up to the Russians, being courageous, not too complex, joyfully murderous, and quite capable of skinning a prisoner this week and killing him the next. Whatever one thinks of the war, events in that somber land are not amusing, not a fit subject for dilettantes with too little to do. Perhaps a guerrilla movement is not the best focus for the maternal drives of a woman who badly needs a child or a cat.

An astonishing amount of policy in this city is made by people with the complacent arrogance of the rubber boat, by people writing about baffling problems they do not understand in remote regions they cannot find on a map. The truth is that most people in this administration could not distinguish between a helicopter and a hand grenade with fewer than a half-dozen guesses.

I am reminded of the cartoon showing an English literary fop saying indignantly to his mother, "One doesn't write *about* anything, Mother, one simply writes. There is nothing particularly Republican about this woman s colossal fatuity. Hobbyism runs rampant everywhere in Washington. The underlymg premise here, as important in its utility in saving labor as was the cotton gin in the Old South, is that at the higher levels one does not need to understand anything; indeed, the time spent in learning is better used in self-promotion.

For example, an acquaintance of mine is a catamaran liberal, the sort of Presbyterian minister who has a sailboat, believes that God is a pervasive force for community organization, and yearns to boycott South Africa, wherever it is. The man is positively Newtonian in his predictability, a boiling, narcissistic assault on the doctrine of free will. A sort of jackleg sociology I favor holds that a Methodist is a Baptist with shoes, a Presbyterian a Methodist with a Buick, and an Episcopalian a Presbyterian with a stock portfolio. Somewhere between shoes and Buick, politics tilts from right to left. A repressed and angry vanity then discovers that celebrity is after all possible, given the proper venues of demonstration; God is quietly dropped as an embarrassment, and crusades fill the gap. Besides, ifs boring out in the suburbs. Here is the origin, and substance, of liberal religious politics.

The minister and his wife know nothing about anything at all, fervently attend rallies for Nicaragua, and have all sorts of indignant bumper stickers which I suspect they view as reference work. I once showed them some slides I had taken of the Marines in Lebanon before the advent of the unfortunate truck. "How awful," said the wife. And what ocean is that on? One simply writes.

Slipping toward the bar thorough the surging extraterrestrials, I heard someone say, Dick Allen. Did you see Allen?...Dick Allen was here, I think he left. "Dick Allen. Did you see Dick Allen? Lynne Nofziger. Did you see Nofziger?', I didn't have a clue who Dick Allen was, although Nofziger brought to mind a particular sort of beard, presumably attached to Nofziger, that I had once seen on television. It didn't really matter who Nofziger was, or Allen. Every couple of years there is a new Dick Allen, who struts and frets, slings his arrows, and dives back into the law firm.

To normal people, the terrible importance of knowing Dick Allen is hard to grasp. An administration does not consist of normal people. The people who make up an administration seem to have no existence of their own, no particular qualities other than a consuming desire to be obviously important. The danger is that such derivative people, measuring themselves as they do by their propinquity to the radiant candle of the presidency, consumed by a desire not to do anything but merely to have influence or its appearance, will not make reasonable decisions. And, of course, the closer to the president they are, the better. Thus the prevalent photographs of Me in the Oval Office, shaking hands with the latest haberdasher to rule the country. Never mind that most presidents, on their merits, would seldom be invited to more than a Shriners' barbecue.

I talked for a moment to a pleasant fellow, a giant clam, who on president Reagan's long march from Sacramento had been a technician of some sort—an advance man, a pollster, someone in the mechanical trades. (People do not make good clams, even when they are from California. At bottom, clams do not have legs.) He was young and vivacious, pleased with his lot, and bright without having a thought in his head.
I tried **to talk about Nicaragua, but found he knew nothing of the third world, tried to talk of Star Wars, but found that he thought it was extremely important without knowing what it was, tried...without success.

"I'm just a politician I guess," he finally said, Clearly proud of being just a politician. He seemed quite aware of having the world by the handles, of having inexplicably reached the top of the heap. After spending a few years as minor lawyers and aspiring pols, such as he sweep into office on some presidential bow wave. And they make the great discovery that the exercise of power requires no qualifications. All you need is the power.

Years ago I thought of such people as being Ostrogoths, fingering with brash incomprehension the scrolls of Rome. Now I think it fairer to regard them as children who have taken over the controls of the amusement park. It is not true that Democrats cannot be distinguished from Republicans. Republicans these days seem brighter than Democrats, and crazier, or at least crazy in ways promising a higher yield. "Don't you think the MX missile is crucial?" I heard someone say at the bar. «Why?" carne the sumptuary response. "We haven't even used the missiles we've got yet." The remark was original with John Lofton, I think, but in any event epitomized a certain outlaw brashness of the current occupiers of Washington. No Democrat would have ventured such a luminously fey thought.

The reason is probably that the Democrats must genuflect to so many solemnities as to make mental movement difficult, and a decent insanity virtually impossible. They must reverence the poor and the black while going to great lengths to avoid them; curtsy to the old, the brown, and the female; pretend insouciance with regard to money while accumulating as much of it as possible; eschew elitism while furiously practicing it; and condemn any foreign policy more virile than the international distribution of powdered milk-although, come to think of it, they are against powdered milk. Theirs is a hard row to hoe.

Further, I decided, a Republican always looks expensively dressed, even when disguised as an octopus. Democrats look like dope dealers.

Having made a last foray to the hors d'oeuvres tray (it is possible in Washington to live entirely on hors d'oeuvres), I left. Enough is enough, and sometimes too much. If government is not possible, I reflected, neither perhaps is it necessary. And if the citizenry knew how they were governed, and by whom, those with a sense of humor would buy radiation suits and a ticket to Switzerland and the rest would head straight for the Mexican border.

A high school student in sports jacket and bow tie got my car, looking as I suppose Christopher Buckley must. It was true, we had not yet used all the missiles we had, and there was much of worth to ponder in the ornithological interpretation of the Afghan war: All those little fuzzy ducks, grim of mien and bent under machine guns, quacking toward Kandahar. *The truck bomb used by terrorists to kill 241 Marines in Beirut **Star Wars: A technologically improbable anti-ballistic-missile system proposed by Reagan and more discussed than built. ***The sale of powdered milk was much condemned because mothers in the third world watered it excessively to make it last and thus starved their offspring. This piece was originally published in *Harper's* magazine.

[1]

[FR1]

ABOUT THE AUTHOR

Fred Reed

Fred Reed describes himself as a keyboard mercenary and part-time sociopath living near Guadalajaraa, Mexico with his splendid wife Violeta Gonzalez and three useless but agreeable street dogs. The son of a mathematician working for the Navy Department, he grew up, or at least got older, mostly in the small-town South and later fell into journalism because, he says, it didn't require any credentials, which is how many he had. He has written for Soldier of Fortune, Harper's, the Washington Post, the Wall Street Journal, Playboy, and suchlike riffraff. He offers no apologies.

BOOKS BY THIS AUTHOR

A Brass Pole In Bangkok

Another collection of Fred's Fred on Everything columns, seditious, outrageous, inflammatory, evilly funny. Fred dislikes everything he is supposed to like, and likes everything he is supposed to dislike. He likes downscale bars, thinks bar girls are decent human beings, approves of dogs, motorcycles, and really loud blues. He detests wars, which he has seen several of, loathes ugly feminists with politically significant hairy armpits, believes that congressmen would serve well as skeet, and proposes to tie everyone on Wall Street to an anvil and drop it in a river. Obviously he is a benefactor of humanity, like Gandhi.

Curmudging Through Paradise

Fred Reed, who has referred to Oprah Winfrey as looking "like five hundred pounds of bear liver in a plastic bag," takes a jaundiced and highly irreverent view of all things sacred-journalism, marriage, affirmative action, federal scams, governmental uselessness, women, men, fellow reporters, and popular culture. On the other hand, he has a kind word for drunks, bar girls, and children. Neither a liberal nor a conservative-- he describes these as "twin halves of the national lobotomy"-- he is just Fred. He figures it is enough. Anything more would be multiple-personality disorder. Fred has spent many years doing things your mother wouldn't want you to do, such as living in alleys in Taipei, Bangkok, and Saigon, with some of the strangest people ever to crawl this weary earth. Once a war correspondent in Viet Nam and Cambodia, then for years a police reporter in places the media don't admit exist, he spent most of a decade writing a syndicated column on matters military. While he tends to write with wit, he has seen, he says, a lot of ugly things, and doesn't like the people responsible. He says so. Fred may charm or offend, but he'll keep your attention. "Funny, sharply observant and often deeply poignant, Fred Reed writes what a hell of a lot of Americans are thinking, but are afraid these days to say. He is delightfully beyond category for anyone with an open mind, which is probably why he lives in Mexico, far enough away that the politically correct of both camps cannot strangle him." --Joe Bageant, author of Deer Hunting with Jesus

Nekkid In Austin

Essays on America, life, politics, and just about everything, The author chronicles among other adventures an aging stripper in Austin, dressed in a paper-mache horse, who had with her a cobra and a tarantula like a yak-hair pillow with legs and alternately charmed and terrified a room full of cowboys sucking down Bud and.... Fred was an apostle of the long-haul thumb during the Sixties and saw...many things. He tells of standing by the big roads across the desert, rocking the wind blast of the heavy rigs roaring by and the whine of tires and dropping into an arroyo at night with a bottle of cheap red and watching the stars and perhaps smoking things not approved bye the government. He tells of...well, that's what the book is for. Join him.

A Grand Adventure

More outrage and sedition from the internet's leading curmudgion. Sardonic, funny, savagely irreverent, Fred trounces everything and everybody except children, drunks, and bar girls, for whom he has a soft spot. He also likes dogs. This is the man who who described Oprah Winfrey as looking like "five hundred pounds of bear liver in a plastic bag." A former Marine and war correspondent, he loathes war, the Pentagon, and the military budget, and thinks the Marines can do the world a favor by staying home. Dentists like this book as it makes people grind their teeth, but they also applaud. He asserts that after he writes about feminists, Republicans, Democrats, evangelical Christians, or atheists, a lynch mob forms outside his house in Mexico, but he may be stretching the truth a bit. In case he isn't, you may want to buy a rope before ordering A Grand Adventure.

The Great Beer Storm And Possumsquashing Of 1962

Fred's reflections on America as it was and isn't. In the title essay he tells of his rural Southern boyhood, driving a 1953 Chevy the color of two-tone dirt, an aging wreck serving as heraldic emblem, codpiece, bar and, far less fy than he would have liked or admitted, love nest. It usually started but remembered compression as an aging gigolo recalls the ardors of youth and on the night of the possum-squashing, with Bobby on the roof and Itchy in the trunk and a great many empty beer cans.... Well, you get the idea. It was another country, says Fred, and he would like it back. Never happen.

Triple Tap

Robert Dawson, a free-lance police reporter in Washington, DC, ex-Marine, ashen-souled cynic after seeing how the world actually works, finds himself and his girlfriend, AAttila the Liberal, who works for one of the three-letter spook agencies, involved in a weird web of genius dweeb Carol Oslieber, plus a couple of ex-Special Forces nut-jobs, and various drug dealers, who want to...well, that's the story. Written by a veteran police reporter who has actually been there, this is hard-boiled police fiction, not the wine-and-cheese unisex variety common now. If you liked Raymond Chandler, you will like Triple Tap. If you want nicenesss and political correctness, find another book.

Killer Kink

Robert Dawson, police reporter for the Washington Herald, hard-drinking ex-Marine with a sardonic view of practically everything, finds himself first covering and then involved in a string of truly bizarre murders involving grotesque mutilation and apparent Satanic rituals. Then his girlfriend, Attila the Liberal, who works for one of those super-secret three-letter spook agencies, begins receiving body parts from the murderees. Somebody, it seems, doesn't like Dawson. Riveting fiction by an author with eight years experience of covering Washington's police department.

Au Phuc Dup And Nowhere To Go

A wacky novelette by a Marine veteran of Viet Nam who says he finds it easier to laugh about the war than to assault the Pentagon with a back hoe, which would be his preference except that he doesn't have a back hoe. Follow the adventures of Major Egglesby, the worst fighter pilot in the Air Force, and Sergeant Anesthesia Remingham, a black Marine from Alabama who invents the Torpedo Rat and nearly brings the war to a halt, and the concert with the rock band Klok Mortuary and the Gadarene Swine and...and....